Comments About *Memories of Maggie*
Martha Raye: A Legend Spanning Three Wars

From a General

8 November 1996

Dear Noonie:

Yours is an interesting book about an American Legend—at least in the memory of thousands of military Veterans—Martha Raye. Indeed, it is well done.

Martha was a real trooper in every respect. Thank you for telling an important story—in fact recording American history. Best wishes.

Sincerely,

W. C. Westmoreland

Comments About *Memories of Maggie*

From the White House

January 2, 1996

Dear First Sergeant Fortin,

Thank you so much for the inscribed copy of *Memories of Maggie.* I was proud to award Martha Raye the Presidential Medal of Freedom, and your book is a wonderful reminder of her valiant work on behalf of America's armed forces. I appreciate your generosity and kind words and send my best wishes.

Sincerely,

Bill Clinton

COMMENTS ABOUT *MEMORIES OF MAGGIE*
BY NOONIE FORTIN

"I just completed your wonderful biography. Very well done. Thanks for writing about this truly remarkable woman."
—Richard E. Goldsberry, U.S. Department of State

"Noonie Fortin has completed a labor of love in this book. It makes interesting reading as it also traces the trials of the author and her friends in the pursuit of appropriate recognition on a national scale for a real Trooper, Colonel Maggie."
—AJJ, *SABER*—1st Cavalry Division

"You did a wonderful job. It is easy to read and follow...it's like a gift from God."
—Melodye Condos, daughter of Martha Raye

"Noonie Fortin has captured the essence of Martha Raye."
—Al Hemingway, *VIETNAM* Magazine

"It's wonderful and really tells her story. Wonderfully done."
John "Top" Holland, President of AFFA
(Americans for Freedom Always)

"This book is the first one in a long time that gave me that warm feeling. It was positive, upbeat, and told it like it was."
—Jim Tucker, OCSA, The Pentagon

"...this is a must have book. I'd advise you to send for it right away if you can't get one signed by the author at the JFK Special Warfare Museum."
"Tom Squier Looks at Books," *Spring Lake News*, NC

"The descriptions of how much warmth and caring could come from this woman offers readers a book that begs to be held in your lap and read..."
—Meribeth Jones, *Veterans' Voice*

"Noonie Fortin, a wonderful writer, leaves us with memories of the good that was America in Vietnam."
—Chris Noel, Armed Forces Radio Vietnam 1966-71

Potpourri
Of
War

Potpourri Of War

LABORS OF LOVE REMEMBERED

NOONIE FORTIN

LANGMARC PUBLISHING • San Antonio, Texas

POTPOURRI OF WAR
Labors Of Love Remembered
ByNoonie Fortin

Cover: Michael Qualben

Back Cover Photos: Susan Christiansen and Noonie Fortin.

Purple Heart provided by Faith Shorey and SGT Jim Boguszewski.

Published by
LANGMARC PUBLISHING
P.O. BOX 33817
San Antonio, Texas 78265-3817

Library of Congress Cataloging-in Publication Data
Fortin, Noonie, 1947-
    Potpourri of war : labors of love remembered / Noonie Fortin.
        p. cm.
    Includes bibliographical references and index.
    ISBN 1-880292-24-6 (pbk.)
    1. United States--Armed Forces--Women--Miscellanea. 2. United States--Armed Forces--Women--Anecdotes. 3. Women and the military--United States--Miscellanea. 4. Women and the military--United States--Anecdotes. 5. Raye, Martha--Miscellanea. 6. Raye, Martha--Anecdotes. I. Title.
UB418.W65F67 1998
355' .0082--dc21
                                       98-14954
                                         CIP

DEDICATION

To Benita and Arden

To all Veterans of our country,

Gold Star Mothers, Fathers and Siblings,

POW/MIA'S,

the eight women on The Wall,

and all civilian women
who died serving our country

IN MEMORY OF

Marcia Oropallo, an Army Veteran
born 5/5/61 Albany, NY—died 1/11/86 Loudonville, NY

Raymond William Tymeson Jr., USMC
born 3/31/48 Troy, NY—died 12/2/68 QuangNam, VN

Paul Joseph Baker, USMC
born 8/23/48 Troy, NY—died 3/29/69 QuangTri, VN

Peter Mathew Guenette, USA
born 1/4/48 Troy, NY—died 5/18/68 QuanTanUyen, VN

We know that in everything God works for good with those who love him, who are called according to his purpose.

Romans 8:28
King James Version of the Holy Bible

Memorial at Camp Smith, Peekskill, NY. Photo by Noonie Fortin.

The willingness with which our young people are likely to serve in any war, no matter how justified, shall be directly proportional to how they perceive the Veterans of earlier wars were treated, and appreciated, by their nation.

George Washington

CONTENTS

FOREWORD

Thirty-three years ago on a makeshift stage atop a sand dune at Chu Lai, South Vietnam, Martha Raye brought several hours of America and sanity to a group of scared and lonely Marines, Seabees, and sailors. After the show Martha and her small troupe ate the same field rations that we were eating. She walked among us, talked to us, took pictures with us...she brought us a bit of home. I only had one group picture taken with her...but how can one forget those unselfish, loving moments of hers?

OCTOBER 20, 1994:

I cried! The brief article on the front page of our local newspaper announced that Martha "Colonel Maggie" Raye had died. I couldn't finish my breakfast. I just got up from the counter, paid the check, and headed to my school. As I signed the teacher check-in sheet, the principal noticed that something was wrong and invited me into his office. Once again I openly wept. I never expected this to happen...I don't cry easily or publicly. The loss I felt was real and hurt like everything. As I left his office the principal asked, "Are you OK?" I answered, "Yes, but I just lost a friend...America just lost a friend!"

Noonie Fortin's first book, *Memories of Maggie,* told of such brief encounters with Maggie three-plus decades ago along with many, many other loving remembrances of a great lady. *Potpourri Of War* is not only a continuation of the "Colonel Maggie" legend, it is an important chronicle of a segment of our population that has served this country in both military and civilian capacities with dedication and bravery, yet has gone essentially unnoticed...namely, American *women* amidst our wars!

Potpourri Of War is one of those books that you hope never ends. You just want to keep reading, savoring the contents. I thought *Memories of Maggie* told the whole story, but *Potpourri Of War* has proved me wrong. As I read *Potpourri*, I began to understand that Noonie had just begun to record Maggie's story in *Memories of Maggie*. I don't think that she realized just how much of Maggie was in the hearts of America's veterans until *Maggie* was published.

At each book signing or veterans event, Noonie listened to many new stories and made contact with people who would send her letters and pictures of their experience with Martha Raye. Oddly, stories about other women began to surface in significant numbers. It became evident to Noonie that though Maggie might be the focal point for a second book (*Potpourri*), the story of other American women who served their country in war settings needed to be told.

Potpourri Of War is an important work because it starts to paint a picture of the many women who have served in or alongside our military forces "in every clime and place" in every war, conflict, or police action of the 20th century. The women Noonie writes about are military personnel, USO, Red Cross workers, Hollywood stars and relatives of veterans.

Most of these women went to war in a significantly different way than men did, but just the same they went to war. Sharon Lane didn't carry a gun or fly a combat mission, yet she lost her life in Vietnam trying to save those that did. A Gold Star or POW/MIA mother did not shoulder a weapon, yet she suffers a fate almost worse than death itself. The women killed in Operation Babylift never humped the boonies, yet paid the ultimate price on the fields of Vietnam. Journalist Georgette "Dickey" Chapelle was killed at Chu Lai, while I was there, by a Viet Cong booby trap. The chapter "Brave

Women" is a stark and moving reminder that the horror of war is not gender specific.

Potpourri Of War is just that—a potpourri of accounts and reminiscences, but it is also a history. Noonie Fortin's simple and straightforward style makes *Potpourri Of War* a wonderfully easy book to read and remember.

The chapter written by Susan Christiansen alone is worth the price of the book!

Noonie has given us the story of Maggie and all those other great ladies in a format that will last. She has given this country a plethora of heroic women at a time when real heroes—male or female—are few and far between. Just maybe it should be required reading for all of our young people!

Bless you, Noonie!

Semper Fi

Gil Woodside

* Line from the Marine Corps Hymn

PREFACE

Martha Raye's mission in life was two fold: (1) To lift the spirits of her beloved troops for a few minutes or hours throughout three wars and (2) To entertain audiences around the world.

My mission is five fold: (1) To keep Martha Raye's memory alive by telling Americans about her involvement with Veterans, and how others like her have served—with little or no recognition. (2) To urge students to learn about and remember the Vietnam War and its Veterans. (3) To help renew a sense of patriotism and a renewed interest in America's military history, geography, and writing. (4) To help keep the POW/MIA issue alive. (5) To honor women and men who served and died in Vietnam.

As I traveled over 35,000 miles from coast to coast the past few years, much of my time was spent on trains, buses, and in my car. Thoughts about how I could best share my experiences prompted writing this book.

By age forty I thought I had achieved my life goals. That is, until October 1987. There was no way to anticipate I would get so deeply involved as I did in Maggie's life and career.

Memories of Maggie was about Martha Raye's life, how she served and impacted our Veterans, and why she deserved the Presidential Medal of Freedom. Full names, ranks, and branches of service of each Veteran who wrote to me about their encounters with Maggie were cited when provided. Just as Jan Scruggs wanted full names on The Vietnam Veterans Memorial (The Wall), I used full names and titles in the book.

Veterans don't usually talk with others about their wartime experiences, so I was thankful they were willing to share their stories about Maggie. Some Vets wrote or talked extensively, while others were very brief. Some were eloquent and insightful; others were barely understandable. It was difficult for some Vets to bring up all over again some things they endured. It reveals just how much Maggie meant to them that they are willing to talk or write about their encounters with her.

After reading the first draft of *Memories of Maggie*, her daughter, Melodye Condos, gave her opinion. "You did a wonderful job. It is easy to read and follow. I am really impressed with the work you did. Mom's life was so scattered, I'm amazed at how well you put it together. It's like a gift from God."

This book describes other women and men who served our country proudly. My own encounters with Maggie's troops and the painstaking process of what it took to get *Memories of Maggie* published and distributed internationally are discussed. Some reviews and comments about that book are included in this one.

Many Veterans and their families contacted me after reading *Memories of Maggie*. They had seen their friends' names in it and wanted to know how to reach them. Added to this book is a "Buddy Search" that lists names of those we are trying to locate. If you know any of these people, perhaps you can inform me of their location so their buddies can contact them.

As most researchers do, I consulted numerous books and periodicals to compile material. New terms and acronyms are found throughout both *Memories of Maggie* and this book, so a glossary is included in each volume.

An index for easy location of names, places, or events is in the back of *Potpourri Of War*. Suggested activities for students fifth grade and up are included.

My life now revolves around educating Americans about those military experiences that aren't taught in schools. Students need to learn about what makes ours a free country and why we come to the aid of other countries to help safeguard their freedom. While doing presentations to groups, my chief goal is to emphasize what is *good* about America. Martha Raye did it so well!

BLESS YOU, COLONEL MAGGIE!
Noonie Fortin

ACKNOWLEDGMENTS

Thank you to the military and civilian Veterans who have served our country. To honor them, as always, I capitalize the words Veterans and Vets throughout this book.

A special thanks to Arden Davenport, who allowed me to use her computer, phone, and spare room whenever I was in Texas as well as assisting with transportation. I am really a stubby-pencil person, but I soon realized to be professional I needed the use of a good computer.

Thanks to Benita Zahn who provided Maggie and me with television time. She gave me the idea for this book's subtitle.

To Susan Christiansen who, without realizing it, gave me the title *Potpourri Of War*. While discussing at length what to name this book, we eventually came up with the title. I asked Susan to write the words *Potpourri Of War* vertically. When she read the first three letters POW, she realized its deep significance. A special thank you to her for sharing a chapter of her life in this book.

Thanks to Charles Fake and Lillian Eagle, former Lansingburgh High School teachers, for teaching me *why* we should study history and share it with others so mistakes are less likely to be repeated in future generations. Now I speak to groups of all ages to share history.

Those who helped with transportation, contacts, and speaking engagements: Robbin Agard, Brenda Allen, Melodye Condos, John "Top" Holland, GeorgeAnne Schultz, Jim Spitz, Janie Torres, LeEtta Waldhausen, Terry Waterston, Gil and Jewel Woodside Jr.

To Faith Shorey and SGT Jim Boguszewski who found a Purple Heart for this cover.

To Melodye Condos and Susan Christiansen whose lives have also been changed by Maggie. We have become more like sisters than friends.

Special thanks to Lois, James, and Michael Qualben of LangMarc Publishing for taking a chance on an unknown first time author with *Memories of Maggie*. Their assistance, love, and commitment helped me with my first book as well as with this second book.

To all those who have shared a small segment of their lives and how they were affected by Martha "Colonel Maggie" Raye, I want to say thank you. As time passes and we alter our lives, we sometimes change history to what we perceived it to be. Both this book and *Memories of Maggie* contain stories and other people's perceptions; if they are not totally accurate, I sincerely apologize.

Martha "Colonel Maggie" Raye may be gone but I believe that *Memories of Maggie—Martha Raye: A Legend Spanning Three Wars* and *Potpourri Of War: Labors of Love Remembered* will keep her memory alive for years to come along with the memory of other women and men who are mentioned throughout this book.

Noonie Fortin

INTRODUCTION

Labors of love are not financially motivated but rather heartfelt gains. In most situations they require much sacrifice. What you are about to read tells of labors of love of many individuals I have come to know who have been to war for America.

When I compiled *Memories of Maggie*, many Veterans had communicated toward the goal of having Martha Raye receive the Presidential Medal of Freedom. After the book was published, Vets said that although the war was long over they still wept when they read a page or two about their beloved Maggie.

Some Vets were unable to approach us at book signings. Some would look with tears in their eyes at the book cover. Many were unable to express their feelings. The painful memories—even nightmares—still return too often for too many of these sons, husbands, brothers, daughters, wives, and sisters.

Why in 1998 are some of these people still waking up in sweats? Why are some Vets reluctant to tell children about our wars? During presentations, I ask students how many of their parents served in our nation's military. Those who did said their parents did not talk about it. Curiously, female Vets seemed to talk less than male Veterans.

I have learned that Americans don't do as well as other cultures do with keeping important memories alive. Few customs from the old country (our ancestors) are handed down to our young. But how else will our children learn our families' heritage if not from their adults? We need to tell the stories—Grandpa, Grandma. What was it like for you in World War II? In Korea? In that strange place called Vietnam? If you don't tell us, will we repeat your mistakes?

Too many Vietnam Veterans still experience Post Traumatic Stress Disorder (PTSD). Regardless of honorable service in the armed forces of our nation, they were often spit at and called names. When they returned home, they were not accepted with honor from friends and neighbors, sometimes not even from their own families. Too many turned to alcohol and drugs to blot out the horrors they saw or experienced. To this day—their demons rage on.

Americans need to know these things didn't just go away. Parents could not just "stop" their depression when sons or daughters were lost. We all deal with loss in different ways. If we fail to educate our children, they will experience similar problems in the future.

The theme of this book is to remember the labors of love of so many women and men who have served our country, either as military personnel or as civilians. This mixture of people shows their many sacrifices. Their stories, more memories of Maggie, and my own personal experiences are woven throughout this text. I did this in the hope of showing everyone that many diversified people have served our country in many ways.

We should honor our Veterans and their families, every day —not just on Memorial Day, Fourth of July, or Veterans Day. They deserve our love, respect, and devotion. Without them, we might not be the free country we are today.

1

A Woman "Goes Military"

My dream was to join the Army. I came from a patriotic family. My mother's father served with the Army in World War I. My stepfather served in the Navy during World War II. Mother's brother served twenty years in the Air Force flying in and out of Korea and Vietnam. My mother refused to let me enlist. Many of my friends were going to a place called Vietnam to serve our country. Three of them died there—many were wounded. Maybe my motives were their memories, in addition to my own patriotism.

The first forty years of my life were ordinary enough. During school in Troy, New York, I was in a dance review, active in sports, and played violin in the orchestra. I went to college and work.

After I married and was divorced, Mom no longer decided my fate. I enlisted in the Army Reserve. For twenty-two years I served in the military before retiring as a first sergeant. Military pay helped to complete college and make mortgage payments.

Anonymous work in a warehouse followed. Then I worked for the New York State Department of Motor Vehicles for over twenty years.

In 1987 my life changed—forever. In September I joined the Tri-County Council Vietnam Era Veterans in Albany, New York. Belle Pellegrino, who served with the Women Marines, and I were the first two women who actually served in the military to join this group. The other female members were spouses of Veterans. The group treated us well, and we loved them dearly. I also became a firefighter, emergency medical technician, and driving safety instructor with my local fire department and rescue squad.

In October 1987 I was asked to assist in obtaining the Presidential Medal of Freedom (PMOF) for Martha Raye. Between 1987 and 1989 I collected information about Maggie related to her military affiliations. From 1989 until 1993 Belle and I co-chaired the Medals for Maggie Committee to have her honored for her involvement with the armed forces. After Maggie received the PMOF, I researched for two more years and collected more information about her personal life and career.

After organizing the information I had, along with the background material Maggie and her daughter, Melodye Condos, provided me, I began writing a manuscript entitled *Memories of Maggie.*

MEMORIES OF MAGGIE: A BRIEF SYNOPSIS.

Memories of Maggie pulled together the flood of information—much of which was sent to us by Veterans—about Martha Raye. I traced the uphill battle to have "Colonel Maggie," as Vietnam Veterans called her, honored as a recipient of the PMOF.

While *Memories of Maggie* is not a complete biography, it touches on many features of Martha Raye's early life through her death, and how her efforts came to focus on personal service to our troops throughout World War II, the Korean War, and the Vietnam War. It includes personal remembrances from hundreds of people that demonstrate why she so richly deserved the Presidential Medal of Freedom.

Maggie made two requests: that I tell the truth as I know it, and that I not publish her story until she was gone. My actual writing task began in November 1993 after she received the Presidential Medal Of Freedom. I began looking for a publisher in March 1994. I vowed to keep my promise to not have the book published until after her death. She passed away on 19 October 1994.

In July 1995 LangMarc Publishing of San Antonio offered me a trade publishing contract. Rewrites, editing, and blue lines followed. The finished product came on the market in December 1995. It seemed fitting that my first book signing was on Pearl Harbor Day.

After *Memories of Maggie* was published, I thought I was done writing—wrong! Stories and photos continued to pour in. Maggie's involvement with the armed forces began before World War II officially started, and it ended when she was buried at Fort Bragg, North Carolina. My involvement had just begun!

Benita Zahn of NBC's WNYT-TV13 in Albany, New York, has been a friend since the day we met. She and the television station she works for gave our cause for Maggie excellent coverage in the Albany area. Each time I saw Benita, she pointed out that what we were doing for Maggie was a labor of love. To put aside

Benita Zahn
Contributed by Noonie

everything to get someone else honored was something few people had done, she observed.

During a television appearance with Benita in October 1995, I told her about the publication of *Memories of Maggie*. When I decided to write a sequel, Benita's phrase "labor of love" would be just right for a subtitle.

Two framed letters hang on my wall: President Clinton's letter and General Westmoreland's letter. I was honored that President Clinton felt the way he did and that he again took the time to write to me. And it had never occurred to me that *Memories of Maggie* was a "history" book, as described by General Westmoreland.

During my years in the Army and with the Department of Motors Vehicles I was asked to speak to groups. Since *Memories of Maggie* was published, I have spoken to groups of all ages about Maggie, what it took to get her honored, how difficult it was to get published, and how my life has changed. Writing, speaking, and traveling consumes most of my time these days.

I have met many fascinating people, traveled to places I had never been, and learned so much more about the women and men who have served our country in so many ways.

Roy Benavidez Pins a Medal

Martha Raye received her Presidential Medal of Freedom (PMOF) in November 1993. Congressional Medal of Honor recipient Master Sergeant Roy Benavidez (Army Special Forces) pinned it on her twenty years after the Vietnam War ended.

Roy, who had served in Vietnam, was so badly wounded that he was thought to be dead. Most fellow soldiers he had attempted to rescue that fateful day in

Cambodia were dead. Roy had thirty-seven shrapnel wounds; his intestines were exposed. He heard the sound of the snaps on a body bag being closed around him. Had a comrade not recognized Roy, he would have suffocated in the body bag. When a doctor finally checked for a heartbeat, Roy managed to spit in his face and got the doctor to realize he was still alive. Even so, the doctor did not expect Roy to live.

In February 1981 President Ronald Reagan awarded the Congressional Medal of Honor to Roy after an uphill fight to get Roy recognized for his actions. His CMH was awarded to him many years after his actions in Vietnam and Cambodia. Why did it take so many years for him to be honored? From the Nixon administration onward, our government didn't want to admit we had military operations in Cambodia.

In 1989 I wrote to Roy seeking his assistance in obtaining stories about Maggie's role with our troops. He was the first person to endorse the Medals for Maggie Committee. We exchanged many letters and phone calls over the years. He was so generous to mention the committee, our goal, and me in his book, *The Last Medal of Honor*.

Audie Murphy Luncheon

As many times as Roy and I had spoken and corresponded, it would be over five years from our first contact before we met in Copperas Cove near Fort Hood, Texas, where I was living and working on *Memories of Maggie*. Roy came to Fort Hood to address Audie Murphy Club inductees. He invited me to be his guest at the luncheon. What a thrill to sit next to Roy at the head table!

I had read two of the three books about Roy's experiences in Vietnam and stateside. I was in awe of this man. As Roy spoke, the inductees' faces reflected their respect for him and what he had been through.

After his comments, Roy introduced me by saying I was largely responsible for getting Maggie honored by the President and that I, too, should be honored for persevering. He encouraged the group to read *Memories of Maggie* when it was available. Roy also suggested that I be invited to address a future inductee group since I was a retired first sergeant. This elite group of soldiers all had to be superior non-commissioned officers, meet some stringent rules, and aspire to be like Audie himself.

Who was Audie Murphy? He was a Texan who became the most decorated soldier of World War II. Born in 1924, he was inducted into the Army at age eighteen despite being only five feet four inches and weighing 120 pounds. After basic training in Texas, he had advanced training at Fort Meade, Maryland.

Audie was assigned to the Third Infantry Division. He fought in North Africa, Sicily, Italy, France, and Germany. He was on the frontlines at least four hundred days. Audie earned thirty-three military awards, citations, and decorations for his actions. He received a battlefield commission as a second lieutenant for his combat leadership and courage. Audie was awarded every American medal for valor, including the Medal of Honor. Although he was still under twenty-one at the time of Victory in Europe (V-E) Day, Audie was officially credited with having killed, captured, or wounded 240 Germans.

Audie's story was portrayed in his book and a movie, *To Hell and Back*. He returned to the United States after the war and became a movie star. He died in 1971 in an airplane crash and was buried with full honors at Arlington National Cemetery.

The Audie Murphy Club has a chapter on each Army base. Members' main goal is to follow in his footsteps with leadership and courage. They also pledge to help fellow soldiers, regardless of rank.

What a privilege to be among these men and women who continue such an inspiring heritage!

2

GETTING THE STORY TOLD

Martha Raye authorized only three people to write about her: her daughter Melodye, Veteran correspondent Susan Christiansen, and me. Melodye would write about the personal side of Maggie's life. Susan would write about how and why civilian women became involved with the armed forces. My "shot" was to write of Maggie's role with our troops, stateside and overseas.

I assumed it would be easy to find a willing publisher for a book about Martha Raye. I was keenly aware of my first-time author status. But, after all, Maggie was a Hollywood celebrity. She had just received the highest civilian award our President can authorize. There shouldn't be roadblocks to getting *her* story published. Guess again!

Although many of my articles appeared in newspapers, magazines, and journals, writing and getting a book published is an entirely different world. I read books about formatting manuscripts for publication, obtaining agents, copyrights, contracts, self-publishing, and marketing. Then, there is the difference between a "trade" publisher (who takes all the risks and foots the production bills) and "subsidy" presses. Subsidy or "vanity" presses charge the author all—or most—of the book's production costs. It occurred to me that if I couldn't find a "trade" publisher that I'd have to publish it myself. These days many books are self-published.

After completing the manuscript, I wrote query letters to agents and publishing houses. My goal was to mail twenty letters a week. I wrote to nearly 450 publishing companies between March 1994 and July 1995. My file box filled with rejection slips. Only twenty-four of those publishers—barely five percent— asked to see my proposal. More rejections. Twelve publishers requested the complete manuscript. More rejections. Each time I opened one of those letters my heart sank. Didn't anyone care about Maggie and her life story?

I wrote to more than a hundred literary agents. More rejections. I stopped contacting them, since I was already doing what agents would do. I continued contacting publishers myself. However, without an agent I couldn't get a foot in the door of large publishing houses. Oh well!

Then on 10 July—nearly nine months after Maggie's death— I received a phone call from Lois Qualben, the president of LangMarc Publishing in San Antonio. She was interested in seeing my proposal and manuscript. Lois phoned me three days after receiving it and asked if we could meet. She drove to Copperas Cove on 15 July, and we talked for five hours. Lois liked what she and her senior editor had read, and they were interested in publishing Maggie's story.

When I saw LangMarc's logo (a whale), I knew it was destiny that Lois read my query letter. My home is filled with whale statues and photos. I even wore a whale necklace that day and now I have a whale bracelet. Whales are my favorite mammal—next to cats. Lois offered me a contract that same day and said I could have a finished book in about six months. A few days later, after some deliberations by phone with Lois, I signed a contract with her company. I have never regretted doing so.

Lois and I worked closely together through the first two rewrites. We discussed military terminology, ranks, numbers, and cut the original manuscript from over eight hundred pages to a more workable four hundred pages. Then she turned over the manuscript to editor Debra Innocenti. James Qualben, LangMarc's senior editor, helped me with historical background as well as the book's structure and "flow." Michael Qualben designed the cover. Through conversations, he had caught the essence of Maggie and her involvement with the armed forces.

Following the editing process and formatting came the "blue lines," which had to be checked carefully for errors. We all proofread; corrections were made. In November the camera-ready copy was sent to the printer.

The publisher called me the first week of December when the books arrived. On 7 December 1995 I was in San Antonio autographing books for people who had ordered them ahead of the actual publication release. Maggie's legacy had come full circle. Martha Raye started entertaining troops before Pearl Harbor and here it was—Pearl Harbor Day 1995—when I had *Memories of Maggie* in hand and was signing it!

AGENTS

Before most agents will approach a large publisher, the author most likely will have to part with several thousand dollars to have a well-known (typically: New York) editor work on the manuscript. Regardless of which type of house publishes your book, an agent will charge ten or fifteen percent of the author's royalties.

Three agents said they would represent me if I found a publisher. Why should I pay them a percentage when I did all the work?

An agent may help, but perhaps you don't need one.

PUBLISHERS

Large companies may offer authors an "advance" on a book's anticipated royalties. (This is the exception, by far, rather than the rule, especially for first-time or little-known authors.) They may have a frequent change of editors and each one might insist you change your manuscript to fit their tastes and styles. The large houses usually take one to two years to publish a book, unless you are already well known or the topic is headline news. Most do little or no promoting and marketing for unknown authors. However, the large houses have an advantage in book distribution.

Small publishing companies usually do not offer advance money, and they are unable to spend large sums on promotion and marketing. Many can't get books distributed easily to bookstore chains. However, the publisher and editor are more likely to work closely with the author, and they may be able to publish a top-quality book in nine months to a year.

Few new authors realize the high priority publishers place on the *author's* marketing potential. Colin Powell's contract, for example, committed him to sixty-two days of cross-country book signings. Writing your book is not even close to fifty percent of your work and effort for a successful publishing experience. Slack off on your own marketing efforts and no reputable publisher will consider your next manuscript.

DISTRIBUTORS

Most book distributors don't promote or market books. They are wholesalers who only warehouse and distribute them. The large distributors ship your book to bookstores IF the store orders the book. That usually happens only if an author has a book signing at a store or a customer requests a certain book. If a customer requests a book that the store doesn't have in stock, the store orders it from the distributor.

If the book is not in their warehouse stock, a distributor can order it from the publisher, who ships it (usually at the publisher's expense) to the distributor's warehouse. The distributor then sends the book to the bookstore. The publisher has to wait for partial payment for at least ninety days after "selling" to a distributor at the standard fifty-five percent discount. One begins to understand why books cost consumers so much these days.

Large distributors ship books nationally and internationally. A distributor may order just one book or several thousand books from a publisher. They place the books in their various warehouses around the country only to return some of them in a few months. It is common for certain distributors to return books just prior to a billing quarter's end, only to reorder the same books right after the next quarter starts. Small and medium-sized publishers face an accounting nightmare because of such practices. Many small publishers prefer direct-order sales to customers rather than work with large distributors.

There are some reputable smaller distributors that are more cooperative. Unfortunately, many are regional; they serve a limited section of the country, sometimes only a few communities or one state.

This is only the tip of the reality iceberg. I learned the

realities about publishing, distributing, promoting, and marketing after writing *Memories of Maggie*.

LangMarc's leadership and I attended the Texas Library Association convention in Houston. They had arranged for me to be a guest author at the book signing section of the convention hall. A gentleman approached me at the author's booth. He was carrying documents I had written in 1987. He began to introduce himself, but as soon as he said, "My name is Ed," I filled in the blank. "Baron—Ed Baron of Houston." [1] Ed played in a band and he saw Maggie several times, starting in the 1930s. He was eighty at our Houston encounter in 1996. He spoke of his other encounters with the woman who combined her "Big Mouth" with a warm heart. Later Ed brought Jerry Noble to a store where I had a book signing. Jerry saw Maggie while he was in Korea.

Meeting Ed and Jerry may seem trivial to some who are unaware of "the other side" of Martha Raye. This extraordinary—sometimes heroically so—caring human being gave the best of herself so often over so many decades to America's military men and women. At times, I wonder if this "side" of Martha Raye is one of those best-kept secrets of our nation's past half century.

Perhaps her "secret" has some connection with most citizens' continued confusion and ambivalence about the Vietnam War. Three Presidents and several Secretaries of Defense may have gotten bogged down in a swamp of muddled policies about Vietnam. But Maggie understood what our troops were going through, and she did the best she could to help them through it.

So many times and in different parts of the country, Veterans have introduced themselves as a prelude to recounting their own personal experiences with "Colonel Maggie" and her unique gifts for making them feel like the sons and daughters, brothers and sisters, husbands and wives, and parents they were back home.

Their experiences are part of America's birthright.

BOOK REVIEWS AND INTERVIEWS

Book reviews are crucial for making a book a success. In most cases, reviews have a greater impact than an advertisement. We are deeply grateful for every review and interview that has honored *Memories of Maggie*.

Sharleen Bell from the Copperas Cove *Leader-Press* reviewed *Memories of Maggie* and interviewed me before the book was released to the public. "Fortin has done a credible job in telling Raye's story from the perspective of the soldiers and civilians who knew and loved her."

Meribeth Jones wrote one of the first book reviews, which appeared in the February 1996 issue of *Veterans' Voice:*

> The descriptions of how much warmth and caring could come from this woman offers readers a book that begs to be held in your lap and read, like a puppy who wants a few moments of your love...this is not a definitive buffet of all that she did. It is one big chunk of story and you have the time and the fork. Go for it!

Reviews of *Memories of Maggie* appeared in the *Army Times, Air Force Times,* and *Navy Times* in March, as well as in numerous newspapers circulating near bases around the country. Most had similar phrasing: "Her gravestone reads 'civilian,' but with the nickname 'Colonel Maggie,' one would think Martha Raye was a soldier. She dedicated her life to serving her country and the needs of her fellow man."

Arthur Junot of the First Cavalry Division Association wrote a review that appeared in the March-April 1996 issue of *SABER.*

> Noonie Fortin...has completed a labor of love in this book. It makes interesting reading as it also traces the trials of the author and her friends in the pursuit of appropriate recognition on a national scale for a real Trooper, Colonel Maggie.

The Killeen *Daily Herald* published an article by Elke Hutto along with pictures of me at Fort Hood's Post Exchange signing books.

BOOKSTORE SIGNINGS

Book signings at bookstores are important in introducing a book to the public, but they are hard work! An author needs to leave his or her ego at home, as book signings can be a humiliating experience. Most book stores are pleased if an author sells between six and twelve books at a signing.

Several people who purchased books at signings had stories of their own about Maggie. Milton Wilson worked with Maggie during the early 1950s on her television show and several stage shows. He brought a photo of her with Harpo Marx, Rocky Graziano and himself.

L-R: Harpo Marx, Maggie, Milton Wilson, and Rocky Graziano.
Photo contributed by Milton Wilson.

LangMarc Publishing and I contacted the Army Air Force Exchange System (AAFES) headquarters in Dallas. We assumed they would be anxious to carry *Memories of Maggie* since it was related to the armed forces. They refused to carry the book.

We contacted several base bookstores for direct orders. At first, the signs were encouraging. The Crossed Sabers Gift Shop at Fort Hood carried the book. Their clientele is mainly members and friends of the First Cavalry Division and Association. But when Fort Hood's Post Exchange set up a book signing for *Memories of Maggie,* the Crossed Sabers Gift Shop decided it would no longer carry the book.

We contacted other bases that have museums with gift shops. The John F. Kennedy Special Warfare Museum's gift shop at Fort Bragg, home of the Special Forces and burial place of Martha Raye, has carried the book.

James Napier of Waco, Texas had a segment called "James Corner" on the evening news program on KWTX-TV10. He re-

membered Maggie and interviewed me on his program. He helped arrange my first book signing—at Gladys' Book Store in Waco. Gladys Strakos held an autograph party and notified the local papers. A reporter interviewed me and took some photos for the paper.

During the Spring, I had signings at bookstores in Waco, Austin, Grapevine, Arlington, Killeen, and Houston—just to name a few. Many who came recalled meeting Maggie. Elmer Giese of Copperas Cove remembered Maggie in his area near ChauDoc in AnPhu Province of Vietnam in 1966-1967 when he was with Military Assistance Command-Vietnam (MAC-V) and Lieutenant Colonel Weber was his commander.

WHO IS YOUR AUDIENCE?

Originally, I assumed that the audience most interested in *Memories of Maggie* would be Veterans communities and people over forty who might remember Maggie from her movies. Much to my surprise, students from the fifth grade through college were also interested—and feeling ignorant about an epoch so important as Vietnam.

Thanks to Dr. Jerry Jones, I addressed his International Relations class at the University of Central Texas in Killeen. Some students were Veterans of the Gulf War; others remembered their parents mentioning Maggie from earlier wars.

Copperas Cove Junior High School students were writing papers that required historical research. Marianna McDonald invited me to speak to them about my research experiences in gathering information about Maggie. They heard about newspaper morgues, how to get information from Army sources, as well as how to procure copies of birth and death certificates.

Authors need to seek opportunities to make their books available to target groups. During Presidents Day weekend, I went to Corpus Christi where USS *Lexington* supporters were holding their annual Canteen Show and Dinner to raise funds for the museum. Since attendees would be of an era to remember Maggie, I stayed for two nights of book signings and reminiscences of Maggie encounters.

Writers groups and reading clubs are eager listeners. Betty Trabue arranged a presentation for me at the Copperas Cove Library. This group of avid readers seemed intrigued with the process of getting published and challenges in marketing a book.

With a wide variety of topics, authors who are willing to speak will have opportunities. I have spoken to Veterans groups, public school and college classes, optimist clubs, women's groups, church groups, and all types of community organizations. These speeches are important for getting out your message and for selling your book.

In March 1996, I attended a meeting of the local chapter of the Special Forces Association in Killeen, Texas where I made a brief presentation. At the request of Earl Trabue, I returned to speak to them in August 1997 and Tom Johnson recalled that he had choppered Maggie around Vietnam. At the Fiftieth Reunion of the First Cavalry Division Association in Killeen, more Veterans shared their Maggie stories. Ken Olson from Golden Valley, Minnesota had seen Maggie at Bon Song in Vietnam during 1967-1968 when he was with the First of the Ninth Cavalry. He already had a copy of *Memories of Maggie*, but he purchased one for his friend, Bill "Deer Hawk" Silverstone of Powell, Wyoming. Bill and Ken have invited me to be their guest speaker in the Minneapolis-St. Paul area for Memorial Day 1999 for another Veterans reunion.

Eddie Pine saw Maggie in QuanLoi during Christmas 1968 while he was serving with Company D, Second of the Twelfth Cavalry. Hugh "Tim" Millar from South Harwich, Massachusetts saw Maggie a couple of weeks earlier both on the ground and in the air near QuanLoi. Tim was with the Third Brigade at the time.

Chaplain Colonel Frank Grieff served with the Seventh Cavalry in Korea. He wrote *The Circuit Riding*

Combat Chaplain; we traded copies of our books. He was interested in reading stories from other chaplains about their encounters with Maggie.

Only four months after publication, *Memories of Maggie* went into its second printing.

3

THREE SPECIAL JEWELS

When I autographed hundreds of *Memories of Maggie* copies in San Antonio in December, 1995, the publisher sent complimentary copies to some special people.

CHRIS NOEL

One book was sent to Chris Noel [2] whom I met in 1993. Her birth name was Sandee Noel; she grew up in West Palm Beach with her sister Trudie. Her father left when she was young; her mother, Louise, remarried. At seventeen, after graduation from Palm Beach High School, Chris opened her own modeling school; at eighteen she went to New York. She modeled for Kodak print commercials and photo shoots for top magazines. Talent agents first changed her name to Liz Barrett, then to Chris Noel so she could retain her family name.

Soon she was off to Hollywood where she became a successful actress. Chris made movies with Elvis Presley (*Girl Happy*), Steve McQueen (*Soldier in the Rain*), Richard Chamberlain (*Joy in the Morning*), Robert Goulet (*Honeymoon Hotel*), Dennis Hopper (*Glory Stompers*),

and Nancy Sinatra with
Chad Everett (*Get Your-
self a College Girl*) just to
name a few. She per-
formed with Robert
Vaughn and Gary Lock-
wood (*The Lieutenant*) and
Ben Johnson (*Wild Ones*)
on television. *TV Guide*
printed a story about her
called "Happiness is a Girl
named Chris." She was
quoted as saying she
didn't really want to be "a

Chris Noel
Photo contributed by Noonie.

famous actress but rather a great personality—a person!"

Singer Jack Jones was her steady boyfriend in the
1960s. He was responsible for her audition with the
Armed Forces Radio Network (AFRN). She became the
first woman broadcaster on this network since Marty
Wilkerson, known as GI Jill, during World War II. For a
couple of weeks Chris was co-host of a program called
"Small World" with George Church III. Soon AFRN
offered Chris her own show, "A Date With Chris." This
program made her an instant hit with the troops in
Vietnam.

"A Date with Chris" was an hour-long program that
included mail from the troops, song dedications, public
service announcements, and interviews with Ray
Charles, Marvin Gaye, Nancy Sinatra, Bobby Rydell,
and many other celebrities.

Chris volunteered to go to Vietnam because she
wanted to do something more for her country. She had
no way of knowing that Vietnam "would become a
dominant force in her life." She would travel many
times to that small country while our troops were there.

Chris arrived at TanSonNhut for Christmas 1966.

Soldiers tagged her "Miss Christmas." She visited troops at Vung Chua Mountain in QuiNhon, Monkey Mountain in DaNang, and Camp Enari on Dragon Mountain. She was at DucPho, LaiKhe, LongBinh, ChuLai, Saigon, Camp Goodman, the highlands, Kontum, and many other areas of Vietnam. For most of her shows she wore miniskirts, white boots, suntanned panty hose and a bush hat; sometimes she would wear fatigues and combat boots. She always said, "Hi Luv."

Chris, like Maggie, went to places where there might be a hundred—or only two—soldiers. She was on board the USS *Ticonderoga*. She was in sandbagged bunkers, on the perimeters, and in morgues.

She was shot at along Highway Nineteen between QuiNhon and Pleiku. She was at places under rocket or mortar attack. Chris survived sniper fire while hurrying to a chopper. She went down in a rice paddy when another chopper had hydraulic failure. She saw death and destruction. But Chris learned to live one day at a time.

Chris had been exposed to Agent Orange since she was frequently choppered into areas that were freshly defoliated. She drank contaminated water. Like so many other Vietnam Veterans, she worries about the effects it may have had on her.

Chris returned to Vietnam several times for AFRN. The Viet Cong offered a $10,000 price on her head, dead or alive. General Westmoreland and Bob Hope each merited a $25,000 price. The price on Maggie's head was even higher.

When Chris returned home after each trip to Vietnam, so-called friends in the entertainment world often turned their backs to her at social events. She was accused of working for the Central Intelligence Agency (CIA), called a hawk—and much worse. She stopped attending such gatherings.

In 1987 Chris Noel wrote *Matter of Survival*, a book that explained how her life was forever changed by the war.

> I join the thousands of Vietnam Veteran brothers and sisters; our struggle in redirecting our lives is a matter of survival, as it should be of concern, understanding and humanity to those who were not directly involved in that war.

Chris was surprised when she read the chapter in *Memories of Maggie* that included Ty Herrington and Maggie's party. [3] Ty, a member of the Army's Special Forces, and Chris met in Vietnam. They fell in love and were married. After Ty returned to the United States, he committed suicide. To see Ty's name after all those years was "a shock and a pleasure." Chris sent me a note:

> Martha Raye, my hero! Maggie introduced me to my Green Beret love. In Vietnam, I watched her in awe as she sang songs, gave love and said 'God Bless' to her guys. Noonie Fortin, a wonderful writer, leaves us with memories of the good that was America in Vietnam.

More than ten years after her last trip to Vietnam, Chris noticed symptoms of mental and physical changes. Her doctors treated her for allergies and anxiety. She became addicted to Valium. No one asked her about Vietnam, the trips she made there, the bodies she had seen, or what she observed in the hospitals there. Vietnam made Chris a fighter, but she soon realized she was a survivor.

Chris is not a military Veteran, but she is a civilian Veteran of the war, as well as the widow of a Veteran. She suspected she was suffering from Post Traumatic Stress Disorder after reading a brochure about it. Chris experienced most of the symptoms: depression, anger, anxiety, sleeping disturbances, emotional numbing, survivors guilt, and others. She sought counseling.

When Chris meets women Veterans, they become sisters just as male Veterans become brothers. She knows the trauma they have suffered. She hugs everyone. It makes her feel good. "It's my way of saying I care." Nurse and author, Lynda Van Devanter, helped Chris; they were "sisters" who had faced the same reactions here and abroad. One Vet said, "You keep me alive. We need each other."

Chris has been married three times. She headed Noel Cosmetic Company, acted in movies and commercials, and attended college. In spite of health problems, she keeps active in all Veterans issues. Currently, Chris is the Executive Director of Vetsville Cease Fire House, a home for needy Veterans in West Palm Beach.

FRENCHY AMUNDSON

Lieutenant Colonel Rolande "Frenchy" Colas de la Nouye Amundson was one of Maggie's best friends. I met her for the first time in 1990 and saw her again in 1991 and 1996. This rare jewel of a person received one of the first copies of *Memories of Maggie.*

After Frenchy read the book, she was eager to talk. My phone number was unlisted so she contacted retired members of the Special Forces and Special Operations to help locate me. Since she knew I lived in Copperas Cove, she called someone in Houston who told her that Colonel Earl Trabue also lived in Copperas Cove. When Earl knocked at my door, he had a message for me from Frenchy to call her immediately.

Who was "Frenchy"? She had served in the Special Air Service of the French Army and became part of the French resistance during World War II. Later Frenchy trained to be a secret agent for the British Special Operations Executive and became a paratrooper. She stood five feet two inches and (in 1943) weighed all of a hundred pounds.

Frenchy parachuted several times into occupied France and Germany and returned important information to British headquarters. On one of these missions, she was captured, tortured by the Gestapo, and sent to the concentration camp at Mauthausen, east of Linz, Austria. There she was repeatedly raped and sodomized. She was liberated on 1 May 1945 and repatriated in September.

Frenchy attended night school and became a nurse. She served as a nurse in French Indochina from 1947 to 1949. She married and bore a son. They lived in a small house in Cholon (the Chinese sector of Saigon) in Vietnam. Her son and maid were killed when their house was mortared by the Vietminh. Frenchy's husband failed to return from a flying mission. She returned to France alone.

Frenchy obtained a job in the American Embassy as a typist, then as an interpreter for General Dwight Eisenhower. She met an American soldier, married him, moved to the United States and became an American citizen in 1958. She and her husband adopted an orphaned girl.

In 1976 she met members of the U.S. Special Forces. These Green Berets had heard of her exploits and welcomed her into their fold. They presented her with an honorary Green Beret and named her a lieutenant colonel. They became her family.

Frenchy and Maggie became close friends. They had far more than Vietnam in common, these extraordinary women. Rising above enormous personal tragedy, they not only achieved much but coupled so much courage with so much caring for others. They attended many functions together. Frenchy became a member of the California State Guard. She lived in Paso Robles and volunteered at the Camp Robert's Historical Museum in San Miguel.

Maggie, Ernest Price, Jr. and Frenchy at the 1990 Drop-In.
Photo contributed by Ernest Price, Jr.

Frenchy died 7 October 1997. She received a full military funeral and was posthumously promoted to full colonel.

BRENDA ALLEN

Brenda Allen, whose real last name is Allacher, is a country-western singer and comedienne who lives in Omaha. Brenda has performed with stars such as Minnie Pearl, Tex Ritter, Sheb Wooley, and Johnny Cash. She was part of The Taylor Sisters singing group. The four young women were not "blood" sisters but were of kindred spirits. Formed in 1964, the group consisted of lead singer Helen Taylor, drummer Patty Brown, bass

Brenda Allen. Photo
contributed by Noonie Fortin.

player Onnie Barr, and Brenda on guitar. They not only played their instruments but sang.

Johnny Cash gave the group their big break when he introduced an agent to them. There were few all-woman bands at that time. The agent began booking them on shows with well-known country headliners.

Sheb Wooley, who played Pete on the television show "Rawhide," recommended The Taylor Sisters to a promoter who arranged for entertainers to perform for the troops in Vietnam. A Korean agency would be responsible for their safety, lodgings, and tour dates during their fourteen weeks in-country during 1969.

Johnny Western wrote many songs, one of which was the theme song for the television series "Paladin." He was in Vietnam when The Taylor Sisters performed; he and Brenda became friends. When Brenda told him about her inclusion in *Memories of Maggie*, Johnny interviewed me on his KFDI AM & FM radio program in Wichita.

None of these four women were prepared for their experience in Vietnam. Brenda recalled that much of Vietnam appeared to be in an earlier century; part of it smelled like a swamp, sapped their energy with its oppressive heat, and was filled with mosquitoes. They were told they would be traveling with two men riding as gunners. They weren't told they would be shot at.

The Taylor Sisters traveled by helicopter, jeep, or boat from one base to another. Many have heard of NhaTrang where the women performed, but they also went to many more remote areas. Typically they stayed at a base for three days and did three shows a day. They were paid $175 a week. When Bob Hope was there— usually at Christmas time—he was flown in daily from Bangkok, Thailand, and then returned to the safety of a Bangkok hotel each evening. Meanwhile, The Taylor Sisters listened to rockets and mortars firing every night.

Yes, these women endured the hardships of actual combat. But no, they didn't complain. The troops tried to do as much as humanly possible for them. Brenda said, "We were everyone's sister, mother, and wife."

Brenda remembered a picture of three smiling soldiers and her standing on the deck of a boat. The Taylor Sisters were traveling by boat to QuaViet near the Demilitarized Zone (DMZ). After landing, they performed on a small stage while their all-male audience sat on the sandy beach cheering. That evening the base was attacked. Two-thirds of their earlier audience were killed that night—including the three GIs in Brenda's picture.

Brenda Allen first wrote to me from Omaha in 1990. [4] She knew the risks that Maggie had taken, and she understood why thousands of Veterans bonded together to get Maggie the PMOF. Brenda and I spoke often on the phone. We finally met in November 1993 in Washington, D.C. She joined Belle Pellegrino, Susan Christiansen, and me as we celebrated the PMOF being awarded to Maggie and the dedication of the Vietnam Womens Memorial. Brenda asked me at that time what was to become of the material I had gathered about Maggie. She suggested I write a book.

While the PMOF campaign was in full swing, Brenda assisted in obtaining many signatures on petitions. She attended numerous Veteran functions in Nebraska and explained what we were trying to accomplish for Maggie. When she heard that *Memories of Maggie* was being published, typical of her generous nature, Brenda asked what she could do to help get the book noticed. She came through! Brenda contacted Veterans groups and talked about the book. She set out on her own quest to find me speaking opportunities in Nebraska.

Brenda has her photo albums and other items to remember those months in Vietnam. She continues entertaining Veterans at various functions and reunions. She treasures the thanks and hugs she receives from other Vets, for she too is a Veteran.

Brenda was one of four Nebraska women who were profiled in a 1991 thirty-minute Nebraska Educational Television Network documentary called "Not on the Frontline." The other women were Reesa Eisler, a Red Cross worker, and nurses Judy Knopp and Marcita Martin.

These women know what it is to serve their country, whether as military members or civilians.

4

SUSAN CHRISTIANSEN

Many civilians have asked me, "Who is Susan Messerman (Christiansen) and why did she write the Introduction to *Memories of Maggie*?"

Susan and I met Labor Day Weekend 1990 in Marina, California at Colonel Maggie's All Services Airborne Drop-In. I knew of her from reading her columns "Vet Forum" and "L.O.V.V.E." (Loved Ones of Veterans are Very Enterprising) in various Veteran publications. Since our first meeting we have become the best of friends.

Since Susan and Maggie were friends, I asked Susan to write the Introduction for *Memories of Maggie*. Many folks, including my publisher, have asked me about Susan. Though known mostly in the Veterans' community, she is an amazing woman who should receive credit for what she has done.

Susan, like Maggie, put her nurse's training to work when she joined the stateside Red Cross. She became qualified for First Aid, Advanced First Aid, Cardio-Pulmonary-Resuscitation, Emergency Disaster Relief, and Trauma Counseling among other required courses for a Registered Nurse degree. This training would be put to use throughout the rest of her life.

Susan has been married and divorced twice. Her two husbands, Chris and Mike (her close friend), fathered her four children: Bryan, Tammy, Ricky, and Keith. Three of the children have suffered from Agent Orange toxins, as has Susan. The first time she married Mike, they were sixteen. The marriage was declared invalid since they did not have parental consent. She married Chris, and then later she and Mike remarried. Both Chris and Mike are Vietnam Veterans and both men have remained a part of Susan's life. Chris served two tours in-country with the Army between 1967 and 1969. Mike served in the Army in Vietnam 1969 to 1970.

A long time ago Susan had mentioned that she was at Kent State University during the student protests and witnessed the shooting of students. Years later she denied having been there, but she had been having nightmares about it. *Why?*

In 1980 Susan moved to Yucca Valley, not far from the Twenty-Nine Palms Marine Corps base where in 1982 she began writing "Vet Forum" for her local paper. She wanted to help Veterans' wives and families deal better with their loved ones who were still suffering effects of the war. She counseled Vets to help deal with their Post Traumatic Stress Disorder (PTSD.) Several other papers carried her column.

In 1982 Susan also became involved with the Agent Orange issue after hearing a radio blurb about Dioxin victims. Susan's children were having physical and mental problems. Three of them have tested positive for Dioxins.

Susan was so involved with the Veteran community in southern California that she went with the Vets to Washington, DC for the dedication of The Vietnam Veterans Memorial on Veterans Day, 11 November 1982. This dedication became known to many Veterans as SALUTE ONE.

Susan met Britt Small for the first time at The Wall. She witnessed the discord among some Vets and watched how Britt soothed them when he began to sing. Britt and his band Festival became mainstays at The Wall. They sang there every Memorial Day and Veterans Day thereafter.

Susan began writing for BRAVO's *Veterans Outlook* in 1984. The editor wanted her to work exclusively for his Veteran publication. He promised to cover her mail and phone expenses as she continued to counsel Veterans and their families. He assured her that he would take her to Vietnam and would give her artistic freedom to run her column. She agreed to that at the time although simultaneously writing for other special interest publications. Her affiliation with BRAVO ended abruptly in 1991.

Susan led the Southern California Honor Battalion delegation in a parade in New York City in 1985. Vets began asking Susan, "Did I know you over there?" She denied being in Vietnam.

In 1987 she attended Rolling Thunder I in Washington, D.C. She had met John "Top" Holland earlier that year after assisting in taping a pilot show of "The New Queen For a Day" with Marian Shelton, the wife of the only POW not declared dead by the U.S. Government. Susan joined Top's group called Americans For Freedom Always (AFFA) and went to work on the POW/MIA issue—her real passion.

Many Vets told her they were glad she got back to The World safely. She kept insisting that she had never been in-country and that they must have had her mistaken for someone else.

But her nightmares had already begun. *Why?*

Susan attended the dedication of the California Vietnam Veterans Memorial in Sacramento in 1990. Some women who recognized her asked her to join them for a photo. She froze and said, "I didn't serve. I don't belong in the picture."

More nightmares followed. *Why?*

When Susan interviewed me for BRAVO's *Veterans Outlook* in 1990, we discussed my motivation for getting Maggie honored. We became friends through many long distance phone calls and letters. We were together in 1993 over Veteran's Day weekend in Washington, D.C. for the dedication of the Vietnam Women's Memorial and celebrated Maggie receiving the Presidential Medal of Freedom. We keep in constant contact.

The National Vietnam Veterans Coalition Breakfast
1993

Chris Noel at the National Vietnam Veterans Coalition Breakfast, 1993.

John "Top" Holland (President of AFFA—a POW/MIA organization) and Adrian Cronaur (AFRN DJ known for his "Goooooood Morning Vietnam").

Photos by Susan Christiansen.

I have not scratched the surface of Susan's life—that's for her to write about someday.

Maggie had told Melodye that Susan was in-country with her. This helped to explain why Melodye, Susan, and I were so connected. Each of us knew a part of Maggie's life, but all three of us had different parts. We had to get together to put those pieces together—like a large picture puzzle. Maggie protected us all in her own way.

I asked Susan about this. As we talked she began recalling things she had suppressed and denied for years. She has suffered her own PTSD, which is certified in her medical records, but didn't realize its severity until our conversations. Knowing how healthy it is for Veterans to talk or write about their experiences, I asked her to write as much as she could recall. It was like the floodgates opened, and she can now begin to understand why for years she has been plagued with nightmares. The following is Susan's story (as only she can tell it) of how she met Maggie, what they did together, how they were able to locate Mike—and how her life has changed.

MAGGIE AND ME

In the Words of Susan Christiansen

For the members of Special Forces,
whom I've known, loved, and lost:
Martha (COL Maggie) Raye
COL Rolande "Frenchy" Colas de la Nouye
Amundson
John Dean Bauer
Wilfred (Mad Dog) Collins
and the one who still acts as an anchor to my "Doc":
John (Top) Holland

Their bravery in combat is surpassed only by their
humanity and sense of justice in civilian life.
God Bless them all.

PART ONE

IT STARTED WITH MIKE

Hollywood in the infamous sixties. Wow! What a time and place. And I was there. Not to be part of the music scene, although I was. Not to participate in either the marijuana culture and "free love" confusion, although I did. Not to condemn and/or hail the war in Vietnam, although I did. I lived in Hollywood in the late sixties simply because that's where I had a great job.

I had passed the tests and been licensed as a primary private investigator. I worked as a skip-tracer for a collection agency. I could find anyone, anywhere, any time. I took pride in the fact that I was one of the best in my field.

Michael John Holmes Sr. My mentor. My guide. My friend. It started, all of it, with Mike. I was an abused child in my native Chicago. I was fifteen years old when we met. I was in Lutheran General Hospital's psych ward as a perpetual runaway. I detested violence and especially being violated. When I met Mike, I had chemical amnesia. He told me my name, where I was, why, and promised to protect me. Even if I were lost in China, Mike promised I could call collect, and he'd find me. He arranged my adoption to my Godparents, Elaine and Larry Messerman. He saved my life, and gave it back to me. He was the single most important person in my life at that time.

After my adoption, the first thing Mike wanted to do was marry me. His parents cheered, as did mine. Not me. (Although, if I had, I still wouldn't have a clue about the war in Vietnam, or ever have really known Maggie.) I wanted to be a beloved daughter, not a young wife. We married at sixteen but it was declared invalid since we didn't have parental consent at the time.

By the time I was eighteen, Mike had married someone else after he'd enlisted in the Army. My wonderful new family moved to California.

I already had three years of RN training behind me. But, I wasn't in the frame of mind yet to become a licensed nurse. Hence, the skip-tracing job.

I had two apartments in Hollywood by the time Mike was sent to Vietnam in 1969. There was the small, single flat, where I actually lived and managed the building. And, there was my boyfriend Tom's place, where I usually stayed. (My father was a real stickler about good old-fashioned morality.)

At Tom's, our penthouse neighbors were Burl Ives, his wife, Dorothy, and her son, Peter. We were all friends who socialized frequently.

One of the Ives' family's best friends was Rock Hudson. His best friend was Martha Raye. There was no social line to be crossed. Friends were friends, celebrity status so unimportant as to never even be mentioned. I knew Maggie was some kind of movie star, and I often heard her sing. In the beginning, that was all I knew of her. Immediately upon meeting, we liked each other and that was that.

Early in 1970, I noticed Maggie hadn't been around for quite some time. Rock simply said, "She's back in Vietnam." How exciting! My friend Mike was over there, too. Maybe they'd run into each other.

In June 1970, Maggie was back in California when I

received the first of thirteen telegrams: "We regret to inform you that 'SP/4 Michael J. Holmes' is listed as wounded, Missing In Action, and presumed dead." The world, as I knew it, ended there. I just didn't know that yet.

Photo contributed by Susan Christiansen. Her 1970 passport photo.

Hey! I'm a skip-tracer. I could find anyone who doesn't want to be found, anywhere in the United States. Surely finding Mike in a place about the same size and shape as California, and his wanting to be found, couldn't be much of a problem. I knew he wasn't dead. If he had been, I'd have felt it.

Mike's mom, Doris, his Auntie Ev, (who co-raised him and was a Veteran herself) and I took the Pentagon's phone number and formed a twenty-four hour phone tree. We called every hour, checking for information about Mike. On the third day, my voice was recognized by a Pentagon operator. He said the words that branded inside me and changed me forever: "Stop calling and bothering us! If there's any new information, we'll call you."

Everything I believed in was smashed to oblivion. How can they presume someone they can't find is wounded? How can they presume he was not only wounded and missing, but dead? Mike and I had just turned twenty years old. I felt a bilious rage I will never have the words to define.

I did what I was trained to do. I called the overseas phone operator, #47, and asked for the area code for Vietnam. Thank God, a lady I still only know as Operator #47, realized I was an innocent, uninformed, terrified kid.

Operator #47 led me into a quest that would control the rest of my life. If I'd have known what I was getting into, I'm not sure I would have proceeded. The point is, I did. Going by the last APO number I had from a letter from Mike, we began calling bases all over Vietnam.

Each call was an education unto itself. The guys, 16,000 miles away, were wonderful. Every single one gave us a follow-up phone number to try and locate Mike. Operator #47 and I always stayed on the phone as long as the transmission held. We laughed with the guys. We took phone numbers to assure their loved ones they were O.K. We answered questions about what was happening in The World—and learned how to lie with the best of them! Still, no Mike.

I finally went to Burl's. Maggie was there. "You sick or something?" she greeted me. I told her Mike was missing. I told her the government was not cooperating in trying to find him. I asked her what to do.

"Find him and get him out!" she replied. I'd never heard such commanding certainty.

I sought out a drug dealer everyone in Hollywood knew could obtain anything, and anything was for sale, at that time, in that place. John assured me he could obtain papers to get me to Vietnam—for $2,400.

Mike's Aunt Reen's church raised $1,900. We couldn't come up with the rest. I was losing too much time at work trying to find Mike by phone. Mom and Auntie Ev couldn't work, because they were sealed at home, awaiting word of Mike's fate.

I took my frustration to Maggie. "I can get to Vietnam," I explained, "but, we still have to raise another $500." Dead or alive, Mike was an American soldier and I couldn't live with the notion of never knowing what had happened to him in a place I couldn't even find on a map.

Since 1970, to this day in 1997, I remember every moment up to that point. For all these years, the story I have told as to how I found Mike and got him back to America has been that, eventually, Operator #47 and I found him by phone.

It's not a lie. It's just the way I remembered it. And, to this point, the memory was accurate. The phone calls are real. I did find Mike and get him home. Only—it wasn't until 1997 that I remembered how I actually did it.

It wasn't by way of any help from the government. It wasn't by way of long distance telephone. It was by way of Maggie.

A truth I had suppressed, for twenty-seven years

surfaced. They say, "The truth shall set you free." Or destroy you. It did both to me.

Note: Several physicians, four shrinks, and a king's ransom later, I finally understand what each and every one of them patiently tried to explain: Once someone's brain has been chemically altered (as mine was the eight days I endured clinical amnesia in Lutheran General Hospital, Park Ridge, Illinois), that part of the brain is forever weakened.

When a mental trauma occurs too severe to be dealt with, without intense therapy the mind retreats to the familiar: mental amnesia. The trauma is then in a category not yet fully explained nor understood by health care professionals—"Suppressed or Repressed memories."

The amnesiac (me, in this instance) is truly unaware the trauma has taken place.

Very few amnesiacs can suppress a memory their entire lives. However, something else in the course of living must trigger the memory. In rape survivors, it is usually a sexual incident.

In my case, it was the dedication of the Women in Military Service for America (WIMSA) Memorial.

There are always hints of memory repression. Mine were nightmares. Recurring nightmares. Always the same. Always terrifying. Always there, trying to remind the brain of what it is afraid to remember. It doesn't go away until the memory emerges.

The doctors believe bringing the suppressed memory into real memory is the beginning of the healing process. Unfortunately, they neglect to tell you that when the memory surfaces, it is not just a memory. It is as though the traumatic incident has just happened.

It is only since Noonie asked me to write this chapter that my time in Vietnam is surfacing, bit by anguished bit.

In my mind, I have just returned to The World from the hell of Vietnam.

PART TWO

Maggie and Susan do Vietnam

I was to leave for Vietnam in two weeks. In the meantime, I'd continue the endless phone calls with Operator #47. In two weeks, I knew I'd find some kind of way to obtain the additional $500 I needed to go to Vietnam. Somehow.

I opened my door to find Maggie in full uniform. "I didn't know you were in the military." She'd never mentioned that. I thought she went to Vietnam for USO shows. I was with the Red Cross. I counseled families with a loved one in Vietnam or returning home. They wouldn't send me to Vietnam because civilian women had to be twenty-one years old. Too bad the same wasn't true for men. They got to go as their senior trip, before they were even old enough to vote.

"Come on," Maggie ordered, dryly. I followed her outside, where a military Jeep was parked. Maggie handed me the keys and told me to drive her to Burl's.

I don't care how much of a couch-potato you are. Never on TV, or in any movie, have you witnessed a car chase as hysterically funny, or equally dangerous, as me trying to drive Maggie around in that Jeep! Only Guardian Angels and God Himself can explain how I didn't end up killing us both.

I had no idea what Maggie thought of this. She never uttered a word during the drive. Now, I guess, I understand she was probably too scared.

At Burl's, Maggie headed straight to the bar, pouring herself a tall glass of booze and sucking it down like water to someone stranded on a desert finding the last oasis.

In a few minutes, after silence, Maggie looked squarely at me and asked, "Is there *anything* you can do to help in Vietnam?" I told her about my Red Cross training, as well as my previous nurse's training.

Maggie slowly shook her head. "That'll do." She nodded to a uniformed soldier I hadn't noticed until then. He came up to me and said, "Come on. I'll take you home." I looked toward Maggie, but she didn't look back or acknowledge me or the soldier. In fact, she poured another drink and didn't say another word to me that evening. I left with the soldier, and he drove me back to my apartment in the same Jeep I had left in.

I grabbed my mail on the way to my apartment and, exhausted, I dumped the pile on my desk. After a shower, a call to Mike's mom, and a good cry, I turned on the TV next to the desk. The corner of a letter was sticking out from about the middle of the pile. It looked like the kind of envelope Mike sent his letters to me in.

I must have stared at that envelope for quite some time. It was from Mike. A message from the grave? I was afraid to open it and terrified not to.

"Dear Susan," it began, "Don't tell no one because no one's supposed to know. But, tomorrow, we go into Cambodia." I sat down, stunned, clutching the letter. Finally, I noticed the TV was on.

Suddenly I was looking into the eyes of President Nixon, pointing his finger, directly at me, "We have not committed troops to cross the border into Cambodia." I let out a scream, pulled the phone out of the wall, and threw it at the TV.

I believe it was the next day, although it may have been two days later when Maggie again showed up at my apartment. In uniform, she handed me a fairly full duffel bag. In it were Army green uniforms, the pockets stamped with the name, "HOLMES."

"Get dressed," Maggie ordered, pointing to the bag. On my way to the bathroom, I silently handed Maggie this last letter from Mike.

Once I was in uniform, Maggie nodded her approval.

She told me to add two civilian outfits to the bag, as well as items for personal hygiene. I did what I was told, without question. I locked the apartment and followed Maggie outside.

There, the same Jeep, with the same driver, waited. On the road, Maggie handed me a sheaf of military papers. "Read them. Memorize them. Live them."

Although we remained friends, my newly-found relationship with Tom had fizzled out. My sole focus was on finding Mike.

I was now Susan Holmes, sister of Michael Holmes, (his divorce was not yet final, and I couldn't claim wife status when the Army had a record of his actual wife) and born in 1948, not 1950, aging me to twenty-two years old. Old enough to go to Vietnam. I was listed as "Special medical escort, detached to Martha Raye: destination Vietnam."

We were driven to a military base, where a plane was being loaded with equipment and soldiers. Panicked, I begged Maggie, "What do I say? What do I do? They're going to know I'm not trained for the military!"

Maggie shrugged. "You outrank the grunts and flirt with the Brass." O.K. I climbed the ramp behind Maggie. We were going to Vietnam. Greetings. I was now considered, for all practical purposes, as a member of the armed forces, a nurse, assigned as medical personnel to Martha Raye, on special assignment.

I do not like to fly. No matter what I was taught about aerodynamics, I can't see what's lifting that heavy plane up or what's holding it up.

I didn't especially want to go to Vietnam. I just wanted Mike to come home. But, if he wasn't coming to me, I never gave a second thought about going to him.

I was scared half to death on the military transport plane. Commercial airplanes were frightening enough. This was white-knuckle horror. Although I didn't say anything about it, as usual Maggie knew what was happening anyway.

"Relax," she suggested, "this is the easy part."

Oh yeah.

Yeah.

Over an ocean that I was sure covered most of the globe, Maggie turned to me and asked casually, "You don't have any weird phobias or good habits, do you?"

I took it seriously. I am, to this day, more afraid of any form of rodent than any form of gunfire. I have been found up flagpoles, on top of other people's trucks, on roofs, and a host of places I don't care to admit to—after seeing a mouse, a rat, or even a hamster on the loose.

Maggie shook her head in great understanding. "Don't worry. You'll get over it in Vietnam."

"The phobia," I asked, "or the good habits?"

"Both," she answered, while the men within hearing range had themselves a hearty laugh.

My first memory, upon actually seeing Vietnam is twofold. How could some place so exquisitely blanketed with a million hues of pristine greenery be such a threat to my country that we were committed to destroying it? Secondly, somewhere, hidden in that natural beauty was Mike. Could he sense I was near? Was he in pain from wounds the government was not telling us about? Were the people of this exotic land hiding him from me? If I couldn't find Mike by jumping around with phone numbers, how could I tramp through this cramped world of large jungles and small villages and find him? My questions had no answers, and I remained silent.

The transport plane put down in Bangkok, Thailand.

I don't (yet) remember how we got there, but I remember a short stay in DaNang. Maggie was greeted like everyone's long-lost love. She and the troops laughed, threw puns, drank, smoked, and joked. This was not the same Maggie I knew in Hollywood, California, U.S.A.—if, indeed, there really was such a place. I was having a difficult time figuring out what was real and what wasn't. I didn't trust my own mind. Mainly, I simply observed, quietly.

When I was brought into a conversation, I reacted on automatic pilot, taking my cues from Maggie. I could laugh, joke, talk, smoke, etc. But, it seemed like I was watching someone other than me do it.

I wondered if Mike had felt the same way. Or, had actual military service prepared him for what I was completely unprepared for? And, where was he, anyway? Could someone please produce him, right NOW! So we could go home???

Instead, Maggie and I boarded a Huey headed for ChuLai (about seventy-five miles northeast of the Vietnam/Cambodian border) on our way to the last place Mike wrote he had been.

Leaning forward, I looked over Gunny's head, marveling at the living post card below us. Little villages, without telephone poles or electrical wires. Buildings, homes, made of the land's own material. I thought of the Native American Indians. They, too, had lived in harmony with the land—until, of course, the "new" Americans showed up. We took the land. We took the heritage. We killed those that disagreed. We kidnapped Africans, also living in harmony with their land. We enslaved them, in the name of "freedom," to work the land we took from the Indians.

I just couldn't imagine how small people in handmade homes, living off their land, 16,000 miles from our own, could be a threat to our "National Security." I wondered if they even knew of America before we showed up to...what? Give them our technology? Show them a better way? To do what? Or, the worst thought of all—were we simply doing to Vietnam and its people what we had done to America and Africa and their people?

On and off during various discussions in Vietnam I asked those questions. Not once did anyone have a single answer. This is what was going through my mind as the Huey glided through the air.

Then I started to see little puffs of smoke rising. And muted crackles, definitely not coming from the helicopter or any of us in it.

I didn't see or hear the ground fire that hit Gunny in his shoulder. He was shooting at the ground while bleeding in the chopper. I grabbed my medical kit and applied pressure while Maggie tersely watched.

The whole thing takes longer to tell than it did to happen. As suddenly as the shooting began, it stopped. There was general relief, and nervous laughter. If I felt or thought anything at all, it must have been, "Is this normal?" Or, perhaps, "What's 'normal'?"

I'd been shot at by the National Guard during the Chicago riots, just because I was there. I'd been shot at by the National Guard at Kent State, just because I was there. And that was in America, by the American military. So, who and why was I being shot at now? Americans or Vietnamese? I could no longer define reality. What was, was. That's all.

Soon, we landed at ChuLai. No fuss. No muss. An easy landing. Gunny gave a half-salute and headed toward the largest building in sight. The rest of us meandered off in different directions.

Then it hit me. There were buildings here. Not exactly Chicago skyscrapers. Certainly not the pastel dwellings in California. But, buildings they were. Somehow, I derived a sense of well-being in that.

Maggie and I had a place to store our duffel bags, sleep, and take shelter. She told me when to eat and when to lay down. I helped out whomever I could, whatever was happening.

Not much was. Mainly, I was bored. Bored was better than riding on what passed as dirt roads in the back seat of a Jeep. Boring was better than being shot at while in the air. Boring was better. Period.

Bored, Maggie and I were sitting on piles of sand-bags, smoking, talking to some of the guys that were sitting around with us. She asked the questions. She had all along. "Seen another Holmes around?" she'd ask casually. "Susan's brother is over here." The guys liked that. But, no one remembered a six foot five-inch blonde with green eyes, by the name of Holmes or any other name.

I was sipping a warm soda when everyone on the bags scattered. I slid to the ground and stood there, taking in all the very sudden, very unboring activity. Maggie had been the first one up and on the run. She hadn't even glanced at me as she sprinted toward the largest building.

Then, I could hear it. You only have to hear artillery fire once to recognize it forever. And that's what I was hearing. In the distance I could hear the roar of multiple choppers, too. A soldier with an M-16 in one hand pushed me hard from behind, screaming at me as he ran, "Go!" I could have taken the Gold at the Olympics when I ran for the hospital Maggie had entered only seconds before.

The hospital didn't look anything like any hospital I'd ever trained at. I wasn't surprised—I just happened to notice.

In front of me were tables, all filled with blood-soaked soldiers. Behind me, litters were piling up, more blood-soaked soldiers on each. The sounds of the heli-copters landing, taking off, landing, blocked out most other sounds.

Elbow deep in the blood of a teenager on a table, Maggie screamed at me, "Set up triage! NOW!!"

"Triage" was not yet a word used commonly in hospitals in the United States. In fact, I never heard the word before Maggie ordered me to set it up. But, somehow, I suddenly knew, without question, what I was supposed to do.

I went from litter to litter, spending mere seconds assessing the condition of their occupants. I pulled whoever I considered the most seriously wounded, but still capable of sustaining life, to the front. The ones I knew couldn't be helped, at least not in time, I pulled further back. I tried to smile, or squeeze a hand, of each man. And I saw understanding, not contempt, in their eyes. When I came across a troop without vital signs, I whispered, "God Bless you. I'm sorry." Then I dragged their litters to the far side of "my" triage area.

I looked into the eyes of the wounded soldier, the ones who could open them, and the faces of every single troop I assessed and/or treated. Every second, in the back of my mind, every single second as I worked was the same identical thought: What if the troop I was working on was Mike? What if the troop I was working on, wasn't? I saw a part of him in each life—and—death—I took care of.

Webster was wrong. Regardless of what definition in the dictionary of torture, it is wrong. THIS is the true definition of pure torture.

Just looking, praying, sorting out bodies and body parts. There was nothing else I could possibly do. It wasn't enough. It was simply all I could do.

There was no one to assist me in separating the wounded. However, different troops rolled the "mended" from the surgical tables to a recovery area. Other troops removed the dead from triage as quickly, as yet others brought more wounded in.

It continued. Endlessly. Throughout that whole night. Into the next day. Then it was night again. Just when I would think things were slowing down, they speeded up.

There were no time-outs. No potty breaks. No cigarette breaks. The only breaks were the bodies of American soldiers.

It seemed to me, at the time, every troop in Vietnam had been wounded, maimed, or killed. I couldn't reason the sheer numbers coming in to be treated.

When things really did begin to slow down, I was in for more surprises. Not shocks, mind you. I was beyond that. Just surprises.

Troops who were brought in to be treated, but who were not mortally wounded, pitched in to help in any way they could function. Many men told me, "I'm O.K. Help him," pointing at someone who the wounded deemed more wounded than himself. Many men wrapped makeshift bandages over their wounds and pitched in with others still waiting just to get into triage.

The first time I heard an accent that wasn't "American" by my experience, I expected to be shot. I was too busy to care, so I kept on working. No one had mentioned the thousands of troops from Canada, Australia, New Zealand, Mexico, Panama, and a dozen other countries who were fighting alongside our own.

In "The World," I had survived race riots. And, I had heard there was a lot of hate among our own people since Martin Luther King, Jr. had been assassinated. I'm proud to say I saw no evidence of this in Vietnam. No one was white, or black, or red, or purple, or green. We were all Americans and that was enough.

When it came to the Vietnamese, that was a different story. We were "round eyes;" they were "gooks." During the day, Vietnamese worked alongside Americans on the bases. They are a beautiful race of people. Polite. Obedient. Hard-working. I was constantly being warned not to make friends; at night they were all the same—Charlie, the enemy.

Finally, when I had decided I was born in Triage, had spent every day of my life in Triage, and would keep going until I fell over dead in Triage, things really did begin to slow down.

Sometime during the night, I'd been dimly aware that this base was under fire. I was nearly deafened by the monsoons and shelling, on top of all the other sounds of combat. There were dings as bullets hit the hospital. You could see the indents in the walls. As far as I know, no one was hit while inside the hospital.

What's astounding is that in the middle of all the confusion and chaos, everyone around me just kept doing their jobs. Without complaint. Without self-pity. Without argument or grumbling.

When I realized no more wounded were being brought in, I began to help out in the surgical theater. Mainly, I put in IVs, cleaned wounds, wrapped wounds, and did some minor stitching. The more serious injuries were being handled by professionals who actually knew what they were doing.

It was daylight when Maggie took my arm and led me outside. It wasn't raining. That was my first thought. My second was, "There's no visible blood!"

Maggie led me, as if I were a small child, to our place. We grabbed some soggy clean uniforms and personal hygiene stuff and headed for what passed as the showers. No hot bubble baths in Vietnam. A rinse. Scrap off blood and everything else clinging to your body, rinse again, for about three seconds, slip into your uniform, and it's someone else's turn.

On our way to grab some food, I walked silently beside Maggie. Without preamble, she squeezed my arm. "Not bad for an FNG, Captain," she smiled her crooked smile.

The papers Maggie provided me listed me as a first lieutenant. I had just received a field promotion. I knew I'd never wear the bars or truly carry the status, but I will always be proud that Maggie was proud of me.

We sat next to each other on a bench. A table was between our bench and the one on the other side. No one looked like a teenager anymore. These were brave men and women who had seen the worst life has to offer. I was awed that I was accepted as "one of the guys," without question.

Maggie's *modus operandi* (MO) again prevailed. She ate, drank, smoked, and joked, her energy limitless. I stirred my food around the plate. There wasn't a single thought in my mind.

I sort of heard bits and pieces of conversation, but I didn't even try to put them together. Maggie suddenly swung around to a man on the other side of our table and a couple of seats down.

"What did you say?" she demanded. I stared at her in utter confusion. I hadn't heard him say a thing, and I was closer. She'd been in an altogether different conversation with someone else. How did she hear anything this man had to say?

"All I said," he looked as confused as I felt, "was Holmes, huh?"

Maggie looked at me. I looked down at the name on my uniform, as though it was the first time I'd ever heard the name.

"Yeah." I said, blandly.

Getting a reaction, the medevac pilot smiled at me and said, "I flew a guy out last night who said his name was Holmes."

"What do you mean," Maggie said carefully, "He said his name was Holmes?"

"No ID," the pilot answered, taking a bite and continuing. "No wallet. No tags. Pretty banged up," he shrugged.

"Big guy?" Maggie asked.

"Yeah. I'd say so."

I was awake and alert again. Now I remembered

what I was doing here.

"Blonde? Green eyes?" I demanded.

"Her brother's over here," Maggie interjected.

"Blonde, I guess," he answered helpfully. "Had his eyes bandaged. Got hit in Cambodia. We'd have popped him here, but you had a hot LZ."

In one crisp move, Maggie was up and out of there, me following. In the radio room, Maggie got through to wherever the pilot said he had taken Holmes. I never did hear the rest of their conversation. I had retreated into myself, afraid of what I might—or might not—hear.

I stood at Maggie's side as she took over. She'd ask the radio man a question. He'd repeat it into the phone. She'd ask me a question. I'd answer Maggie. She'd repeat it to the radio man. He'd repeat it into the phone. And so it went.

We had found and identified Mike.

He was to be taken out of lock-down (no ID, you get locked down). But, Mike's sister, a Captain in the United States Army—according to Maggie—had just ID'd him. Now, he'd be shipped to Tokyo for treatment.

"I want to go to Japan!" I begged Maggie.

"No," she answered.

"Why" was not a question you asked in Vietnam. I wanted to go to Japan. I wanted to be Mike's nurse. I wanted to take him home. Maggie said "No," and I never thought to question her wisdom.

That night began like our first night in ChuLai. We were sitting around on piles of sandbags, gabbing away. The rain had stopped, and there were no in-coming. Looking around, I suddenly spied something I'd never seen before.

"Look, Maggie!" I enthused, "a Vietnamese pig. It doesn't have a curly tail like American pigs!" I was

enthralled, and it wasn't until years later that I understood the soldier's laughter. No one had ever mentioned
three foot-long Vietnamese rats. I have a funny feeling
that if I had known about them then, Mike might still be
MIA today.

Maggie told me to get ready to go the next day. I was
surprised when I found out I was going back to The
World. Maggie would be staying in Vietnam.

"You want to be there when Mike gets home, don't
you?" she asked, without a hint of it being a question.

As we hugged good-bye, Maggie ordered me to
change into civilian clothes on the plane. Put my uniform and dog tags in my duffel bag, and she'd take it
from there. I'd learned to follow orders without question and didn't question them now. She kissed me on
the cheek and whispered, "God Bless."

At the airport, the same driver who had taken us to
and from Burl's, and then to the plane, met me. His
uniform had no name on it. I'd never heard Maggie call
him by name, and I didn't ask. I hadn't even noticed that
before Vietnam. When we reached my apartment he
told me to leave my duffel bag in the Jeep. I did. He left,
and I've never seen him again—that I know of.

PART THREE

THE WORLD

I slept for two days; then I put a call in to Japan.

At first, Operator #47 and I were getting frustrated. No matter how many times our call was transferred, no one would even acknowledge Mike was there.

I finally pulled rank. I addressed everyone as "Private," regardless of their rank, announcing, "This is Captain Susan Holmes. If I do not speak to SP/4 Michael J. Holmes within the next minute, you will be a Private by morning!"

The voice rang through, "Susan?" I hadn't said a word, since I'd told the last man I threatened that I was Mike's sister. (He's an only child.)

"Is this SP/4 Michael J. Holmes?" Operator #47 demanded.

Mike gave his name, rank, and serial number.

"Your party is on the line," Operator #47 sobbed. "Congratulations. Good luck."

I couldn't answer either the operator or Mike. All I could mutter was, "Mike."

He tried. He really tried, to talk to me. After several tries, he finally told me I was hyperventilating. He told me to breathe into my cupped fists. I did.

"Do you know what time it is here?" Mike almost laughed.

My watch was still set for his time-zone. He was impressed I knew it was 4:00 A.M. there, and they had to wheel his bed to the phone.

"How did you find me here?" Mike asked, once he knew I could talk.

"I'll tell you when you get home," I answered tiredly. He never did ask again.

"Let me tell you what happened, so you won't be surprised," Mike offered gently.

"Let me tell *you* what happened, so you will be surprised," I counter-offered. And I did tell him. Again, he has never questioned how I knew.

Then, I told him to stay by the phone. The operator I was working with was going to patch his mother and Auntie Ev through to him on my line. I figured hearing from me first would lessen the shock.

"Mom?" I was slightly hesitant. "I found Mike. He's alive. He'll be coming home soon."

Auntie Ev was patched in by then. "How badly is he hurt?" she demanded in a military fashion.

"He had some superficial shrapnel wounds, mostly to his left arm. And, he has malaria," I added.

"They're not sending him back to that damn war, are they?" Mom demanded.

"Well, no. He's also blind in his right eye. A piece of shrapnel severed his optic nerve." Just what she needed to hear.

It took awhile to calm everyone down, obviously. I asked Mom and Auntie Ev to acknowledge his wounds, but casually brush them off. "Just be glad he's alive," I suggested, I wasn't a mother, yet, but I was a daughter, thanks to Mike. I knew how much worse he'd feel if his family got hysterical.

They talked. We talked. Mike mentioned that he was happily surprised to find out he was being shipped to California, rather than Illinois, where he'd enlisted.

With the $1,900 Aunt Reen's church had raised, Mike's Mom flew out to California to wait with me for Mike's arrival.

Tom had taken me to the airport to pick up Mom. The Jeep was still parked at my apartment, but I knew better than to try to drive it. I figured "soldier no name" would show up to take us to Mike when we got word of what base in California he would land.

For the next week or so, Mom and I walked around

bruised. Every time the phone rang, we'd clobber each other trying to get to it first. When *the call* finally came, Mike wasn't in California after all. He was in Great Lakes; the closest base to where he had enlisted. Mom decided she'd stay another couple weeks with me, as long as she was already in California, and Mike was in a hospital over 2,000 miles away.

"Now," Mom said with heady relief, "things can go back to normal."

I didn't tell her then that there is no such thing as "normal." I wanted to give her the last peace of mind I knew she would ever have for the rest of her life.

When we next ventured outdoors, the Jeep (with my duffel bag) was gone.

PART FOUR

TOGETHER THEN—TOGETHER AGAIN

Life did go on. I flew to Illinois. Mike and I flew back to California. We got married. We got divorced. We never talked about why. We never talked about Vietnam after our first week together. Or rather, he talked. I questioned, innocently, and answered whatever I was asked. Mike was not the same man when he came out of Vietnam that he had been before he went. I guess I was different, too. Neither of us talked about it. The subject of Vietnam never came up again until 1985 when we had both divorced other partners, for the second time. (Not including our marriage to each other.)

I met and married Chris, a two-tour engineer. We had kids. Mike went back to Illinois. Eventually, Chris and I did too, for a short time, before again returning to California. Chris and I divorced.

I hadn't known Chris before he went to Vietnam. But, he and Mike were so much alike as Veterans; I'd often lament they were interchangeable. I didn't yet understand it. And I couldn't live with it.

So, I spent the late seventies and early eighties cooking, cleaning, writing children's stories for my three babies: Bryan, Tammy, and Ricky. I managed the apartment building we lived in. We got by.

Every couple of years, I'd get a Christmas card signed, "Bless You, Maggie."

I hadn't seen or talked to Maggie in years. I was surprised she remembered me from Burl's. It was a pleasant surprise, but slightly unnerving.

You see, from the time I talked to Mike in Japan until 1997, I had absolutely no memory of having gone to Vietnam.

In 1980 I moved my children to Yucca Valley, California. A desert town of about 2,500 people, only 17 miles from the U.S. largest Marine base, in Twenty-nine Palms.

I bought a house on an isolated mesa in the mountains. I did a lot of community service, primarily with Vietnam Veterans and their families.

It got to the point where the sheriff's station and the hospital had me on twenty-four hour standby. If a Veteran went into flashback, especially if weapons were involved, I was called in first. There had already been two firefights under those conditions before I became involved. I didn't want the Veterans to hurt the cops, not the other way around as the sheriff mistakenly presumed.

No one ever got hurt that way. When the hospital, sheriffs or Veterans asked how I knew the way to talk a man out of a flashback, I'd answer, "I've been married to two Vietnam Vets, and I'm alive to talk about it."

The negative side to this was a recurring dream: I am riding in the back of a Jeep. There is a military driver and Martha Raye is in the passenger seat. We were riding in the purest black of night, through a jungle on a tiny dirt road. When we'd hit a stone, or large bump, my body would flip-flop around. We hit an enormous rock, and I was thrown from the Jeep into a narrow tunnel. I was merely annoyed, expecting that Ms. Raye and the driver would grab me out within seconds.

Instead, I kept almost floating downward. There was no light whatsoever, and I was completely blind. I reached out to the sides of the tunnel for a root or something to grab onto. The more effort I put into trying to break the fall, the faster I descended, and the wider the tunnel became. I was scared, but, not unduly. My life has been an eleventh-hour save since I was a fetus.

The eleventh-hour came and went. I knew there was to be no rescue when sweat literally poured from me as I saw, not too much farther below, the bright fires of hell.

I knew I would either be engulfed by the flames, or splat when I hit bottom. Either way, I knew I was dead.

That's when I'd always wake up. And my nightie was always saturated with sweat.

Then, I became involved with the Agent Orange lawsuit.

Next, I worked with the Inland Empire Vet Center.

The more I worked with Veterans, the more frequent the nightmares.

With no credentials whatsoever, I began the advice column, "Vet Forum" out of the Twenty-nine Palms newspaper, *The Desert Trail.* Within three weeks, other publications were running my column.

Soon, I joined a Veterans organization, BRAVO, which put out a monthly Veteran magazine, *Veterans Outlook.* And the VVA. And I worked on "Stand Down" assisting homeless Veterans and their families.

Susan Christiansen using Britt Small's equipment to make a keynote address in Washington, DC, 1990. Photo contributed by Susan Christiansen.

Comedian Joey Bishop being interviewed by Susan Christiansen during Stand Down 1991. Joey has been very active in promoting Veterans' causes. Photo contributed by Susan Christiansen.

People stopped me everywhere to ask how I knew just the right answers the Veterans and their families needed. Always my same reply, "I was married to two Vietnam Veterans."

It never occurred to me that my ex-husbands and I had never discussed their experiences in Vietnam. I didn't even realize the most reading I did about the war was my own! How did I know the questions—and answers? I decided not to ask myself.

In 1982, I heard there was going to be an unveiling of a Vietnam Veterans Memorial, in Washington, D.C. I envisioned a huge granite boulder engraved with names, almost like graffiti. My nightmare visited nightly.

So, I took out a loan, sent my children to my mother and prepared to go to "SALUTE."

Here I was writing a successful advice column to and about Veterans without any background or first-hand knowledge. What if "Vet Forum" were successful but inaccurate? Might I actually be doing my readers more harm than good? I decided "SALUTE" was the perfect opportunity to be with a large group of Veterans who could let me know if "Vet Forum" was the right thing for me to be doing.

"SALUTE." The Wall. Britt Small & Festival. For the first time in my life, I felt as though I belonged. I felt an absence of all negativity. Most importantly, I could physically feel the power of God's loving arms encircling us all in one family embrace.

Colonel Earl Hopper (father of LTC Earl Hopper, Jr., USAF MIA 10 January 1968) and Britt Small offering each other support. Photo by Susan Christiansen.

I might be nuts anywhere else but, at The Wall, I was perfect, just being "Susan."

THE VIETNAM VETERANS MEMORIAL...THE WALL.

Photo by Susan Christiansen.

The Wall was—and is—*home* to me. It is the only place on earth I don't have to do anything but be there. It is the safe haven I've sought all my life.

From that point on, if I heard of an event where Vietnam Veterans gathered, I was there. Often, so was Martha Raye.

At one of these events, I was talking with a group of Veterans when one excitedly jumped up calling gleefully "Colonel Maggie!" He tried to introduce us as Maggie recalled meeting this Vet over twenty years earlier. She remembered every detail. I was enthralled with her memory.

"We've met," Maggie addressed me.

"Of course," I answered warmly, "at Burl Ives' place in the sixties."

"Yes," Maggie said softly (especially for her) all the while looking at me so oddly, I felt uncomfortable.

"We'll have to talk," she added.

"I'd love to," I informed her. But I didn't see her again at that event.

When the statute of "The Three Servicemen" was to be dedicated in 1984, I again took out a loan so I might attend. I wanted to be back at The Wall to see if the feelings I remembered were as warm and fuzzy as I believed them to be.

THE THREE SERVICEMEN

Photo by Susan Christiansen.

They were. And, even more so. "SALUTE II" was one of the greatest experiences I've ever had. But something odd was beginning to happen. Veterans started greeting me with, "Remember me? We met in DaNang, in 1970."

"I'm sorry. I was with the Red Cross stateside during the war."

Every time it happened, the Veteran would walk away, looking hurt and confused. I began to wonder whom I so closely resembled.

As more and more Veteran events included me, I was approached more and more often by Veterans who placed me in Vietnam in 1970. I was completely bewildered that the year always stayed the same. The month of June was frequently mentioned. The places—DaNang and ChuLai— were noted.

After I was truly rooted in the Vietnam Veterans Community, I set out to answer the question: "...and, its 1-2-3-, what were we fighting for?"

The quest took five years. The final answers, the real ones, landed in my post office box. The Pentagon, quite by accident, I'm absolutely certain (since they've been trying to get those papers, the originals, back, since 1986), sent me "Classified" documents. In them were the missing pieces. Now I knew *why* we were in Vietnam. And a lot more that I wasn't looking for and didn't particularly want to know.

In 1985, I was working with BRAVO when Mayor Koch of New York City threw the Vietnam Veterans a "Welcome Home" ticker-tape parade. It was decided that I would lead the Southern California Honor Battalion. I was told I was the only woman to lead a delegation. I was the only non-Veteran to lead a delegation. I was the only one who had never served in the military to lead a delegation.

The privilege was so enormous, it was hard to accept. There was one little problem. I wanted Mike at my side in that parade. I hadn't seen him since 1972. However, his mother and I had been in contact all those years. Mike and I had kept track of each other's lives. We were both single parents now. It was time to reunite. Again.

Mike Holmes and Susan Christiansen in Central Park after the parade, 1985. Photo contributed by Susan Christiansen.

We did it together. And we bonded more strongly than in the sixties or seventies. We joked about our once every decade love affair and felt like no time had passed at all.

Mike lived in Wisconsin now with his mother and son, Michael Jr. Mike asked me to spend the summer with him. Again, the kids were shipped off to Nana's, and I was sent off to Mike.

My children were thirteen, twelve, and eleven years old. Mikey was seven. And, against all odds, we had conceived Keith, although we didn't know it yet.

Mike, Mom, Auntie Ev, Mikey, and I decided to drive back to California in two cars.

Mikey and my kids were siblings from the moment they met. For once in our lives, Mike, me, and the kids lived as a real family. And, we were happy and content.

I had to go for a physical. I'd had a mild heart attack right before I left for Wisconsin. My doctor, a woman Veteran, wanted to see if my body was assimilating the heart medication. It was. That would be good for my pregnancy.

PREGNANCY!?

Of all of us, I still don't know who was more in a state of shock. Pregnant at thirty-five? With a career in the Veteran Community I adored? I had to remind us all that God has a sense of humor.

Mike had one more year of college to become a Veteran psychologist. He would take his family back to Wisconsin, have his credits transferred to California, and we would spend our lives happily ever after.

I continued my work within the Veteran Community throughout my pregnancy. I had to. Mike never came back to California, and there was no explanation.

BRAVO founders, Tony and Barbara Diamond, became Keith's Godparents. Mike had wanted to name Keith, Tiberius Wolfgang. I said fine. I wanted his son so badly, I was certain the child would be a girl I'd name Sara Elisabeth. Mike was ecstatic when our son was born, even with the name change.

Now, I was a single parent with *four* children. And I kept on within the Veteran Community. Maggie and I kept meeting at events. We were overjoyed every time we ran into each other. And each time, Maggie would tell me, "We'll talk."

From 1984 to this day, I spend the month of Memorial Day, as well as the month of Veteran's Day, at The Wall. I had joined Americans For Freedom Always (AFFA) by now. Its entire purpose is to change the "Missing Service Personnel Act of 1942," whereby any POW/MIA could be declared dead, without any kind of proof, after one year. What if I hadn't found Mike—by phone, when he was MIA? I couldn't endure other families' pain and loss. Besides, I was now the mother of three sons. The government of the United States of America was not going to do to my sons what they had done to their fathers. Not while I had a single breath left in me.

Maggie and I spoke infrequently by phone all this time when we were between Veteran events. She backed me all the way.

Then, I got word Maggie had never received the Presidential Medal of Freedom. I had done exactly the same thing I detested the government doing—presume she had it. That's when I met Noonie. Together, we worked (primarily her) endlessly to right that wrong.

Noonie and I had visited with Maggie in August, 1990. Everything was wonderful among us. Noonie was with her again in August, 1991. Then, in October 1991, I found out Maggie at seventy-five had suddenly eloped with forty-two-year-old Mark Harris.

First, I phoned Noonie, sending her spinning. Then I called Maggie. Mark answered. I had gotten word that Maggie's beloved Special Forces and her enduring Airborne troops couldn't get through to her. Noonie and I were the only ones who could.

"So you're Susan!" Mark greeted me with enthusiasm. We chatted and Mark offered, "You're one of my wife's favorite people. I know she'd love to see you. Would you consider spending at least this weekend with us?"

This was definitely not making sense. So, I told Mark, "I have a male roommate, and I'd hate to leave him." I had known Mike Deason and his family since 1980, when they'd built my house in the mountains. After our divorces, we'd become roommates. I knew Mike D. would protect me—and Maggie—with his life. And, since I didn't know what Maggie had gotten herself into or what I was about to find, I had no intention of going there alone. It never even entered my mind that when I said "Mike" Mark took it as my ex-husband Mike from Vietnam rather than Mike D. who is the best friend I've ever had.

Mike D. and I set out for Maggie's.

As always, Maggie greeted me with loving warmth.

"We're never together very long," she looked intensely into my eyes and through me, "to get close enough. To talk."

Maggie had had her stroke by then. She didn't get around well, so we spent the first two days playing penny poker, watching her movies, television show videos, and girl chatter. When she heard my daughter, Tammy, was in a private school not too far from her "Team House," Maggie insisted I bring Tammy back with me so she could meet her.

You'd have thought Tammy was Maggie's grandchild by the way they instantly took to each other! I loved that part, as did my daughter and Mike.

Maggie and I spent an enormous amount of time talking about her precious Melodye and my Tammy.

Just two old friends sharing in the delights of motherhood.

On the third day, Maggie and I got into some serious talk. "Melodye, Noonie, and you are the only three people I authorize to write about me. No one else. And, you have to promise not to do it until I'm dead."

This time, I asked the forbidden question: "Why?"

"I don't want to be embarrassed or embarrass anyone else," was her explanation. Of course, I agreed to it. I knew Noonie would. I'd never met Melodye, but I figured her mother knew she'd go along with it too. Maggie had always said, "I only served one tour of labor and motherhood."

Mark knew this. So, he sent Mike D. back to Yucca Valley to pick up my typewriter, Mike's tools, (Mike D. is a licensed contractor, and Mark wanted to make some improvements on Maggie's house) and someone we could trust to help Mike out.

Now, Tammy, Mike D., his sister Pam, and I were all staying at Maggie's.

Mark put us all to work immediately. Mike D. and Pam worked on the house. Tammy sat in bed with Maggie to watch movies. Mark set me and my typewriter at the breakfast nook. "You're the only one my wife will talk to about Vietnam," Mark began, energetically.

I stopped him immediately. "I can't write about that until after Maggie passes away."

Mark took it in stride. "O.K. Let's write about *me*," he offered cheerfully. Within minutes, Maggie sent Tammy to bring Mark and me to her bedroom.

"Susan's here to talk to *me*," she admonished her new groom. "No writing. This is a visit." She told him quite firmly.

Looking at me, Maggie said, "I'm ready for a nap. But as soon as I wake up, you and me are going to have a serious talk."

Before Maggie awoke from her nap, Tammy was back at school. Mike D., Pam, and I were on our way back to Yucca Valley.

Members of Special Forces were keeping a close eye on Maggie, God love 'em all. Mark was making frequent trips to New York. I was notified the next time he was out of town. I called Maggie with Noonie on a three-way call.

Although Maggie was thrilled to hear from us, what she really wanted was to know why we were gone when she awoke from her nap. I told her. She told me how to handle it. This was the last time I ever saw Maggie, as well as the last time we ever spoke.

This is not the format for those details. You can read them in my own forthcoming book.

PART FIVE

THE AFTERMATH

The recurring nightmare became an almost nightly experience. It just wouldn't go away, and I didn't know why.

I was talking to Melodye right before Memorial Day, 1997 and confiding how my life was falling into shambles. The government had illegally seized the house I'd paid for the last fifteen years. Most of my family members had died, almost one a month, between 1995-1997. My older kids had all moved to other states, getting on with their own lives. Mike D. had left the desert. I had another mild heart attack and stroke. I had taken Tammy, my grandson Darrian (I helped deliver him! Sorry. There are just some things worth bragging about), at three months old and my now nine-year-old son, Keith, to Wisconsin, going thousands of dollars in debt. I wanted Mike to meet the son he'd never laid eyes on and see our first grandbaby. I had to do it. At the rate my loved ones were dying, I wanted to do this before one of us died. (Mike didn't know we were coming until I put Darrian in his arms. Ha! Ha! I *earned* that one!)

"Oh, yeah," Melodye exclaimed, after we discussed Mike's reaction. "I wanted to ask you something: my mother told me all about what you and she did right before she died. But, she didn't tell me how you met. Was it in Vietnam?"

"What?" I asked, clutching my heart.

"Was it Vietnam?" she repeated.

"What makes you think I was in Vietnam with your mother?" I asked with a calmness I wasn't feeling.

"She told me all about it." Melodye answered.

"Your mother told you all about what *we* did in Vietnam together?" I was incredulous. Maggie's photographic memory.

All the Veterans over a fifteen-year span that recognized me from Vietnam...in 1970. All the knowledge of that war I had but couldn't explain. The recurring nightmare.

"Can I call you back, Melodye?" I asked.

Of course I could. That's what friends are for, right?

I called Mike's mother. "Mom," I began foolishly, "When Mike was MIA in Vietnam, did I ever go over there?"

"For twenty-seven years I keep telling you both that neither of you have been the same since Mike came back," she said, irritated.

"Yes, I know," I agreed, "but, was it just Mike that came back from Vietnam, or was I there?"

"It's not like you're a Vietnam Vet or anything," Mom sighed. "You were only in Vietnam eleven days."

Shaking, I called my biological father, Mel. He had kept track of my life since my adoption.

"Do you happen to know if I was ever in Vietnam?" I asked, fearing his answer.

"Yes, of course you were. When your husband was missing." Adding, "But you weren't there too long. I never saw combat when I was in the Army."

"Wait a minute!" I yelled. "You were in the Army? I was in Vietnam?"

"Of course," he answered, "don't you know that?"

He must have repeated it several times before it sank in.

I took two Valium and a heart pill and put myself to sleep. When I awoke, my bedroom was a tornado survivor, and I remembered going to Vietnam.

I haven't had the nightmare since.

As of this writing, I still don't remember all eleven days, if indeed, that was how long I was there. At strange times, bits and pieces come back. But, this jigsaw puzzle is far from finished.

The WIMSA Memorial dedication was less than sixty days away. I was invited to take part in the first and only Memorial dedicated to "Women Who Served."

I'm proud of that. But, just as uncomfortable.

I believe all those times Maggie told me "We'll talk" was because she was the only person in The World who knew that I didn't know! I believe she told Melodye so someday I would have a way to confirm it. I believe that's why Maggie and I stayed in touch throughout four decades. I believe that's why I was the only invited visitor to Maggie's Team House after her marriage to Mark Harris.

Now, there's a side of me naked and exposed. I was barely twenty years old when I went to Vietnam. I wasn't trained. I was inexperienced. I was ignorant of the war, itself. And worst of all, at least once, I set up Triage, determining who would be treated and who would wait—possibly too long. How many mistakes did I make? What would I have done differently, if I had known what I was doing in the first place?

Never mind what this new knowledge of my old past is doing to me. What about all those Veterans who recognized me for fifteen years, and were disappointed by my denial? How badly have I messed up their confidence in their own memories?

Then, Noonie called. Could I please expand on my relationship with Maggie and explain about what happened to us in Vietnam for this book? And, as I write, more memories flood my mind.

"It'll help you heal," Noonie insisted. "Get it all out in the open, and you'll begin to heal. Isn't that how you counsel Veterans?"

Yep. That's exactly what I counsel Veterans to do. But, I'm not a Veteran. My most popular column has always been, "John Q. & Jane Z. Wannabee." I took great pleasure in exposing the low-lifes who hang on to the Veterans' earned glory.

I wasn't in the military. I didn't go to Vietnam for patriotic reasons. I wasn't in Vietnam with the Red Cross. I had no altruistic motives of being any use to the troops. I was in Vietnam for the most selfish of reasons: I had to find Mike.

But, I was there. I assumed the role of an Army nurse during a firefight. God alone, and Maggie alongside Him, know what else I did in Southeast Asia.

So, am I a total civilian?

I thought I knew by now who and what I am. Wrong! I don't have a clue to where I fit into today's society.

That's why I am schooled to nearly the point of graduation and "legal" licensing—and quit. I've developed a second phobia—I won't allow any government agency to number and license and control me ever again.

I beg God's and the Veteran's forgiveness for any harm I might have done. I thank God, from my very soul, for any good I may have accomplished.

The Veterans I've spoken to in these last few months have been the biggest surprise of all. I have "confessed" to each that I was there. Every single one had identical answers, "Yeah, I know that. I figured you just don't want to talk about it." Thanks, my Veteran Brothers and Sisters or cousins, or wherever I fit into your lives. You are all loving, tolerant, understanding, and true heroes.

As Maggie would say, "God Bless."

Yes, Noonie. I'll write this for you. But, could you do me one little favor? You tell Mike. He's the only other person that doesn't know.

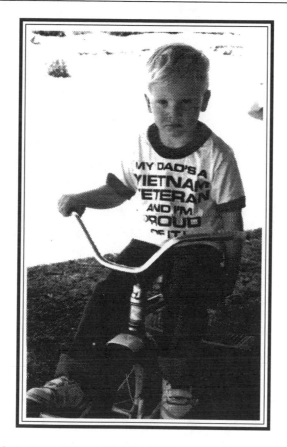

Keith Anthony Edward Michael Holmes, born 13 April 1986,
son of Michael and Susan Holmes (Christiansen).

Photo by Susan Christiansen.

The end result was well worth the journey.

DISCLAIMER NOTE: If draft dodgers can receive amnesty for running, illegally, from their obligation to serve their country, I pray for amnesty in running, illegally, to my obligation to serve my country. If amnesty is not granted me, please consider this a work of fiction. I still have a little son-of-a-Vet to raise.

∽ THANK YOU ∽

SUSAN CHRISTIANSEN

FOR SHARING

THIS STORY WITH SO MANY PEOPLE

Author and Publisher

5

ALL ABOARD

———————————⬤———————————

Writing *Memories of Maggie* has changed my life. My days are filled with presentations, writing, book signings, and traveling. After spending winter in Texas, I boarded Amtrak's Texas Eagle for a trip to my home outside Albany, New York. Train rides provide time to relax. I observed the change from the flat, brown, sunburnt topography of central Texas to green hills in Arkansas. Outside Saint Louis the train crossed the river into Illinois with its farmlands and small communities. My thoughts drifted to two men from Illinois who wrote to me about Martha Raye.

Colonel John Shine from Glenview served during World War II. He retired from the Marine Corps Reserve. John was in the South Pacific when Maggie was there. Richard Largen, now retired from the Army's Special Forces, resides in Bethalto. Maggie was in the last camp he served in Vietnam. It was an "A" Detachment in 1966 at MaiLinh, CheoReo, which was located just south of Pleiku.

In Chicago I changed to the Lake Shore Limited, which follows a course through Indiana, Ohio, Pennsylvania, into New York. When we stopped in South Bend,

Indiana, Vincennes resident Sergeant First Class Cleate Davis came to mind. He saw Maggie in early December 1966 when she visited BienHoa, Vietnam. Cleate, who served in the Army, said that Maggie stayed after her show and talked to the troops in his unit. She was wearing her lieutenant colonel's field dress uniform. She was great at personal visiting, and she was late leaving them. Cleate will never forget her for that. He says it was one of the best days that he had over there.

The train rattled on; sleep came intermittently. When we stopped in Cleveland, I thought of two other men from Ohio with whom I've corresponded. David Joe Hayes from Mount Vernon was stationed in both DaNang and Pleiku between 1966 and 1967. For two weeks he was in the hospital in Pleiku, where he had watched Maggie's show. "She was great! I really enjoyed seeing her. I didn't get to meet her but she put on one heck of a show."

As a child during the 1950s and 1960s, Technical Sergeant Richard Martin watched this magnificent comedic actress on his family's small black and white television. He met Maggie at Ohio's Lockbourne Air Force Base, now called Rickenbacker Air National Guard Base.

> I was a maintenance crew chief on one of the Strategic Air Command's (SAC) finest aircraft. I was pulling my tour of SAC alert when our Base Commander informed us we were going to have a special exercise for a distinguished guest. After this exercise we all went into the debriefing room where we waited with much anxiety as to who this big high ranking officer was that would warrant our Commander blowing the horn.
>
> Well, to everyone's surprise, in walked Colonel Maggie, dressed in her lieutenant colonel Green Beret uniform. All the flight crews were introduced. Then the maintenance crew chiefs were introduced to her. I per-

sonally was the senior crew chief on alert that tour and after being introduced to her, she reached up and gave me one of the biggest kisses that I think I have ever received in my entire life.

To say that you were kissed by the original one and only "Big Mouth," I'll love her forever!

After things settled down, she came into the alert dining room and sat with a few of us maintenance folks just to chat about our families and our commitment to our jobs. She was sincere. You could tell it in her voice and by the way she looked at you. The conversation we had that day will always remain in my heart.

Her troops knew her well and loved her dearly! They respected her and felt very deeply for her. She honestly cared about them as well. If I had the power, I would erect a monument in her honor with her standing in that proud uniform.

The train stopped in Erie, Pennsylvania. Lloyd Moore, James Lauria, and D. David Hayes live in the area. Lloyd, a retired Air Force colonel, saw my request for information about Maggie in a 1989 *Air Force Times* and wrote that she spent several weeks or months at CanTho in the IV Corps area of Vietnam in 1966.

James served with the Army and met Maggie in 1966 at Pleiku. He was a Non-Commissioned Officer (NCO) stationed on St. Barbara Hill and ordered to the airfield a few miles away at Camp Halloway. He remembered Maggie exiting a Huey gunship, smiling and shaking hands with everyone around her. The day was overcast and rainy, but seeing her smile seemed to brighten everything up just a little. James lives in Pittsburgh.

D. David Hayes saw Maggie at Freedom Hill near DaNang somewhere between June and November in 1970. David had already spent about sixteen or eighteen months in-country and had never had an opportunity to see Maggie or Bob Hope until they appeared together at his location.

I was with the Seabees Mobile Construction Battalion Sixty-two (MCB 62) on a detachment on Hill Fifty-five (about fifteen to twenty miles southwest of DaNang). It was also called Dodge City. It was the major infiltration route of the Viet Cong into DaNang.

By the time we got into DaNang to see the show, it had already started and we had to take seats way in the back. A few of us shimmied up tall power poles that were being used for lighting. Being a Seabee, I was well aware of what happens when one shimmies up pine poles—creosote *burns!* Guess what? It didn't matter! We so admired Martha and Bob for what they had done for the troops throughout the years that the burns just didn't matter. We had to see them and cheer them on. There were about eight of us up that pole that sunny hot afternoon. We probably resembled a family of raccoons taking cover up on that pole!

After only about twenty minutes the word came down from our non-commissioned officer in-charge (NCOIC) that we had to leave there in order to get back out to our detachment before dark, so we all left— bummed out that we couldn't stay to see the end, but thankful that we got to see what we did.

Looking back, it seems funny: Bob Hope and Martha were there to show support for the boys in Nam. But most of us (at least from our truck full of guys) were there to show our support and gratitude to the two of them and for what they had done!

God bless them. I'm sure He will when their day comes and they look Him in the eye. He will be smiling at them.

As the train traveled between Buffalo and Syracuse, I thought of Dolores and Michael Dluhos. Michael is a World War II Veteran who said there were numerous times Maggie raised morale for his shipmates. Dolores and Michael went to the Bath Veterans Administration Hospital where a man told them that at the end of World War II, his battle-weary group got leave in Japan and Maggie appeared there.

John Sullivan from Rochester served in the Fifty-fourth Signal Battalion. He was a Radio Telephone/Telegraph Operator (RTO) assigned to Company A. In late 1965 and early 1966, he was stationed at NhaTrang and CamRanhBay. His company was supporting a Republic of Korea (ROK) brigade. He had been drafted in 1964 and by 1965 held the rank of Specialist Four. His photo of Maggie appearing at the "Playboy Club" was in *Memories of Maggie*, but his story was not included. [5]

> I saw Martha Raye perform for the troops during Bob Hope's Christmas tour of 1965. I also saw her perform alone at the "Playboy Club" in a Special Forces camp near NhaTrang. I was so excited.
>
> She put on her usual dynamite performance and all I had with me to record the event was an instamatic camera. The boost she gave to our morale during that time of year was like a gift from heaven. She was sexy, funny, and beautiful. I shall always remember her, and my time spent there, with a great deal of emotion.
>
> She was an exceptional patriot—in addition to being a caring loving human being. She was there for us giving her all.

As our train approached Schenectady, comments from other Easterners came to mind. Donald Conklin from Middleburgh served aboard the USS *Coral Sea* for three years. "Maggie made one heck of a day out of a long, lonely cruise for a bunch of the sailors."

Nelson Darling, Sr. retired from the Navy as a Seabee Master Chief Construction Utility man. Now a resident of Cropseyville, he served in Vietnam from 1965 through early 1969 on various tours from PhoQuoc to QuonTri. Nelson talked to Maggie on several occasions. His group always looked for her performances. They got quite a kick out of her bragging about her "gams." "She was a down-to-earth gal and a superb entertainer."

I've known Jim Davey of Wynantskill for a number of years. He was instrumental in having a memorial built in Rensselaer County in Troy, New York for the men who died or were listed as Prisoner of War/Missing in Action (POW/MIA) in Vietnam. In late 1966, he was stationed outside Pleiku, at the base camp of the Third Brigade, Twenty-fifth Infantry Division. Maggie staged a show for the troops there that he says he "will remember until the day I die." It was the first time Jim had ever seen a "Star" perform. He recalls it was evening and cool, as the Highlands often were. Maggie did a bit where she pretended to be shaving with her microphone. Jim said, "Simple shtick to be sure, but I can see her doing it to this day."

When the train stopped in Schenectady, I was anxious to get on with my trip's purpose. News releases had been sent to newspapers, radio, and television stations that I was going to be in the area doing book signings and presentations. My first presentation was at the William Sanford Library in Colonie. I showed slides and talked about the medal project and what it took to get published. Three old friends were in the audience.

A Patriotic Family

Terry Waterston from North Creek in the Adirondacks and I became friends in 1992. She had enlisted in the Marines when she was seventeen along with her sister Shirley. In the Marines, Terry had gained self-confidence, independence, and a zest

Terry Waterston in 1954.
Photo contributed by Terry.

for life. She continues to serve by being involved with community activities. Terry's first husband is buried in Arlington National Cemetery. Her second husband, Barry, is an Army Vietnam Era Veteran. Three of Terry's four children followed in her footsteps. One son has already retired from the Air Force as a master sergeant and another was a sergeant in the National Guard.

Terry's daughter, Pam, enlisted in the Army in 1989. She served as an Equipment Transportation Specialist, operating heavy equipment during the Gulf War. When her group, the 368th Transportation Company from Fort Story, Virginia, first landed in Saudi Arabia, they lived in warehouses at the port and worked twelve-hour shifts unloading ships. They were located at the Port of Jubail. She was on guard duty when the war erupted. An Iraqi scud missile blew up over their heads, landing less than a hundred yards off the pier that was stocked with ammunition. "There was nothing we could do but watch, wish, and hope." If she had to fight again for her country, "There would be no hesitation."

Terry scheduled me to address the Warren County American Legion members at their district meeting. They were in awe at what Maggie had done. Most of the Legionnaires were World War II and Korean War Veterans.

Noonie and Terry Waterston at Warren County American Legion meeting in Queensbury, New York, May 1996. Photo contributed by Terry Waterston.

Terry Waterston was chosen 1997-1998 Legionnaire of the Year by her peers on a Post, County, and Fourth District level and competed for the New York State Legionnaire of the Year at the Department Convention in July 1997. I saw Terry and Pam at the Women in

Military Service for America (WIMSA) Memorial in October 1997. These are two women I'm very proud to know.

Noonie and Pam Waterston at WIMSA Memorial, October 1997. Photo by Terry Waterston.

I met Benita Zahn at her television station in Albany. She interviewed me for a fifteen-minute spot on her Sunday morning program, "Forum." We discussed Maggie's medal project, the book marketing process, the reason I was in the area, and the photos on the photo board that I carry to all book signings and presentations.

The following Sunday I went to Queensbury for a book signing where Fran Miller and her daughter Barbara met me. When Fran said, "My son Bill wrote to you," [6] I knew who she was. Bill had told me his parents lived in Schenectady; his father has since died. Bill lives in Fort Worth but is suffering from Agent Orange.

HEADING TO OUR NATION'S CAPITOL

The train moved south from Albany along the Hudson River to New York City. The Catskills were beautiful; how I missed those mountains. As I looked across the river at the United States Military Academy at West Point, I thought of other folks from New York who wrote regarding Maggie.

Buddy and Jean Carroll Howe appeared in vaudeville at the same time Maggie did. In 1990, Jean was living in Hartsdale. She said she lost track of her colleagues' activities and that her personal contact with Maggie seemed like a thousand years ago when they were both teenagers just starting in show business.

Harry Edwards was in the British Army when he met Maggie, who was there doing her stuff in London in 1942.

Amy Andrews of Monroe reminisced about Martha Raye's production of *Hello, Dolly!* at the Bronx VA Hospital in the 1960s. Amy's husband was a World War II Vet and a patient there at that time. "He was so thrilled to see Maggie!"

Paul Masi from Bethpage read the article I had written in BRAVO about Maggie. He saw Maggie in Vietnam in late 1966. Paul felt she deserved nothing but the highest honor our nation could bestow.

In New York City I switched trains for one headed to Washington, D.C. where I had scheduled a stopover. It was the week before Memorial Day. As the train went through New Jersey and Maryland, I thought of Joseph Cappozzoli, who had coffee with Maggie in LongBinh in 1966. He had watched her movies when he was growing up in New Jersey. He knew she was an honorary lieutenant colonel with the Army but felt they should have made her a four-star general. "She was one in a million." Joseph retired in 1968.

Blairstown, New Jersey is now home for Ed Hultberg. Ed was in Staging Battalion on his way to Vietnam. In late 1966 or early 1967 he was stationed with the First Marine Division in DaNang, assigned to drive Maggie's USO troupe with his three-quarter ton truck. Maggie rode in the front seat with him. She autographed the only thing he had with him—a ticket stub from the play *The Greatest Story Ever Told,* which he saw in April 1966 in Oceanside, California. Bill Griffin from Westminster, Maryland was in-country April 1968 through April 1969. He boarded a bird as Maggie exited.

Lieutenant Colonel Richard Lynch, now retired from the Air Force, was with the Fifteenth Bomb Squadron

(Light) during World War II. He had written in his diary that his unit arrived at Ain Taya Rest Camp in Algeria on 14 January 1943, and they were entertained by Carole Landis, Kay Francis, and Martha Raye. His squadron was delayed by a bomb attack and that held up the women's performance. This event was depicted in the movie *Four Jills in a Jeep*. In 1946, Richard took one of his crews to Miami, where they attended Maggie's show at The Copa. She remembered the bomb attack in 1943 and insisted on paying all expenses for that evening.

Colonel Daryle Baxter has retired from the Army. He met Maggie in 1965 or 1966 when she visited Saigon's Koepler Compound, which he then commanded. That was a personnel processing center for some in-country arrivals; such folks remained there nearly a week before moving elsewhere within the country. While Maggie did not entertain at that Compound, everyone knew they'd see her in the "Boonies," on the firebases where the big stars (e.g. Bob Hope) would not dare go. "The presence of such a star overwhelmed any memory of why she was there," Daryle said.

Senior Chief Petty Officer Frank Cirino has retired from the Navy and lives in Virginia Beach. In 1966-1967 he was in Mobile Construction Battalion Forty, The Fighting Fortieth Seabee Battalion was based in the I Corps, ChuLai at Camp Shield. It was there that Maggie put on a show. His unit outfitted her with greens, and she seemed to like the Chief Petty Officer. When she learned that Frank was of Italian decent, she said she was Italian and gave Frank a big hug. Even though Camp Shield was under fire a few times, Maggie stopped there anyway. "She was a wonderful lady."

By the way, according to Maggie's birth certificate, her father was from England and her mother from Montana. But her death certificate stated her father was from Ireland and her mother from Wisconsin. Maggie sometimes gave conflicting information.

Loretta Gibson's husband served two tours in Vietnam. Both times he raved about how wonderful Maggie was. "She was never too busy or in a hurry. She took a lot of time talking to our Servicemen, no matter what rank they held or what job they did."

THE PENTAGON BECKONS

Susan Christiansen May 1996.
Photo by Noonie Fortin.

In May I did a book signing at the Pentagon Book Store and at Reprint Books in L'Enfant Plaza. These events were just before Memorial Day weekend. Susan Christiansen contacted John "Top" Holland, President of Americans For Freedom Always (AFFA) and arranged for us to have a booth at The Vietnam Memorial (The Wall) over the weekend. Susan flew from California. When we arrived at the Pentagon Book Store, we met many interesting people including Jim Tucker, who works in the Office of the Chief of Staff of the Army. He talked to Susan about a memorial

Jim Tucker, the Pentagon Book Store, May 1996. Photo by Susan Christiansen.

for civilians. After reading *Memories of Maggie* he commented, "This book is the first one in a long time that gave me that warm and fuzzy feeling. It was positive, upbeat, and told it like it was."

Eugene Hayunga, one of my Army Reserve officers during the 1970s, was working for the National Institute of Health when he stopped by the Pentagon Book Store. We hadn't seen each other in at least ten years.

The next day Susan and I were at Reprint Book Shop at L'Enfant Plaza in Washington, D.C. Jim Glenn from Congressman Mike McNulty's office brought a bouquet of flowers. Mary Stueland, the Community Relations Coordinator at Reprint, was surprised that so many people stopped by to share their remembrances of Maggie. Reprint Book Shop has new books and reprints.

Noonie, Susan, Belle Pellegrino and the Energizer Bunny near The Wall Memorial Day Weekend, May 1996. Photo contributed by Susan Christiansen.

Memorial Day weekend happened at The Wall. John "Top" Holland had arranged for a spot for us. Top said, *"Memories of Maggie* is wonderful and really tells her story." Susan had brought her now famous Energizer Bunny with her, and we used it on our table. This bunny has been a part of the POW/MIA issue since Susan first received it. After all, the bunny keeps going and going—just like the POW/MIA issue. Her bunny drew a lot of people to our booth. We placed POW/MIA stickers on all the books.

Many stopped by our booth to get *Memories of Maggie,* including Al Hemingway from Connecticut. Al is a contributing editor with *VIETNAM* magazine. His review, which appeared in the October 1996 issue, said, "Noonie Fortin has captured the essence of Martha Raye." Jack Murphy from Pennsylvania was visiting The Wall that day. Jack had recorded a beautiful patriotic song called "The Promise." He gave me a cassette copy and asked if I would play it for groups to whom I speak.

This weekend also was my first opportunity to experience Rolling Thunder. Motorcyclists from across the country gather for a rally to keep the POW/MIA issue alive. Veterans, spouses, family members, friends, and supporters ride their motorcycles to Washington, D.C. every year a few days before the Memorial Day weekend. They gather at The Pentagon's parking lot on Sunday morning to form a line.

The weather had turned cold with drizzling rain, but it didn't stop these determined cyclists. Thousands of them rode their motorcycles from the Pentagon across the bridge and around The Wall. Each bike carried an American Flag or POW/MIA Flag. What an awesome sight! They keep the issue alive in hopes of getting Congress to continue looking for our POW/MIAs from all wars, past and future. No one should be left behind.

Rolling Thunder
Photo by Susan Christiansen.

Susan Christiansen and her son Bryan at the Rolling Thunder IX starting point in The Pentagon parking lot, May 1996.

Photo contributed by
Susan Christiansen.

After the parade of motorcycles ended, drivers and riders descended upon The Wall. I saw several old friends from New York and met new ones from around the country. What a joy it was to meet these people and talk with them about Maggie.

LangMarc Publishing had received orders for *Memories of Maggie* from Veterans stationed around the world. But I had not expected to sign books at The Wall for people from foreign countries who were not American Veterans. Two women from Canada, followed by two people from the Philippine Islands purchased copies. One of them couldn't speak English. A journalist from Portugal asked for a copy. He remembered Maggie.

Memorial Day 1996 was cold and damp. Susan and I were up early since we wanted to present a copy of *Memories of Maggie* at The Wall. I wrote a message on the book's first page. Susan wrote comments on her page.

At 9:00 A.M. Susan and I walked from one end of The Wall to the other, then back to the vertex of The Wall, as we always did. We each took a deep breath and then began our own little presentation. It was strange how quiet everything became. The people around us had stopped what they were doing. Susan read aloud what I had written. I then read what she had written. I placed the book inside a clear plastic bag and sealed it. Together we placed the book at the base of the vertex, stepped backed two paces, saluted, and did an about face. The group had given us room to do our presentation, listened, and shed tears along with our own. The crowd parted as if they were the Red Sea so that we could walk away from the vertex. We each felt Maggie's presence touch us as we walked away. It was as if she had said "thank you for a job well done."

I hated leaving The Wall, Washington, Susan, old and new friends. There was, however, some solace knowing that *Memories of Maggie* would be placed in the archives of items left at The Wall. Perhaps one day it will be displayed with other items that had been left there.

Susan and I signed many books during the three days we were at The Wall. But it was time for Top to drive me to Union Station to board the Capitol Limited heading for Chicago.

As the train moved through West Virginia, I thought of retired Army Lieutenant Colonel Louis Longanacre from Lewisburg. He was in Vietnam during 1965-1966 and again in 1971-1972. In 1965 he was headquartered in NhaTrang. He remembered seeing Maggie on several occasions and got to know her rather well. "She was always in fatigue uniform and wearing the insignia of rank for a lieutenant colonel. She was a joy to see and was always on the 'job.'"

I began jotting notes about my experience in Washington, D.C.

The Display Board that accompanies Noonie
to her book signings and speeches.

6

THE SOUTHEAST TOUR

In June 1996 I traveled by car across the southeastern part of our country with signings at military bases along the way.

As we drove across Texas, through Louisiana, Mississippi, Alabama, Georgia, South Carolina, and into North Carolina, I thought of several people in each state who spoke of their encounters with Martha Raye.

Malcolm J. Marsh thought Maggie was long overdue for the honor she deserved. He was a Veteran of World War II. He said it was a shame that Maggie, who had done so much for the lonely, sick, and crippled GI's, had been forgotten by citizens of the country she so loved.

Lieutenant Madelyne Curtiss retired from the Army Nurse Corps. She was a first lieutenant Army nurse who served throughout the European Theater of Operation (ETO) during World War II. She recalled United Service Organization (USO) teams there entertaining troops and how much Maggie did for their morale.

Al Fred Daniel, formerly of Jackson, Mississippi, served in the Navy. In 1943 his squadron had to pick up their planes at Lockheed, and they had liberty that night. He recalled how his buddy L. Bradbury came in on cloud-nine after an enjoyable evening with Maggie and her friend. Both had "adopted" him as an orphan, alone in a strange town.

I thought of Army Master Sergeant Ernest Eldredge, retired and living in Gulfport, Mississippi. He was in Pleiku from 1967 to 1969. Ernest attended a *Hello, Dolly!* show there. Less than an hour after Maggie's performance, Ernest returned to his quarters and saw Maggie in her fatigue uniform. She was headed for a visit to an adjacent hospital.

Specialist 7 Bill LeMay is now retired from the Army and lives in Hartselle, Alabama. He was at a First Cavalry Division base camp near AnKhe sometime late 1965 or early 1966. He and his first sergeant were manning the Operations/Intelligence center for the Eleventh Aviation Group.

> The phone hanging on the tent pole rang. A major said I should come to his mess tent since Miss Martha Raye wanted to meet me.
>
> I was baffled since I had no idea how she knew I was there. I handed the phone to my first sergeant (Top,) who did what he did best—you know—"Yes Sir...will do, Sir."
>
> Top then told me that he would watch the telephones, teletype, Intelligence Reports and Situation Map and that I should go to the Fifteenth Medical Battalion Officers' mess tent.
>
> When I arrived, I saw her talking to two majors. She excused herself and came over to me. We sat at a table for ten or fifteen minutes until someone else arrived. She showed me a plot of places she planned to go to see people. One of those LZ's was hot. I remember I pointed out that could be a good way to get her tail shot off. She said simply that if the pilots would take her she would go.

Retired Navy Lieutenant Commander Ray Cooper of Madison, Alabama remembered Maggie as not only a funny woman but also a caring person. One of his prized possessions from Vietnam is a picture of the two of them taken in January 1972. Military uniforms have the person's last name over the right breast pocket. This picture was taken to show their uniforms read "Raye" "Cooper."

Maggie and Ray Cooper in Vietnam, January 1972.
Photo contributed by Ray Cooper.

Ray Cooper in 1996.
Photo contributed by Ray Cooper.

Ray was stationed at a tiny base in the far south of Vietnam. Having a famous personality come to Vietnam, a war zone, and to spend so much time with troops was heart warming.

Major William Smith, Jr. was a Special Services Officer for the Army's First Logistical Command in 1967-1968. His responsibilities included planning the itineraries and care of USO entertainers "in-country." Maggie and he became good friends during the months she spent in Vietnam during his tour. He is now retired, living in Phenix City, Alabama.

Sergeant First Class Elmer Rogers (retired) met Maggie on two occasions. His first tour of duty was from July 1965 to November 1967. He was assigned to the 232nd Signal Company, Thirty-ninth Signal Battalion MAC-V, Cong-Ly Street, in BienHoa. Elmer said:

> Maggie brought joy to the men and myself who at that time were very far from home and needed a mother figure during those trying times. If anyone deserved a medal for helping morale—she sure helped mine and she risked her life doing it.

Ernest Quinn of Chickamauga, Georgia served his tour with the Fifty-fourth Signal Battalion (Headquartered in NhaTrang.) For over half his tour he was a member of Detachment One attached to the First Cavalry Division in AnKhe. He made many trips back and forth between AnKhe and NhaTrang.

> I caught a flight out of AnKhe Christmas 1965 to go to NhaTrang to see the Bob Hope Christmas show. Martha Raye, though not a regular member of the Bob Hope troupe, took part in that show. I remember she got her mouth hung up on the microphone. I drank a beer or two with her at the Crossbow Club at Camp McDermott on one occasion. Also drank a few beers with her at the Fifth Special Forces Playboy Club in NhaTrang. This was late 1965 and early 1966. She was traveling from camp to camp and was a lot of fun.
>
> I had the opportunity to see quite a few entertainers during my tour in Vietnam, but without exception Maggie was my favorite. I also remember that even though she was well into her fifties she had as good looking pair of legs as any of the younger stars that did USO shows. I guess only a soldier would have noticed that!

The Reverend Wilfred Hunt ran into Maggie in VungTau in 1965. He was a Warrant Officer and an advisor to the Vietnamese in III Corps at the time. He and Maggie had a pleasant visit, and he had his picture taken with her.

MUSEUM OF AVIATION

When I arrived at Warner Robins, Georgia, I went immediately to the Museum of Aviation about a mile from the Air Force Base. June Lowe, Executive Vice President of the museum's Foundation, and the museum's staff gave me a warm welcome. Robert Dubeil, Director of Public Relations and Marketing, was thorough in his efforts to obtain excellent newspaper coverage. Skip Korson, a reporter for *The Herald,* contacted five of the men from Georgia mentioned in *Memories of Maggie* and published their stories in the paper.

The museum's curator was Darwin Edwards, whose story appeared in *Memories of Maggie.* [7] The next day Darwin gave me a tour of the museum and introduced me to Peggy Young, Director.

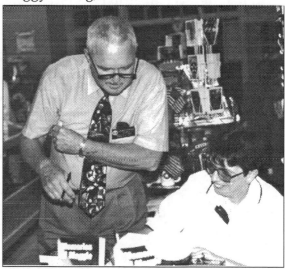

Darwin Edwards and Noonie at the Museum of Aviation, Warner Robins, GA, June 1996. Photo by Julio Rodriguez.

A most rewarding experience awaited me at the Museum of Aviation's gift shop. Among the interested customers were Darwin and three other men mentioned in the book: Julio Rodriguez, Robert Siebenmorgan, and Michael Moehlenkamp.

Julio Rodriguez and Noonie at the Museum of Aviation, Warner Robins, GA, June 1996. Photo by Mary Rodriguez.

Julio's wife, Mary, was also there. Julio had seen Maggie in NhaTrang, Vietnam in 1965. [8] He suggested to Darwin to add a section in the museum about women who served like Maggie.

Noonie and Robert Siebenmorgan at the Museum of Aviation, Warner Robins, GA June 1996. Photo by Julio Rodriguez.

Robert saw Maggie in 1968 when he flew her from TanSonNhut airport to the Mekong Delta region. [9] When Julio and Robert identified each other and discussed why they were there, they shook hands, embraced and said, "Welcome Home."

During this encounter I spotted a blond-haired man strolling back and forth. Each time he glanced at my picture display board, his eyes filled with tears and he walked out the door. But he kept coming back. As soon as I had a free moment, I approached him. Michael, who told me to call him Mike, kept repeating, "She didn't have to go there, but she did." He was talking about Maggie being in NhaTrang during Christmas 1971. [10] We embraced. Here I was a retired Army first sergeant hugging a retired Air Force colonel.

I introduced Mike to Julio, Robert, and Darwin. The four of them talked about their personal encounters with Maggie. They soon learned that they live less than four miles from each other.

They were brought together on this day. They had common bonds—the Vietnam War, Maggie, the book, and the community in which they lived. Julio and Mary took photos of everyone.

My day of surprises wasn't over. Although Dr. Sam Patton wasn't there, his brother Joe came. He introduced himself, "I'm Sam's brother." I finished by saying, "Joe Patton." We discussed Sam's story about meeting Maggie. [11] Joe and his wife apologized that Sam couldn't be there.

Books were purchased as Father's Day gifts for Vietnam Veterans, for birthday gifts, and keepsakes. A woman purchased a book for Max Cleland, who was hoping to replace retiring U.S. Senator Sam Nunn on the Armed Services Committee. Max has written the book *Strong at the Broken Places*. It is about his life and brush with death in Vietnam where he became a triple amputee. A month after I was in Georgia, I received an autographed copy of Max's book in the mail. His is an inspirational story. Max won election to the U.S. Senate on 5 November 1996. Furthermore, he was selected for the position on the Senate Armed Services Committee.

I was introduced to General Robert Scott, who served in the Air Force during World War II. He wrote *God Is My Co-Pilot*, which later was made into a movie. He continues to pilot aircraft and volunteers at the museum. He remembered Maggie. We exchanged books.

General Robert Scott and Noonie at the Museum of Aviation, Warner Robins, GA June 1996. Photo by Julio Rodriguez.

I signed more books in those two hours in the gift shop at the Museum of Aviation than I did in Washington, D.C. Elaine Holt, the gift shop manager, asked me to leave her some of the books I had in my car. She had already sold everything LangMarc Publishing had sent.

Once again I hated leaving my new-found friends. However, it was so rewarding to know that Julio, Robert, Mike, and Darwin had met each other.

It had been a long ride from Copperas Cove, Texas to Warner Robins, Georgia but well worth every tedious mile.

Fort Gordon

My next stop was at Fort Gordon near Augusta, Georgia. Tina Pondy had scheduled a book signing for me on Thursday at The Regimental Bookstore on base. Chief Warrant Officer 5 Charlie Smith commented that the troops at Fort Gordon were too young to know who Maggie was. True, but if they bought the book they could learn about a true legend.

Sergeant First Class Bob Reynolds had met Maggie in NhaTrang in 1967, 1968, and 1969. He showed me a photo he had of Maggie with his group. His wife Annie met her in Scottsdale, Arizona when she and Bob saw Maggie perform in *Everybody Loves Opal*. Bob suggested that I write a book about Frenchy Amundson. I mentioned an article about her that appeared in *The Retired Officer* magazine and that Steven Spielberg was considering doing a movie about her life. Bob first met Frenchy in a market many years ago.

I had hoped to meet Fred Trafton and Joseph Meehan from Augusta at my book signing. They had contacted me about Maggie. Fred met Maggie in 1942, 1947, and again in 1966 while he was serving our country. Joseph is a retired Army sergeant first class, who served in Vietnam 1966-1967 with the Twenty-fifth Infantry Division in ChuLai and in 1970-1971 with Advisory Team Six. He saw Maggie frequently.

The next day in an effort to kick back, I visited the Columbia Zoo. In examining a map I noticed that Rock Hill, where retired Army Lieutenant Colonel Jack Miller lives, was just north of Columbia. He'd read about the PMOF effort in the July 1990 issue of *The Scottish Rite Journal*. He was appalled that Maggie had not been honored with that decoration before then. Jack was the Sector Advisor in Pleiku from May 1966 to April 1967. Maggie visited his sector and stayed several days and nights with the ThuanAn District Advisory Team.

If ever there was a way to boost morale and affect soldiers in a wholesome and friendly manner, Martha Raye discovered it by her visits to small outposts and

sharing life with the men in them. To this day, I cherish
a photo, hanging on my office wall, of myself with this
grand lady who did so much for all of us.

My next stop would be Fayetteville, North Carolina,
home of Fort Bragg. I had been planning this trip for
some time because this was the weekend for the annual
Special Forces Association (SFA) convention. While
riding towards Fayetteville, my mind wandered to several Veterans from North Carolina who had met Maggie
over the years.

Beaufort is where Colonel Bert Kurland settled when
he retired from the Army. He first saw Maggie in a show
on Luzon in the Philippines in July 1945. He saw her
again in CoCong, Vietnam between 1965-1966 and at
the Special Forces camps in KienPhong Province, Vietnam in 1967.

Gunnery Sergeant Harold Ritchie is now retired from
the Marines. During the summer of 1965, he was a
member of Headquarters Company, Headquarters Battalion, Third Marine Division in DaNang. Maggie visited his unit before November 1965. He recalled that it
was before they moved the Division Headquarters up to
Hill 327.

Maggie had made an unannounced, unscheduled
stop at their NCO club. It was part of an old French
Barracks, and you could still see the bullet holes in the
ceiling and walls. Maggie entertained them for about
forty-five minutes. Then she visited with the Marines.
Since they were on a two-beer ration per man, Harold
gave Maggie one of his. "She was one of the troops, a
fine entertainer, and gave us something to talk about for
days to come."

Former Marine, Major Charles Olson of Havelock
remembered Maggie very well. He had several encounters with her. [12]

Martha Raye will always be one of my favorite people. I've enjoyed her performances since the forties, spanning the entertainment spectrum of stage, screen, radio, newsreels, and television. Her achievements in her art as a comedienne, actress, and performer are the obvious accomplishments known to most Americans. Her dedicated service to our country, her magnificent warmth, and courageous performance of duty aren't as well known. I suspect that was because of her admirable reluctance to capitalize on the publicity she justly deserved, as it would conflict with standing for what she believed. In her words, she was "just doing my job." She seemed to relish the sobriquet "The Big Mouth."

Thank you for telling the story of Lieutenant Colonel Raye, her love of our country, her service through World War II, Korea, and Vietnam, and the tender loving care she provided to untold numbers of her fellow Americans who served in the Army, Air Force, Coast Guard, Navy, and Marines.

I'd like to share my memories of a real lady. Whenever I see an old movie, newsreel film clip, or segment of television tape, and she's in it, I get this warm feeling of friendship. She always brightens my day. I expect you'll receive more comments about Martha's unforgettable nature.

I was a Marine Pilot. When Marine Air Wings deploy in combat, they're usually spread out to take advantage of available facilities, runways, and be where they're needed to support the ground Marines—The Grunts. It was that way in Vietnam. Visiting dignitaries didn't have the time, opportunity, or transportation to get them to every Marine outfit. They had full itineraries anyway, doing the best they could. USO folks did a great job, without a doubt, but they could only stop off at randomly, or operationally selected Marine units, so the average Marine didn't see much of the visitors. Most Marines felt left out.

Marine outfits were located on the western side of the DaNang Airbase, fronting on the shacks and tin roof checkerboard of the Asian ghetto we dubbed: Dogpatch. Marines were crammed into every available building, which were drab reminders of the French occupation, but most of us lived in tentage between the runway and the base perimeter. The old French barracks, officers' quarters, and out-buildings were dilapidated, rundown, and very small. The quality of food depended upon the latest Longshoreman's strike and what you could scrounge from Navy ships unloading at the docks across the harbor. About what you'd expect in a Marine combat zone.

On the opposite side of the Airbase was the Air Force compound. The Air Force really knows how to go to war. They had new barracks, efficient messhalls, Post Exchange, and a theater, not to mention stateside furniture, new equipment, and all the conveniences.

I believe that Martha may have been approached by some fast-talking Marine who convinced her nobody loved the Marines on the other side of the Airbase. Martha agreed to make a full tour of the Marine facilities and to meet as many Marines as she could. She went from the orderly world of the Air Force to the Marine side of the Airbase featuring its early Salvation Army decor.

Whenever Martha visited anywhere, she was dearly appreciated. She found out where people lived and worked, seemingly by instinct, and intuitively found the youngest and the loneliest wherever she went. She sought out anyone she could find to talk with and, for many, it was the first time they had seen—let alone visited one-on-one—with a celebrity. Martha had the knack of putting people at ease, allowing the conversation to flow, and to make folks feel as if they were talking with an old friend from their hometown or neighborhood. At Martha's request, there was never any limelight or fanfare.

I don't remember any word being passed concerning Martha's arrival at the Command Post and the Air Force triangle. As was her way, she just seemed to pop in.

Sergeant First Class Gene Smith is retired and lives in Sneads Ferry. He met Maggie several times between 1967-1968 while he was stationed with the Fifth Special Forces Group in NhaTrang. He also had the pleasure of meeting her again at Fort Bragg when she attended a reunion of the Fifth Special Forces Group.

Thomas Harwell retired from the Navy Reserve and lives in Greenville. Maggie went to his combat base in the Northern I Corps near the Demilitarized Zone (DMZ) and put on *Hello, Dolly!* for the 121st Seabees and components of the First Marine Division. "What a performance! I still remember it vividly, as I am sure many other Seabees and Marines do." It was a clear evening with gleaming stars punctuated by 105mm and 155mm outgoing artillery, and later by incoming mortars. Thomas remarked that Maggie and her troupe were "regular folk." He continues to have great admiration for her and her efforts. " I saw her, on the front line of freedom."

Retired Lieutenant Colonel Charles Abbey of Winston-Salem saw Maggie at Blackhorse Forward in QuanLoi around January 1970. There were only a few places that she didn't visit.

FORT BRAGG

Saturday morning I was ready to sign books at the SFA convention. This would be a great place to sell books, I thought. These were Maggie's boys. At the convention a local bookstore was to have a table where I was scheduled to sign books. But the vendors weren't allowed to set up, so we went to their store in Fayetteville, where I signed some books before leaving for another bookstore signing. Faye McLemore, a writer for Fayetteville's paper, *The Post,* interviewed me at this second signing and said she would write a review of the book for the paper. And indeed she did!

I headed for Fort Bragg and the cemetery. As I approached the Randolph Street entrance, a flood of memories came back from October 1994 when Maggie died and was buried here. I recalled her wake and all the people who attended it, as well as those who came to her funeral. I could clearly see members of the Special Forces carrying the casket to her final resting place. I could hear the music the Eighty-second Airborne Band played during the ecumenical funeral service.

I recalled Melodye sitting just in front of where I was standing and how much I wanted to reach out in her grief. I'm so glad that Melodye and I have become friends. It has helped both of us deal with the loss of her mother. Although Maggie's funeral was a year and a half ago, when I was at the cemetery it seemed like only yesterday.

I walked among the rows of military headstones and soon came upon Maggie's, site 780-B. Someone had already placed fresh flowers on her grave.

Front of Maggie's headstone, Fort Bragg, June 1996. Photo by Noonie Fortin.

There was a note lying next to her headstone from one of her boys—he missed her. I said a prayer, stepped back two paces, saluted, did an about face and felt her touch me once again. Was I imagining it? I felt her presence at The Wall and again here.

I drove back to my hotel still feeling Maggie's presence. I felt calm. I wondered if she was becoming my guardian angel. There is no real way of knowing that, of course. Still...

Betty Amker of the JFK Special Warfare Museum's Gift Shop helped me set up next to her booth the following day. The halls of the hotel were full of Veterans. I felt at home. When my picture board went up, folks gathered like bees to a hive. They scoured the photos. They were looking for friends with Maggie's photos. Some wanted to talk with me; others shied away. Again I saw the memories of long ago flash across their eyes.

Bill Williams from the St. Louis Chapter (named after Maggie) bought a book. Nick Giordana from New York asked me if I remembered Rick Johannes. The two of them were trying to change their Veterans group name to include Maggie. Dale Libby, chairman of the SFA Convention to be held in 1998 asked me about conducting workshops there. The 1997 convention had been in Colorado Springs; Melodye was there.

Kenneth Plante and his wife, Kathleen, from Baltimore brought a photo of Maggie and Ken together in Vietnam. [13]

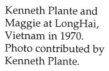

Kenneth Plante and Maggie at LongHai, Vietnam in 1970. Photo contributed by Kenneth Plante.

We began to correspond more
frequently when Kathleen asked
about my family's background.
It seems there were Fortins listed
on Ken's family tree, and she
wondered if we might have been
related. Unfortunately, we were
not.

Kenneth Plante at Fort
Bragg in 1996. Photo
contributed by Kenneth.

Earl and Betty Trabue from Copperas Cove, Texas
attended, as did John "Top" Holland from Washington,
D.C. and Mike Karr from Bothel, Washington. Mike and
I have corresponded for awhile now. He met Maggie
during 1966 at the Advisory Team Twenty-eight Team
House in TuyHoa, PhuYen Province, Vietnam.

Mike Karr with Maggie in TuyHoa, Vietnam in 1966.
Photo contributed by Mike Karr.

Mike recalled that Maggie had arrived at the Team's
area accompanied only by a guitarist. The Team's Ad-
ministrative officer, a young captain, introduced Maggie

to them and made a remark that didn't sit well with her. Maggie gently put the captain in his place with a firm voice, much to *his* chagrin but to the delight of Team members. Her show consisted of several songs, a dance or two, a lot of jokes, and good music. After the show Maggie was escorted to the Officers' Club where she remained for a short time, then to the Enlisted Club. "Her smiles, words, and even her presence made a lot of troops forget the war, at least for a short while."

Mike was so enthused about *Memories of Maggie* that he ordered it by the dozens and sold them to his friends. He is not the only one to do that. Clayton Hough Jr. from Holyoke, Massachusetts has been a marvelous promoter. Clay, who was mentioned several times in *Memories of Maggie,* [14] donated books to schools, Veterans groups, and active duty troops.

Steve Sherman from Houston and Clyde Sincere from Oakton, Virginia, introduced themselves along with many others. Steve had helped Frenchy Amundson locate me and brought Earl Trabue to my door in Copperas Cove. He publishes *The Green Beret Magazine* and provided me with James Fisher's photo of Maggie which appeared on the cover and inside *Memories of Maggie.* Clyde was interested in having me speak to the Special Operations Association reunion in Las Vegas.

In *Memories of Maggie* I wrote about Sergeant Michael B. Dooley, who was killed in Vietnam. His sister, Olive Justice of Montana, wrote to tell me that Maggie escorted Michael's remains home. [15] Again, I was overwhelmed by Maggie's caring heart. While in Fort Bragg for the SFA Convention, I met Michael's brother who shared more about Michael's early years and background.

Tom Squire wrote an article for the *Spring Lake News.* It appeared a few days before my weekend in Fayetteville. He said, "Martha Raye is chiseled in marble on a Veteran's headstone at Fort Bragg's military cemetery and burned into the hearts of untold legions of Veterans and other admirers. Her stories and theirs are entwined here with plenty of photographs, making this a must have book. I'd advise you to send for this book right away...if you have a scheduling conflict that prevents you from getting one signed by the author at the JFK Special Warfare Museum."

Faye McLemore's article appeared in *The Post.*. Faye wrote:

> This book is a biographical tribute to a woman whose life, when examined, makes her seem almost incredible...This is a great reading experience. It moves along easily...The outcome is a beautiful portrait of the kind of person we all need in our lives. The lives she touched will never be the same. She was a friend to the frightened and lonely, a mentor to the young, a nurse to the infirm, but most of all, she was, and is, "Colonel Maggie."

After returning to Texas I received the July 1996 issue of *The VVA Veteran.* In it, Mark Leepson's review of *Memories of Maggie* said:

> Noonie Fortin offers a heartfelt tribute to Martha Raye, as well known for her unwavering loyalty to America's fighting men and women as she was for her work on stage and screen....

While some people were learning about Maggie by reading my book or hearing me speak, I realized that students of all ages needed to learn more about the various wars. I found their general disinterest disturbing.

7

A History Lesson

Memories of Maggie was written especially for the Veterans of our country; it was filled with their stories. In my travels, I have spoken to various age groups. I've discovered that many young people know and care little about history. It is particularly appalling to see how little they know about Vietnam. This chapter is targeted for our younger generation. It is a short lesson in geography and history to show what our brave men and women had to face on a daily basis in Vietnam.

Smaller than California in size, the country of Vietnam is located in Southeast Asia. It was divided into two sections: North Vietnam, known as the Socialist Republic of Vietnam, and non-Communist South Vietnam, called The Republic of Vietnam.

American soldiers were in Vietnam as early as 1945 when the country was governed by the French. Between 1955 and 1962, the U.S. government supplied South Vietnam with two billion dollars in aid, a portion of which was earmarked for military aid. The U.S. also assigned 685 military advisors to South Vietnam; however, by the end of 1961 that figure had risen to 2000.

These advisors were to help the South Vietnamese raise and train an army to protect themselves against communists from the north.

One part of South Vietnam is a rugged, remote, mountainous area known as the AShau Valley near Vietnam's border with Laos. The people who live in the area are called Montagnards or "mountain people." They were part of the civilian defense group trying to keep the North Vietnamese from advancing into their country through Laos.

Other parts of South Vietnam are hilly. Some have paddy dikes for the rice fields. There are many streams throughout the jungle. The canopy in the jungle was often referred to as triple-canopy because it is so dense. The southern area of the country is quite swampy. Although there are some cities and towns, most communities are little more than hamlets and each hamlet is different. All in all, the terrain makes standard military tactics dangerous.

During World War II, soldiers' average age was twenty-six. But during the Vietnam War, American soldiers' average age was only nineteen. Most soldiers were fresh out of high school. Viet Cong soldiers were even younger and were assisted by children and women.

American advisors to a Vietnamese army unit were often young men who had undergone specialized training. They might go for weeks at a time without seeing another American. A marine helicopter would bring in food and mail to the remote areas. Soldiers patrolled the country for days or weeks searching for the enemy.

The Americans wore steel helmets with camouflage covers and green fatigues with suspenders connected to web belts. Attached to the belts and suspenders were ammo pouches, grenades, and two canteens. Pants legs were stuffed into boots and sewn up tightly to keep out jungle critters. A poncho doubled as a waterproof shelter. A ruck pack had a quick release catch that allowed it to be dropped at a moment's notice.

Marines and soldiers often slogged through swamps, over mountains, into valleys, and through jungles. Their shirt sleeves were worn full length to protect their arms from razor-sharp elephant grass. Bloodsucking leeches didn't just live in the water; they frequently fell from trees and dug into soldiers' flesh. They also had to be very careful where they put their feet to avoid land mines that could maim or kill. Some of these mines were called "Bouncing Bettys."

Pits dug and camouflaged often held Viet Cong booby traps. Some had sharpened poisoned bamboo stakes called "punji sticks." The point was so sharp it could easily puncture a combat boot. Some booby traps featured these sharpened bamboo sticks tied together in a bunch. If you triggered the mechanism, you could be impaled on the sticks and die instantly.

Dwight Eisenhower was President of the United States prior to the unofficial start of the Vietnam War. His administration thought North Vietnam was planning an armed attack across the Demilitarized Zone (DMZ), similar to what had happened in Korea ten years earlier. President John Kennedy's administration, which followed Eisenhower's, believed that South Vietnam's armed forces—Army of the Republic of Vietnam (ARVN)—needed a plan to deal with more of a local war waged by guerrillas at the village level.

By Christmas 1962 there were 11,000 U. S. advisors in Vietnam. One year later, when Lyndon Johnson took office following President Kennedy's assassination, there were 16,000. Although President Kennedy had planned to withdraw our troops from Vietnam, President Johnson raised the level of U.S. involvement. By 1967 there were more than 536,000 American men and women in-country. Our death toll was already at 16,000.

During the Tet Offensive in January 1968 there were more than eighty thousand Communist forces attacking prominent communities such as Saigon and Hue. It took more than three weeks for the ARVN and U.S. forces to retake these cities. This caused a significant change in U.S. strategy. By mid-Spring, Johnson's administration was persuaded that a total victory was not worth the cost of American lives on the battlefield or on the home front during the anti-war protests. Reluctantly, they decided to seek a settlement at the negotiating table.

Meanwhile, the American public was told very little about what actually was going on in Vietnam. Although it was receiving coverage on the nightly news and newspapers, few real details were told. Protests against the war took place around the United States.

Richard Nixon won the November 1968 presidential election. His administration hoped to end the war and strengthen the South Vietnamese government and armed forces in the event settlement negotiations failed.

Cambodia and Laos are countries located to the west of Vietnam. In March 1970 the Cambodian government was overthrown and replaced by a military government. Until this happened, the Communists had used Cambodia as both a sanctuary and to transport and store weapons, supplies, and forces for use in neighboring Vietnam.

In April President Nixon approved a plan to invade the eastern section of Cambodia. This invasion created more problems in the United States. Protesters against the war believed this invasion widened the war. Protest marches became more common.

Meanwhile, in the Vietnam province of QuangNgai, soldiers played hide and seek with the enemy. It seemed the Americans gained ground during the day, only to lose it at night. Our soldiers attempted to root out and destroy command and communication posts. They searched for and tried to capture weapons and supplies. They were constantly harassed by snipers, mines, and booby traps. Sometimes they engaged in firefights but more often they had to settle for dangerous and deadly cat-and-mouse games of hit and run.

Soldiers worked seven days a week, often under heavy enemy fire. In November 1968 members of the Eleventh Infantry Brigade (to which [then] Captain Colin Powell belonged) discovered twenty-nine North Vietnamese base camps near QuangNgai village. They captured one of them just outside the village on 15 November along with enemy maps, documents, and weapons.

More than 58,000 Americans died in Vietnam. Many Americans thought they never should have been there in the first place. While soldiers fought in a jungle thousands of miles from home, many people back in the United States marched in protest against the war.

Ron Tansley, who now resides in Albany, Oregon, wondered about the protests. When he was drafted and sent to Vietnam in 1967, he lived in tents for about four months in the middle of nowhere. It became very important to him to be able to buy something—anything. He was told there was a Post Exchange (PX) at a hospital on the coast a little north of CamRanhBay.

> During some free time I got a ride, then walked for miles and somehow came out at the hospital. The Army had been so brutal that I didn't feel like a human and was sure I wasn't supposed to be there. I was afraid to ask where the PX was, but I knew that if I looked like I knew where I was going and stayed in the background no one would bother with me.
>
> None of the buildings were marked but, after a lot of walking, I saw a larger building with men going in and thought this must be it. I matter-of-factly walked in, and there was Martha Raye doing a show for, perhaps,

forty men. It was neat to see a performer with no warning, no hype, nothing, just bang—there she was. She was very good and held everybody's attention. One line that got lots of applause went, "I don't think those anti-war protesters are good enough to lick your boots!"

As I walked back to the compound, I thought about Martha's remark. "What's an anti-war protester? Someone who protests war? Isn't everyone against wars?"

Over and over I worked on it. I hadn't seen a newspaper in a year and a half. Were they protesting North Vietnam's invasion and VC terrorist acts? Then it crossed my mind, were they protesting us? No, that's preposterous. The American people would never turn against their own soldiers in the field.

Still, I remembered what we had been told in advanced training. "If the American people take to the streets regarding the war, the Communists will smell victory and the war will go on and on." That seemed like an odd thing for the Army to say to us. It didn't make any sense. Why would people take to the streets? I decided to check into it, and I soon learned the truth.

I've always wondered if Martha Raye knew what she had revealed? You might think that she shouldn't have told us about the protesters. But the way I see it is that Martha was the only honest person that I met in Vietnam who knew the facts. The movie *Good Morning Vietnam* really had it right. I felt very foolish that I'd written home to my wife and mother saying I thought I would be home by Thanksgiving, then Christmas, etc. when I realized that they knew it wasn't going to happen.

After that I became a much better soldier because I knew I would be there the whole year. I stopped expecting to leave any day.

After I returned from Vietnam I wrote my story for

myself to help me deal with this war experience. I also wrote of Martha Raye. I doubt that you will find a truer view of Martha:

The USO shows that came around also boosted our morale. There were Jayne Mansfield, Nancy Sinatra, Roy Rogers and Dale Evans, Phyllis Diller and Bob Hope at Christmas time. They were all great. BUT, the one that really stands out in my mind was Martha Raye. I saw her several times. I was not able to speak to her, but I consider her a true friend. She really went that extra mile. Her love of servicemen was really special. This must have been very carefully thought out in order to keep it separate from such an unpopular war. To be sure all the stars put their best foot forward under very harsh and sometimes impossible circumstances. It was a welcome relief from the hardships we were enduring.

The 1960s and 1970s were turbulent times. Young men were being drafted and sent off to war in a country they had never heard of before while others wanted to join for the sake of democracy. Women volunteered to join the military to serve their country. Not everyone shared their feelings.

Thousands of people of all ages participated in protesting the war. There were demonstrations, sit-ins, and protests around the country. Singers such as Joan Baez, Arlo Guthrie, and The Beatles were singing songs about peace, and Abbie Hoffman was becoming known for his protests. College campuses had to cope with demonstrations. It reminded me of earlier civil rights demonstrations and riots. At times college protests got out of hand.

College campuses became focal point for rallies and "teach-ins" comprised of lengthy series of speeches attacking the war. Marches on Washington, D.C. began in 1965 and continued sporadically, peaking in 1968 and again in 1971. Suspecting that the peace movement was infiltrated by Communists, President Lyndon Johnson ordered the Federal Bureau of Investigation (FBI) to investigate the movement and the Central Intelligence Agency (CIA) to conduct an illegal domestic infiltration. These inquiries proved only that the radicalism was homegrown.

Led by Students for a Democratic Society (SDS), student protests focused attention on the plight of blacks in the U.S. South and the growing conflict in Vietnam. Tactics became increasingly radical as the war effort grew. Some student elements stateside (and some of those abroad) eventually veered toward terrorism. Incidents of official overreaction culminated in 1970 with the deaths of students at both Kent State and Jackson State universities at the hands of armed authorities. Some of the nation's universities were virtually shut down by protest strikes.

KENT STATE

Kent State University (KSU) in Kent, Ohio, founded in 1910, offered arts and sciences, business administration, education, fine and professional arts, library science, and nursing degrees as well as graduate degrees. How sad that it would become known as a killing field.

Students at Kent State, like many others, were protesting against the bombing of North Vietnamese base camps (where Viet Cong were being trained) in Cambodia and other war-related U.S. foreign policy measures. These bombings, which were led by American B-52 bombers, were illegal. The administration of then President Richard Nixon repeatedly lied to the American people about these bombings.

Four protesters died during the march on the Kent

State University campus. What started out as a peaceful war protest turned ugly. On Friday 1 May 1970 some students demonstrated by burying a copy of the U.S. Constitution in front of the Victory Bell on the KSU Commons. This burial was to symbolize its "murder." The Victory Bell was ordinarily rung after athletic victories. The students planned another meeting for the following Monday noon.

That Friday evening was very warm. Some students were drinking and became more indignant over the invasion of Cambodia. A crowd soon formed and the group moved toward the center of town. A few people in the crowd began breaking windows along the way. Students and other participants were met by police at the corner of Main and Water streets. Local police wearing riot-gear closed the bars and forced the crowd back to the college campus by using tear gas. The city's mayor, LeRoy Satrom, thought there was a radical plot afoot. He declared a state of emergency and called the governor at 12:47 A.M. Saturday morning for help. Governor James Rhodes sent a National Guard officer to the scene. Everything was quiet by 2:30 A.M.

By Saturday noon, it was determined that everything was under control and did not require the presence of the Guard. Students assisted with cleaning up the town. However, there were more rumors of radical activities and threats to city merchants. The students were asking the merchants to post signs that protested the war in Vietnam and Cambodia. Reports surfaced that members of the extremist Weathermen faction of SDS were in Kent and/or on the university campus. Rumors circulated that there were weapons and possibly a sniper on campus. Reports claimed the post office and Army Recruiting office in Kent, as well as the Reserve Officer Training Corps (ROTC) building on the campus, would be burned. Kent State officials had notices distributed to all students prohibiting damage to buildings on campus.

Local law enforcement agencies advised the mayor they could not provide substantial assistance to protect the city and its residents. Mayor Satrom called Governor Rhodes at 5:28 P.M. formally requesting assistance from the National Guard solely for the purpose of assisting the civil authority. The Guard was dispatched, although at no time was martial law declared.

That evening over a thousand people surrounded the barracks housing the Army ROTC on the campus. Shortly after 8:00 P.M. a few radicals managed to set fire to the building. Although the fire department responded, they were hampered in fighting the fire when their hoses were punctured and slashed by protesters. By midnight the National Guard cleared the campus. They forced both students and non-students into the dormitories, where they all spent the night.

National Guardsmen occupied the city and campus. On Sunday both were calm. Several meetings were held that resulted in misunderstandings between state, local, and University officials. Later that evening a crowd gathered at the Victory Bell. They failed to disperse when asked to do so by the Guard. At 9:00 P.M. the so-called Ohio Riot Act was read and tear gas was fired into the crowd. I say "so-called" as no one has been able to produce a copy of it to this day—only a copy of the General Laws of the 180th General Assembly of the State of Ohio that discusses "disrupting orderly conduct of a college or university."

The demonstrators reassembled in Kent blocking traffic at the corner of East Main and Lincoln streets. They thought officials would talk to them but no one arrived. They became hostile and about 11 P.M. the Ohio Riot Act was read again and tear gas was used —this time a number of guardsmen and protesters were injured.

The events of the evening caused resentment among everyone involved. Classes resumed Monday morning. The protesters vowed to hold their planned rally at noon, even if prohibited. The National Guard said they would disperse any gathering.

Although many students knew the rally was banned, more than two thousand demonstrators gathered near the commons by noon on Monday 4 May 1970. Students who commuted didn't know about the ban. The Guard ordered them to disperse. Their orders were met by chants, curses, and stones. Tear gas was fired into the crowd. The Guard, with fixed bayonets, moved towards the unruly crowd forcing them to retreat. They walked up the hill past Taylor Hall onto an athletic practice field. There the protesters were fenced in on three sides. The guardsmen fired more tear gas and the protesters responded with more stones and verbal abuse.

The guardsmen then retreated, followed by some of the protesters at a distance of from 20 to 250 yards. Near the crest of Blanket Hill, 28 of the guardsmen turned and opened fire on the protesters with live ammunition. In thirteen seconds they fired between sixty and seventy shots into the crowd. When the air cleared, four Kent State students were dead and nine other students were wounded. Later, Ohio's Adjutant General S.T. Del Corso would call it a "survival incident."

The four students killed were Jeffrey Miller, Allison Krause, William Schroeder, and Sandra Scheuer. The nine students wounded were Joseph Lewis, John Cleary, Thomas Grace, Alan Canfora, Dean Kahler, Douglas Wrentmore, James Russell, Robert Stamps, and Donald MacKenzie. Dean was permanently paralyzed from his wounds. Two of the victims allegedly were not even participating in the demonstration but were peacefully walking off campus at the time of the shooting.

Remaining students couldn't believe what had happened. Disbelief, fright, and attempts at first aid gave quickly to anger. Two to three hundred students gathered on a nearby slope but were ordered to move. Faculty members finally persuaded them to disperse. The president of the university then closed the campus. Students were told to pack their things and leave the campus. The university was closed until the summer session began.

The following day one of the largest demonstrations ever was held on the campus of California State University at Long Beach. The crowd spilled over onto Seventh Street. Students not only protested the Cambodia bombings but also the killing of students at Kent State.

No one had expected the Kent State protest to become a major news story, so no publications had assigned photographers to cover it. John Paul Filo, a student photographer on the campus yearbook staff, was present. He snapped several photos, one of which he took to a local paper. The *Valley Daily News* not only published the photo, but they sent it out over the Associated Press (AP) wire. The picture of Mary Ann Vecchio screaming as she knelt over the body of slain student Jeffrey Miller became a Pulitzer Prize winning picture.

Twenty-five years later this photo came into question when it appeared in the May 1995 issue of *Life* magazine. The 1995 reprint had been airbrushed by someone who removed the fence post from behind Mary Ann's head. David Friend, *Life*'s Director of Photography, said the fence post-less photo had apparently appeared in various publications dating back twenty-three years to a *Time* magazine article on 6 November 1972. No one knows who altered the photo. The airbrushed photo sparked quite a bit of conversation over the Internet.

Phil Irving of Kemptville, Canada wrote that the result of the airbrush incident is an image which "looks better." He felt it was easier to discern the central images: the student dead on the street, the woman kneeling over him, her companion with a turned head, the woman walking behind her, and the man with his back to the camera. The casual air of not being involved—as though divorcing themselves from the disaster—of bystanders seems as disturbing as the grief of the kneeling woman and the stillness of the dead student. Against these central figures, he felt the background became insignificant.

Mary Holmes commented that by removing the pole, you remove the fence; by removing the fence, you remove the reality of the Kent State University's control of public spaces and at that time, 1970, students' access to them. The whole question of the pole relates to the control of public space. The university had put up a fence to stop people from demonstrating. Mary would argue that erasing that pole erased that fact. Along with control of the public space issue remains that of how the state controlled the crowds that tragic day in 1970. Removing the pole from the photo, Mary believes, amounted to that moment in American History being whitewashed and smoothed over.

I agree with Mary's words "The reality is we will distort the truth in order to make something look better. We will dress up a documentary to fulfill our slant on history and keep within the bounds of professionally accepted norms of aesthetics and practices. All to conform. But at what price?"

JACKSON STATE

Eleven days later a similar incident occurred at Jackson State College in Jackson, Mississippi. Local police officers and National Guardsmen responded to a nearby bonfire and ordered students into Alexander Hall, the women's dorm. Emotions were running high. The college's predominately black students were upset to see authorities on their campus following what had happened at Kent State. Some female students joined male students in jeering the officers.

This confrontation seemed to have passed when a commuting sophomore, Gene Young, noticed he missed his curfew. He began to jog homeward when he heard gunfire. He headed back to the dormitory and found chaos. Two people were killed and a dozen wounded, following the firing of 460 rounds of ammunition. The two dead students were Jackson State junior Phillip Gibbs, who was preparing for law school, and James Earl Green, a high school senior who was on his way home from a part-time job at a local store. Later police said they had responded to gunshots they had heard in the area. Officers from the city of Jackson denied they had fired on the students. Others claimed they had seen a sniper in the dormitory.

Campus officials were unable to calm the students. Gene Young climbed onto a table and began to speak. Using a bullhorn borrowed from Jackson State President John Peoples, Gene used the words of Martin Luther King Jr. calling for peace and prayer. A hush fell over the crowd.

After exams and graduation were canceled, Gene organized a walkout at the city's largest black high schools. The schools were closed until the two slain students were buried.

Questions arose as to the sniper theory. Was it the same one some officials claimed was at Kent State? Little attention was paid to these events at Jackson State. Was it because of the history of the South and Mississippi in particular? Which was it: a racial or anti-war problem? To this day, there are no answers. No officers were ever prosecuted. In 1995 the bullet scars were still visible on the walls of Alexander Hall.

In November 1970, an Ohio grand jury blamed twenty-five students, not the Guardsmen, for the entire incident at Kent State. The jury's report said: The Guardsmen fired in self-defense and they are not subject to criminal prosecution. This report was greeted with dismay but life on campus continued much as usual.

While some people were demonstrating in the United States, others were serving our country overseas. Sergeant First Class Edward Linker was still on active duty when he contacted me. He served in Vietnam with Company B, 158th Aviation, 101st Airborne in 1971 and in 1972 with the 386th Transportation Company, Fourth Transportation Battalion. Martha Raye's words helped him realize he was doing good.

> I remember Maggie as being one of my War Time Heroes in the 1970s. She helped me through a critical period of my life by stating a few kind words in a time of great need. Maggie said to me, "Young man, there are people back in the states that are not fit to even shine the boots that you wear, or for that matter, even walk in your boots, because you are doing what is required of you; you are in Vietnam."
>
> Believe it or not, these few words carried a powerful impact on how I felt about myself and Vietnam. It was a time when few realized what they were doing in Vietnam. There was much unrest in the United States. Those few words spoken so many years ago have made me proud of being a Vietnam Veteran and to this day still have a powerful impact on my life.

27 JANUARY 1973: IT WAS OFFICIAL—
THE WAR WAS OVER

The Paris Agreement signed by President Richard Nixon on January 27, 1973 ultimately ended our involvement in Vietnam. It was official: the war was over. The U.S. would withdraw its troops and Hanoi would return all captives during a phased program code-named Operation Homecoming. Our men and women came home. The United States did not militarily "lose" the war. But returning Veterans had no welcome home parades or heroes' welcome. They had no victory to celebrate. The only celebrations held were when American POWs stepped off their Freedom Birds. But not everyone has been accounted for to this day.

During the war there were mixed attitudes about the men and women who were serving our country. Flower children and "peaceniks" protested the war in peaceful manners while others participated in loud and mean-spirited actions.

Few soldiers had chosen to go to Vietnam; most were drafted. As they returned home, some of them were called baby killers, others were spit upon. Few were welcomed with open arms except by their loved ones. They felt shoved aside, virtually forgotten, alienated. Many Americans shrugged off Vietnam Veterans as losers or warmongers. They were written off as drug users, alcoholics, psychotics, and criminals. While it is true that some became addicts and criminals, far more have become teachers, lawyers, doctors, nurses, or successful in other worthwhile careers. In my opinion they are all heroes and should have been welcomed home a long time ago by all the American people.

THE WALL

In 1955 the first American soldier was killed in Vietnam; however the first name listed on The Wall in Washington, DC is from July 1959. The unofficial start of the Vietnam War for America was in 1961, but the official date is still listed as 1963.

The ending date listed on The Wall is May 1975. The names are in chronological order according to the date of casualty. Within each day the names are listed in alphabetical order. Beginning at the vertex on the East Wall (dated 1959) is the following statement:

In honor of the men and women of the armed forces of the United States who served in the Vietnam War. The names of those who gave their lives and of those who remain missing are inscribed in the order they were taken from us.

The first two names on The Wall are for 8 July 1959. They are Dale Richard Buis and Chester Melvin Ovnand. Names continue from that point to the end of the East Wall.

Starting at the tip of the West Wall, the names continue—ending at the vertex. The last two names on The Wall are Elwood E. Rumbaugh and Richard VanDeGeer. Their date of casualty is listed as 17 May 1975. At the bottom of The Wall is this statement:

Our nation honors the courage, sacrifice and devotion to duty and country of its Vietnam Veterans. This memorial was built with private contributions from the American people November 11, 1982.

The Wall in Washington, DC was designed by Maya Ying Lin of Athens, Ohio. This black granite wall is 493.5 feet overall, each side is 246.75 feet and the vertex is 10.2 feet high. As of June 1997 there were 58,209 names on The Wall. Eight of those are women (seven Army and one Air Force) and sixteen are Chaplains.

During the dedication of The Wall in 1982, Britt Small and Festival began singing "America" in an attempt to settle a commotion that had been brewing among some

Veterans. Since then Britt Small and Festival have been all over the country. Although they sing a variety of songs, most are patriotic songs. One very special song, aptly named "The Wall" is about a Gold Star Mother whom Britt had met at The Wall. With Britt's permission, here are the lyrics to it:

∽ THE WALL ∽

Lyrics by Lyle Zoerb
Music by Ray Roth and Britt Small

"In this place of honor
        to what is best of man—
I found a crying mother
        with flowers in her hand.

"She said that she was there, because,
        her son was ten years gone.
Another life that was not spared,
        in a place called Vietnam.

"She turned to me, and said,
        'Young man, please take me in your arms.
And walk with me, on past The Wall,
        I want to see them all.

"A special place, this is to me
        but, its taken them so long.
To say his life was not in vain,
        in a place called 'Vietnam.'

"The monument here, shows me
        that the nation has some pride.
To say they really care about
        the ones who've fought and died.

> "So you can stand here, with me, now
> and hold me while I cry.
> The price we pay for Freedom, son,
> it hurts me deep inside.

> "The price we pay, for 'Freedom,' son,
> is the highest price of all.
> The price we pay for 'Freedom,' son,
> is written on The Wall.'

> "In this place of honor
> to what is best of man—
> I found a crying mother
> with flowers in her hand."

It took America twenty years to recognize the heroes of Vietnam. What a sad commentary. Men and women answered when their country called, served bravely, sacrificed much and gave their best for duty, honor, and country.

General Colin Powell spoke at The Wall after Desert Storm in 1991. He said:

You need no redemption. You redeemed yourself in the AShau Valley...at Hue... DauTieng...KheSanh, in the South China Sea, in the air over Hanoi, or launching off Yankee Station, and in a thousand other places. The parades and celebrations are not needed to restore our honor as Vietnam Veterans because we never lost our honor. They're not to clear up the matter of our valor because our valor was never in question. Two hundred thirty-six Medals of Honor say our valor was never in question. The 58,175 names on this wall say our valor and the value of our service were never in question.

General Powell said it all in that speech. But if we don't pass on our experiences to others, they will never know the sacrifices we made. I encourage everyone I address to ask their family members about such past experiences.

We must keep these memories alive.

8

KEEPING MEMORIES ALIVE

Soon after moving to El Paso in August 1996 I headed north to attend the Twelfth Annual Nebraska Vietnam Veterans Reunion '96 (NVVR '96) in Hastings, Nebraska.

Since I don't like to fly, I traveled by Greyhound bus. To my surprise, a Border Patrol officer entered the bus at the first stop in Alamogordo, New Mexico. I would have expected to see the officer along the U.S.-Mexico border, but we were over a hundred miles from that border. With his hand on his weapon, the officer told everyone to produce identification (ID). This was my first experience of having to prove my identity. I didn't like it!

During our forty-five-minute layover in Albuquerque, five local police officers rode into the station on their bicycles. While I sat there I thought of Colonel Knute Lawson, who lives in Albuquerque. He was Chief Logistics Advisor of Air Force Advisory Team Seven. He was responsible for the Vietnamerication program for the Air Force in the II Corps region of Vietnam. He remembers that Maggie came by to cheer them up at NhaTrang on 31 December 1971.

By December 1971, CamRanhBay was closed so we were unable to enjoy any type of Christmas show since the big names went to DaNang or TanSonNhut. In a previous tour we had everyone from Bob Hope to Miss America, but in late 1971 few if any performers paid much attention to the "backwash" of the war. There were only thirty-five Americans in this Air Force Advisory Team commanded by Colonel Elvin O. Wyatt. He had made some comments in Saigon about entertainment and Martha came up by chopper to visit us.

We appreciated her morale-building exercise. Elvin Wyatt opened a bottle of Cold Duck that was left over from an operation at Pleiku...Martha did not forget us. I can remember her laugh to this day.

I enjoyed the gorgeous scenery in Colorado. As we passed the signs for Fort Carson, I thought of Sergeant First Class Ernest Bradley's meeting with Maggie during the Christmas holidays of 1965 while he was stationed in NhaTrang. He and Maggie exchanged Christmas cards the next twenty-five years. When I last heard from him, he was still on active duty stationed at Division Artillery Headquarters at Fort Carson.

As we approached Denver, I noticed signs to Aurora. Leslie Gorsuch, a Vietnam in-country Vet, lives there. He met Maggie in NhaTrang in 1966 or 1967 at a USO show. He felt she was long overdue for national recognition.

Bill "Doc" Hoffman served with the Seventh Regiment, First Cavalry Division. He was in LongBinh and saw Maggie late 1967 or early 1968. "God love Maggie for all she did for us, and Noonie as well for a book that has brought tears of gratitude several times already." One of his relatives sent him a copy of *Memories of Maggie*; he and I have been corresponding regularly. He has put me in touch with several other Veterans and organizations. He was living in Colorado when we first began corresponding, then he moved to Memphis, then back to Longmont, Colorado.

Nebraska Vietnam Veteran's Reunion

The theme for this reunion was "Keep the memories alive." Truly, my motive for writing *Memories of Maggie* was to keep her memory alive, so I felt very much at home attending this event.

Richard Goldsberry, who works for U.S. Department of State in Washington, D.C. wrote:

> I just completed your wonderful biography *Memories of Maggie*. Very well done. Thanks for writing about this truly remarkable woman. It is sad she has passed on, but this book will keep her spirit alive as long as there are wars to be fought and Vets to care for.

I am touched by just how deeply others felt about Maggie, her caring heart, and about keeping her memory alive.

There were two people who would be attending NVVR '96 whom I could hardly wait to see: Brenda Allen and Britt Small. (Brenda is one of the "Jewels" discussed in Chapter 3). With her generous nature, Brenda came through once again! She contacted Veterans groups and talked about *Memories of Maggie*; she set out on her own quest to find me speaking opportunities in Nebraska. She arranged for me to attend the Nebraska Vietnam Veterans Reunion '96.

Britt Small and Festival

Remember that man who sang at The Wall to quiet an unruly crowd? As many times as Britt and I have been in the same place, we had never met.

Britt Small & Festival, 1996.
Photo contributed by Noonie Fortin.

When Britt returned from Vietnam, he vowed to keep his family together—especially after seeing how Veterans were being treated by the American public. He and Festival began as a family group of seventeen members; now it numbers seven. I highly recommend his group for any Veteran-related or community activity.

When I arrived in Grand Island, Nebraska, Gene Schmitz and Vi Trausch were there to take me to Hastings.

The next morning Lee and Judy Daily, chairpersons of NVVR '96, arrived at the hotel. The 8:30 A.M. radio interview which had been scheduled for Saturday morning, was moved up to Thursday morning. Bill Rinehart of KHAS-AM1230 Radio interviewed me at the hotel. Judy took me to Grand Island for a noon television interview. Paige Kelton of KOLN-TV10 in Lincoln had arranged for a link-up interview to be conducted in Grand Island. Later that day, KHAS-TV6 broadcast another interview. Such interviews are greatly appreciated and very instrumental in promotional efforts.

Nelda Alexander was hostess at a women's luncheon attended by thirty-six women. Two of the women (Pat and Norma) were nurses who served in Vietnam. Norma was stationed at BinhThuey. After the luncheon, I presented a workshop about Maggie. Jay McIntire, a doctor who now specializes in Post Traumatic Stress Disorder (PTSD), attended. Both he and his wife Carol served in Vietnam.

That evening I waited eagerly for Britt Small and Festival to arrive. During a break in their wonderful performance, I approached Marty, Britt's son, and asked to speak to Britt. Marty spotted my name tag and said, "You're the lady who wrote the book. Come with me. My Dad's waiting for you."

Britt came off his bus and gave me the biggest hug. We spoke at length about Maggie. He still has Maggie's last tattered flag. Britt had served with the 173rd Airborne in Vietnam and received a Purple Heart. He invited me to speak in his hometown of Skidmore, Missouri for Freedom Fest '97.

Following Britt's fantastic performance, Brenda Allen sang, played guitar, and told jokes till way past my normal bedtime.

The NVVR '96 held a parade through Hastings on Saturday morning. They drove me in a convertible that had my name written on both sides of the car. The parade ended at the Hastings Airport, where Lieutenant Colonel Jerry Yeager spoke about the Phantom aircraft, which is on permanent display at the entrance. Jerry was an Air Force pilot in Vietnam.

I asked Jerry if he and Charles "Chuck" Yeager were related (He is not.) Chuck entered the Army Air Corps in September 1941 as a private and rose through the ranks to brigadier general. During World War II he flew sixty-four combat missions—downing thirteen enemy aircraft. In one day he shot down five ME-109s in one dogfight, making him an Ace. He was also responsible for shooting down a German ME-262 jet fighter from his propeller-driven Mustang. However, Chuck really made a name for himself on 14 October 1947 when he became the first person to break the sound barrier when he flew the Bell X-1 over California's Mojave Desert. Fifty years later on that date, 14 October, Chuck returned to Edwards Air Force Base to reenact his history-making event. He was awarded the peacetime Congressional Medal of Honor in 1976.

That afternoon I conducted another workshop about the Maggie project. At one point I showed the group my prepared speech, then threw it away. I have difficulty following a set pattern when it comes to addressing a group about Maggie. Her life and career were so diverse, but she followed scripts only for movies and television.

During this session I mentioned feeling a presence watching over me. During the PMOF campaign, Belle and I often felt someone above was leading us in the right direction. Susan and I felt it at The Wall on Memorial Day. As though she were a guardian angel, I believe Maggie still guides our efforts on behalf of her Veterans.

Lil Montgomery, who was at the workshop, said she also believes in angels. She handed me a beautiful pen with an angel attached to the clip. She told me to keep it and always trust in angels to lead me the right way safely. Well, Lil, I still have that pen and it stays with me wherever I go.

Also in attendance at the workshop was David Spry. He expressed interest in having me address Lincoln and Omaha area Veterans who couldn't make it to the re-union. Brenda Allen will be instrumental in making arrangements.

After a barbecue there was a 1950s-1960s rock-and-roll band and dance complete with poodle skirts, pony-tails, blue jeans, white socks, and oxfords.

Several people with whom I had been in contact attended the reunion. Chuck Folsom [16] drove from Fremont to meet me. Patty Skelley, who represented Colonel Earl Hopper and the POW/MIA issue, was at the reunion. She said she was flabbergasted when she read Susan Christiansen's "Introduction" about the blind Veteran in *Memories of Maggie*. Patty was present at that encounter! "Earl and I witnessed that incident. I was wearing a pink dress. Earl was wearing a blue suit. We saw the whole thing," Patty said. They had just returned from dinner and as they walked into the lobby of the Bonaventure Hotel, they saw Susan talking to the blind Veteran. They watched in awe as Maggie walked to-ward the blind man. He had waited patiently for Maggie to have a few free minutes to speak with him. When she approached him, he began to describe when they had met. Maggie filled in the rest. The Vet wanted to thank her for staying by his side after he was hit in Vietnam. Twenty years later, the memory of that encounter was still very moving.

Patty asked if we ever located the man. Susan, LangMarc Publishing, and I contacted "Unsolved Mys-teries" for assistance in locating him. We want him to know what a profound impact he has had on so many lives. "Unsolved Mysteries" declined to help. We have also requested help from the Blinded Veterans Association in Washington, DC. We will continue to search on our own until we find him.

After four fabulous days in Hastings, I left for Denver and two book signings. I thought about another Veteran from Omaha who knew Maggie. A retired Air Force Technical Sergeant read an article I had written in *The Nebraska Legionnaire* listing Maggie's service. It brought back vivid memories of the entertainers who went to Korea and Southeast Asia. "Their mission—to entertain the troops—never once that I heard, did they complain of conditions, combat hazards…" He and other Vietnam Veterans felt some national recognition was in order for those living entertainers who went there! He requested I not use his name in this book.

> I met her at DaNang and though I'm not sure if it was 1965 or 1966, I did get her autograph. This was in the wee hours of morning. We weren't sure how many performances she had done, but after taking time for autographs and chatting with our small group, she was headed for a remote area. This autograph has been passed onto my son, who is a member of the U.S. Army Special Forces (Airborne). My son, his wife, and I saw her beret on display at Fort Bragg when I visited during Christmas 1989.
>
> Perhaps the entertainer with most recognition is Bob Hope. Others that I remember besides Martha Raye were Raymond Burr, Hugh O'Brian, Willie Mays, Rowan and Martin, and George Jessel. In the group with Mr. Jessel was a female, singer, dancer, comedienne who fell solidly on her rear while performing on a makeshift stage. After Mr. Jessel and a few others filled in for about five minutes, she was back to finish her routine and apologized for the interruption.
>
> It was difficult to explain to my wife what it was all about in Vietnam, having spent more than one tour in

Southeast Asia. Recalling the dedication of the entertainers, the trying conditions, and explaining how well
they did without elaborate stage lights, sound system,
dressing rooms, showers, etc., things all came back as
though it was yesterday. I was in Vietnam the first time
April 1965 to May 1966, and the last time in 1973.

DENVER

In a bookstore on South Colorado Boulevard, I met
two women with whom I had corresponded for a number of years. Bonnie O'Leary, a retired Air Force major,
was wearing a Colonel Maggie T-shirt. Roberta Frye is a
retired Army sergeant first class. Later, Bonnie gave me
a brief tour of Denver and drove me to my next bookstore signing in Lakewood. She contacted a radio station where an announcement was made about the signing.

While I was signing books, the store manager told me
I had a phone call. It was from a woman I had met at the
Texas Library Association convention in Houston in
April. She tracked me down to tell me her company was
interested in putting *Memories of Maggie* on audio cassette. This would be a way for more people to learn of
Maggie's generous deeds. With failing eyesight, many
senior citizens and Veterans can no longer read easily,
so audio books are appealing tools. People also listen to
books as they drive to and from work or school.

Bonnie sent me photos of Bertie, Bonnie, and me that
had been taken at the bookstore in Denver. Sadly, she
also included an obituary notice from the *Rocky Mountain News*. Bertie passed away on 5 October. Bonnie and
I may have the last photos of Bertie.

At the dedication of the WIMSA Memorial in October 1997, it was a thrill to see Bonnie there.

L-R: Roberta Frye, Noonie, and Bonnie O'Leary in Denver, August 1996. Photo contributed by Bonnie O'Leary.

GOOD-BYE EL PASO—HELLO CALIFORNIA

For months Jim Spitz and I had communicated while he was preparing for the Labor Day weekend 1996 Colonel Maggie's All-Services Airborne Drop-In reunion. He invited me to attend and made all the arrangements.

During the long train ride from El Paso to Los Angeles aboard the Sunset Limited, there was a horrible rain storm. As I peered out the window, I recalled some of my correspondents telling me tales about Maggie and rain storms. Clyde Bensenhaver settled in Moorefield, West Virginia after he left the Army. In October 1965 he was in AnKhe where Maggie performed in a USO Show. He was serving with the First Air Cavalry at the time. Clyde recalled that it was raining that day. The troops sat in the pouring rain and watched while Maggie and her group performed. "She did a very good job of entertaining the troops."

Colonel Harlan Jencks of Monterey also had a rain story. He now has his doctorate and is currently serving in the Army Reserve Special Forces. Harlan saw Maggie four times. Two of those were mentioned in *Memories of Maggie*. [17] Here are his other encounters.

In Vietnam in October 1966, I transferred from the First Infantry Division to the Fifth Special Forces Group (Airborne). When I arrived at Detachment B-Forty-one in MocHoa (KienTuong Province), the annual flood was at its height. Most of the province was under water, including three of the four A-Camps.

I was shown a photograph of Martha Raye at Camp KienQuan II (A-412). She was standing armpit deep in muddy water. She had visited the province only the week before, including all of the submerged A-Camps. People, rats, and snakes were living on the tops of walls and roofs, but she had actually put on some sort of a show at each camp!

A few months later, I met Maggie at the Seventh Army Republic of Vietnam (ARVN) Division MAC-V Advisory Detachment in MyTho. She couldn't put on a show that evening because she had laryngitis so bad she was (for perhaps the only time in her life) completely speechless. So we watched a film of one of her TV shows and adjourned to the "club" (such as it was) for a party. Next morning, she and I caught the same helicopter heading north to MocHoa. She was alone, wearing the jungle fatigue uniform of a lieutenant colonel of the Army Nurse Corps. I was really impressed that she was going back to a God-forsaken place like MocHoa, but I had underestimated her. When we stopped at MyPhocTay (northern DinhTuong province) to deliver the mail to the two American advisors there, Maggie got off! I don't know how long she stayed, but there were exactly three Americans in that whole district as I flew away: a captain, a sergeant, and Maggie.

By August 1967, I was Commanding Officer of A-414 near MocHoa. This time Maggie arrived accompanied by a couple of other entertainers (I only recall a pretty girl dancer). Maggie came out to the A-Camp and put on a full-fledged show for my team—about twelve Americans—and the Vietnamese Special Forces and their strike force. It started raining in the middle of the show, but they carried on until the microphone shorted out, giving Maggie a nasty shock. We crowded everyone we could into the team house, and she sang for us. I never hear "Little Girl Blue" without thinking of Maggie and how happy she made us on that monsoon night.

Richard Ray retired from the Marine Corps in 1988. He had served twenty-three years and settled in Jacksonville, North Carolina. He saw my notice in the February 1990 U.S. Marine Corps Combat Correspondents Association Newsletter. It brought back a flood of memories to him.

As most of us do, we reminisce about people, places, and events that were indelibly stamped into our conscious and sometimes subconscious. Martha Raye was one of those people.

During my first tour in Vietnam, I kept a journal of sorts. After seeing your notice I dug out book one of that journal as I had a pretty good idea when Miss Raye put on a show for us.

I was a young private first class and assigned to Force Logistics Support Unit-Two (FLSU-2) at PhuBai just south of Hue. It was a cold, dark night on 14 November 1966. We were told there was to be a USO show that night and that was about it. So we were all standing in front of a makeshift stage that was put up in the entrance to the motor pool butler building. Suddenly there she was, Martha Raye—full of life, laughing, joking and genuinely making us feel that she cared for us. There's a fuzzy memory that she was accompanied by Dianne McBain and Tippy Hedrin, but Miss Raye was the only one that registered with me and the only one to make it into my journal.

Those of us who saw her perform stood outside in a driving rain, enjoyed her jokes, smiles, and enthusiasm for us. I had grown up enjoying her comedy through seeing her movies on TV. There were other stars that made the trip to Vietnam to entertain the troops, and they were probably better known, but they wouldn't come to a place like PhuBai because it wasn't considered safe enough. But there was Maggie.

One of the things that impressed me was that a number of Hollywood celebrities would not travel north of DaNang, because it was considered unsafe. She was there and I've never forgotten her smile as it lit up the throng of Marines that stood there that night, oblivious to the cold and wind.

I could envision Maggie in each of these places. She didn't let anything stop her when it came to being with the troops. She was terrified of snakes, rats, and the monsoons; but if our troops had to endure those things, so would she.

As the train rattled on, I recalled three other Veterans who live in Arizona. Sergeant First Class George Davis, now retired from the Army, lives in Sierra Vista. David Jackson III had been working in the Phoenix area. James Rhodes resides in Yuma. George served two tours of duty in Vietnam, 1966-1968. He was fortunate to work with Jonathan Winters, whom he loved dearly. He also saw Bob Hope. He respected both of those great entertainers but said they pretty much played the larger compounds that were relatively safe. George remarked that Maggie was out there beating the bush with the rest of the troops. He served his second tour as a drummer with a Department of Defense soldiers show. Because they were soldiers (entertainers), they were sent into the "hot" areas to entertain, but Maggie always seemed to be one step ahead of them on their tour.

David Jackson wrote that the director of the Upward Bound program at Arizona State University had a photo of Maggie that he took somewhere in I Corps when he was with the 101st Airborne. Maggie was riding in a Jeep through their rear area at the time. He saw one of her performances somewhere in the Highlands a couple of years later.

James Rhodes served with an Air Force Search and
Rescue squadron in Pleiku, DaNang and CamRanhBay.
He was a combat crew chief and only nineteen years old
between 1968 and 1969.

After exposure to chemical agents employed against
the enemy, as well as exposure to Agent Orange, I
began to bleed from my nose, regurgitate blood, and
pass large volumes of blood through my intestines. For
this reason I was hospitalized for three days at the
Seventy-first Evacuation (EVAC) Hospital in Pleiku.

It was under these conditions that I first met Martha
Raye. I remember she came to my bed and inquired
how I was doing. I recall being extremely aggravated
and hostile to her rank. In retrospect, it is evident that
she realized I had nothing against her as a person. She
handled the situation quite well. Without becoming
upset, she requested that I shower and shave—in an
attempt to make me feel better. Since it really was an
order, I did so. I had the opportunity to lash out against
authority and she saved face, as well as sparing me, by
her wise actions.

However, this is just the beginning of the story.
Since I was extremely tense and agitated, it would have
been very easy for Martha to forget this insulting young
enlisted boy; but, she did not!

Early in the morning, on my second day in the
hospital, I was wide awake inasmuch as my anxiety
prevented me from sleeping. Martha sent over a female
second lieutenant. The lieutenant seized me by the neck
and shoulders and said, "Airman, you are really tied up
in knots!"

I acknowledged the obvious fact that I was indeed
tense.

Then the lieutenant asked me if she could attempt to
massage the anxiety out of my neck and back. I could
not believe this! She had to repeat her request, which I
gladly granted.

Not only was this a compassionate gesture on
Martha's behalf, but an extremely wise move. Martha

probably assumed I had little to no regard for officers; therefore, she sent over a second lieutenant who also was a very lovely woman.

That massage was the first time I had been touched by a woman in almost a year—and she was an *officer*! I was grateful. I (almost) began to realize that officers were people, too! I was moved.

At the end of the next day, Martha sent a Red Cross worker to see me. Her name was Dolly Hasslewonder from Oklahoma. I immediately fell in love. Although Dolly would not give me the time of day and I never saw her outside Vietnam, my mental condition had greatly improved.

I began to view the situation on the brighter side and for that I am grateful; perhaps it saved my life, I do not know. As I'm sure you realize, that lowly second lieutenant and Dolly Hasslewonder were lifesavers. Martha was a great person. I appreciated her caring and compassion, and I apologize (twenty-one plus years later) for my behavior.

The rainstorm ended and the sunrise was beautiful. I had watched the desert terrain stay basically the same from El Paso through New Mexico. In the morning I was still in a desert, only now it was California desert. When the train approached Los Angeles, it was a relief to see civilization again.

In Los Angeles I switched trains and enjoyed the scenery as the train traveled north along the Pacific coastline. After a twenty-six hour trip, I got off the train and searched the crowd until I spotted Jim Spitz. The last time we were together was in 1991.

COLONEL MAGGIE'S ALL-SERVICES AIRBORNE DROP-IN 1996

After a short ride from Salinas to Marina, we pulled into the parking lot at American Legion Post 694 for the

Labor Day weekend Drop-In. There I renewed acquain-
tances with many Vets and their spouses. Frenchy
Amundson attended along with Brenda Lasarzig. Brenda
was an Army Military Intelligence captain. She gave
many helpful suggestions for promoting *Memories of
Maggie*. Brenda knew folks throughout the Veterans
community and the media. She hoped to help get me
television coverage if I return to the area.

Several folks at the Drop-In had already read *Memories of Maggie*. They thanked me for writing it and seeing
it through publication .

The next day Jim picked me up and we were off to the
post. Jim had ordered copies of *Memories of Maggie* from
LangMarc. He had a table set up with fliers, reviews,
and books. He announced that I was there and would
autograph each book. Before 10:15 A.M., I had signed
more than a dozen books.

This group and city adopted Maggie as their own
and honors her every year. Jim escorted me to a blue-
green Pontiac convertible. This was to be my ride to,
during, and from the local parade. I felt like Cinderella.
They had signs on both sides of the car that said, NOONIE
FORTIN, AUTHOR. Charles and Susan Berg from the
San Francisco area owned the car. Charles was the
president of SFA Chapter XXIII. He snapped together
the back seat shoulder harnesses around my legs so I
was somewhat secure as I sat on the convertible's trundle
cover. As we drove along the parade route, one man
called out, "What are you the author of?" I was so proud
to shout back: "*Memories of Maggie!*" As we approached
the reviewing stand, I could hear Jim introducing the
Veterans units, Frenchy Amundson, and me over the
loud speaker.

Following the parade we returned to the post. Jim
announced that the airplanes and parachuters were in
the air. Everyone gathered in the parking lot to observe

the flyover of World War II aircraft. They waited to spot the chutes. Maggie wasn't there to tell them where to look. Finally someone saw them—five canopies circling toward earth. I haven't been around jumpers enough to realize just how good they are. Each one, in his own time, circled the area, then landed—standing upright— in the middle of the Drop Zone (parking lot.) The last man down carried the American flag. They all jumped at the same time; but landed at different intervals.

By 3:00 P.M. all copies of *Memories of Maggie* were gone. I took orders to fill when I returned to El Paso. During the afternoon there was a karoke session. Several folks got up and sang along with the music. Jim did an especially poignant rendition of The Righteous Brothers "Unchained Melody," dedicated to Maggie.

The group dispersed afterward so the post could set up for the evening banquet, where I was to give a brief speech. I did not know I would have the honor of sitting at the head table next to Jim Vocelka, Marina's mayor, and his wife. Mayor Vocelka's dad served twenty years in the military and had been to Vietnam. Jim commented that when he was a boy he feared that his dad would not return from Vietnam.

The entertainment consisted of men, women, and children performing traditional Samoan, Hawaiian, and Philippine dances. The children danced the Macarena. After the floor show was over, a special tribute to Maggie was conducted. A bagpiper entered playing "Amazing Grace." Jim pointed out the small memorial tribute to Maggie—an overturned place setting, an open bottle of Vodka, and her photo. Then a country and western band played "Peace in the Valley." These two religious songs seemed so appropriate. I wondered if they were randomly chosen or if these musicians really saw inside Maggie's heart. The banquet's attendees were then invited to pay their respects by saluting Maggie's photo.

Butterflies invaded my stomach as I awaited my summons to address the group. As I approached the podium, I asked Jim if he really wanted me to read what I had. He nodded but asked that I try not to cry.

My voice cracked right away so I decided to read Belle Pellegrino's poem about "Colonel Maggie" (in *Memories of Maggie,* on pages 249-250.) [18] I still become emotional when I read it. When I finished I walked to Maggie's setting, saluted her, did an about face and returned to my seat.

Later that evening I located my protégé, Aimee, and her friend Kim. Aimee and I had not been together in four years. Sunday morning we went to the post for breakfast. I wanted to introduce Aimee to some of my friends. She is currently on active duty with the Army Reserve. They met Jim Spitz, Frenchy, and Brenda. Kim surprised Aimee and me when she started conversing in French with Frenchy. Even Frenchy was amazed on how fluent Kim spoke French.

After I turned eighteen, I spent almost every summer on Cape Cod where I enjoyed the sun, surf, salt water fishing, and whale watching. I have not been to the Cape since 1992. But that Sunday morning Aimee, Kim, and I went to Marina Beach on the Pacific Ocean. As we walked along the shore, Kim spotted several black fins not too far from the shore. They may have been pilot whales. What a thrill!

Later, I said my good-byes to Jim, Frenchy, and the others. I hoped I would have an opportunity to see them again.

TRAIN RIDES ENCOURAGE REMEMBRANCES

The train traveled south through mountains and along the coastline. It was a beautiful ride. Someone spoke over the speaker system identifying points of interest along the way. I felt renewed when I saw the Pacific Ocean again.

As the train made its way toward Los Angeles, I wrote about my trip to the reunion. I wondered about other people from California who had written us about Maggie.

Steve "Doc" Scott now lives in Fresno. He served in the Marines and kept an informal daily diary during his 1966-1967 tour. He searched for and finally found it. He soon realized that he did not even document a VIP chopper landing on a hilltop some distance from the air base at KheSanh during Christmas season. It was Maggie. He recalls that he stood in the background, somewhat distracted by his immediate surroundings and tried to hear what was going on over the never-ending chopper noise. He didn't remember any announced schedule of her visit, which lasted only a few minutes. But someone cared enough to come visit a few guys stuck way out there.

> Martha Raye's visit into KheSanh seems to have grown in significance over time to have more meaning now than at the time it happened. I survived my tour and rotated home in spring of 1967. During subsequent years, as I was exposed to all the media coverage of all the folks going to visit the troops I found myself saying, "Yea, but there was only one that came out into the boonies to visit us grunts."
>
> I still have no idea where the closest safe zone may have been, but I'd be willing to bet that other traveling shows were there playing to larger audiences than a platoon still in flak gear and with M-14's close at hand on top of an elephant grass covered hill.
>
> It is strange that after all these years when I sit down alone I still find that I have a lot of hard bitter feelings about the whole Vietnam experience. But this is one

"Thank you" that I can sincerely send as a long outstanding debt from my tour.

Herman Posch, also known as "Jumpin Herman,"
lived in Greenville. During a conversation with an airborne buddy who lived in Phoenix, Herman asked if he
remembered seeing Maggie when they were in Europe.
He did. He told Herman that he, along with three
others, traveled to Luxembourg to get some wire they
had left behind. They also picked up Maggie's piano,
which she had to leave there. They took the piano to
their mess hall in Chalons, France where Maggie then
entertained them before they took off for Operation
Varsity.

Richard Weir of Mountain View was the Commander
of Fremont's American Legion Post 52 when he contacted me. Members of his post agreed it was reasonable
and proper that Maggie receive the Presidential Medal
of Freedom since she served in the European Theater of
Operations (ETO) right along with Marlene Dietrich
(who by the way was never recognized for her efforts
with the troops.) Both women earned the respect and
admiration of GI's everywhere in the ETO.

Fred Wise from Wofford Heights was in Biskra, North
Africa in 1942. Maggie visited his squadron. He contrib-
uted a photo taken by their squadron's photographer of
Carole Landis and Maggie with (then) Major Glen
Hubbard. The photo is in *Memories of Maggie*. [19]

Ernest Price Jr. is a retired Army sergeant living in
Riverside. I met him at the Drop-In in 1990. He drove the
vehicle in which Maggie rode during the parade. Belle
and I were her honor guards and walked beside the car.
He had first met Maggie at The Hippodrome Theater in
New York City in 1943 while he was serving with the
Navy.

Ernest had an interesting career. He survived the

sinking of his ship, the USS *Spaight*, in March 1943 off the coast of Africa. His lifeboat was captured by the Germans and the crew members were held as Prisoners of War. He left the Navy in July 1948 only to enlist in the Army the following October. He served during the Korean War. He retired in 1963 with twenty years combined military service. Then he served as a

Ernest Price, Jr.

civilian military advisor for the Army in Pleiku, Vietnam from June to November 1967. He had a special relationship with Maggie.

Mary Anne Williamson from Fairfield remembered that her husband Dick met Maggie when he was at the Officer's Club in BienHoa sometime between August 1965-1966. Maggie was stranded by her Special Forces escort when he was called to a firefight. The escort dropped her off at the club and entrusted her to a lieutenant, instructing him to buy her a drink. The lieutenant was broke and asked Dick if he would buy him two drinks. Dick asked him who the heck he thought he was and told him to get lost. Soon after, an arm went around Dick's shoulder. A voice said, "Major, will you buy a lady two drinks?" That's how Dick met Maggie. Dick later told Mary Anne that Maggie was there for all of them when no one else cared. "She was a fine lady."

Captain Bob Gragg, formerly from Visalia, met Maggie at HuePhuBai during his tour as Commanding Officer, Company A, Eighth Radio Research Unit in 1965. His widow, Cherrill, still lives in Visalia.

She was a frontline troop person. She gave a great
show, was garrulous, effervescent and just a great lady.
We just loved her. She was genuine. No television
cameras. We all sat within three feet from her. Unlike
Bob Hope! You couldn't get within 300 yards due to
television cameras, generators, cables and selling his
show stateside.

Les Jacobs, formerly from Oxnard, retired from the
Marine Corps in 1973. He was in Vietnam from 1966 to
1967. Les was attached to Embarkation with the Third
Marine Amphibious Forces at the compound across the
river from DaNang, between Monkey Mountain and
Marble Mountain. Les recalled that Maggie signed a
Vietnamese Fifty Dong note to him that says, "Bless
You—Martha Raye."

Maggie visited Les's compound and spent time chat-
ting with the troops. General Lewis Walt was the Commanding General. He and Maggie knew each other
from World War II days when he was with the Marine
Raiders, and also from Korea.

Retired Army Command Sergeant Major Maurice
Zepeda calls Antelope, California home. He met Maggie
on two occasions: in ChiLinh, Vietnam with A-332 in
1967 and in 1972 at Fort Hood when he was with Company A, Seventy-fifth Rangers.

Former Marine Private First Class John Hall lives in
Richmond. He recalled a photo of Maggie in Vietnam.
She was working as a surgical assistant—a soldier was
in surgery—and Maggie was there helping.

The train continued southward. I wondered what
would happen in Los Angeles. I hadn't been there since
1991 when I stayed with Maggie for her seventy-fifth
birthday. Although I had written and talked to Melodye,
Maggie's daughter, since Maggie's funeral, we had not
met except at the funeral. I would be staying at her home
for the next week.

I was anxious to meet Melodye and her son Nick Lancaster. Two book signings had been scheduled. I had written to over ninety people and groups telling them I would be in the Los Angeles area. Would any of them attend the signings or the special dinner that was planned for Friday night?

I prayed everything would go well.

Jack Sprague, Melodye Condos, and Ed Sprague at Special Forces Association reunion in Colorado Springs, CO, 1997. Photo contributed by Melodye Condos.

9

LOS ANGELES
AND SAN DIEGO

As I stepped down the ramp from the train concentrating on where my feet were going, I heard my name called. Approaching me was a woman wearing an Army field jacket. It had chevrons on the sleeves, a gold oak leaf on the collar, Airborne patches, jump wings, and the name tape read: RAYE, MARTHA. Of course the woman was not Colonel Maggie, but rather her daughter Melodye.

We embraced. Melodye may have inherited her Dad's dark hair and eyes, but she had her Mom's smile, quick wit, and love for people. As we walked arm in arm, we chatted all the way to the baggage claim area, to her car, and her home in Burbank.

Melodye had a blue 1976 Volkswagen bug. Her dog, Precious, was in the back seat as we drove to her home. Like her mother, she lived in an unpretentious three-bedroom bungalow. She made me feel right at home. We sat up late talking. In fact, we talked all week long!

We discussed Melodye's manuscript about her life as the daughter of a Hollywood personality. I had mailed my original manuscript of *Memories of Maggie* for her approval long before I signed a publishing contract. Melodye asked me to read her manuscript. Tuesday morning she went to work while I read her manuscript. I learned so much more about Maggie's personal life, just as Melodye had learned about her Mom's time with her troops from reading mine. Melodye told her co-author, Jean Pitrone, that she had allowed me to read the manuscript. Jean was concerned I might steal some of the materials. "No Way!" Melodye said. She knew I didn't want to write about Maggie's personal life.

When Nick Lancaster, Melodye's tall well-built son, came home, I noted his structural resemblance to his late grandfather, Nick Condos, Maggie's fourth husband and Melodye's father. He has dark eyes and hair like his Mom. Nick, like his mother and grandmother, is interested in the music business. I learned that Melodye also has a fine singing voice and writes songs.

I enjoyed meeting Nick. Our paths crossed several times during the week. He thanked me for writing a book about his grandmother, whom he loved dearly and missed.

Melodye returned from work, changed clothes, and the two of us were off to my signing at a Burbank bookstore. When we entered the store, there was a sign in the entrance announcing that I would be their guest author. The Community Relations Coordinator (CRC) took us to the cookbook section where she had a table set up for my signing. This was Melodye's first experience with a book signing.

We sat there, just the two of us, for what seemed an eternity. Melodye couldn't believe where we were stationed. How would anyone know where to find us? If they're going to hide us, the least they could do was put us in the biography or military section. Why with the cookbooks? Unfortunately, many stores place authors out of store traffic. Melodye was learning quickly.

Melodye and I took turns talking to the people who came to look at the book. We answered their questions about Maggie. Sergeant First Class Cheryl Patterson and her husband, John, a retired Army master sergeant, stopped by. Cheryl and I knew each other from when she was stationed in Schenectady, New York with the unit to which I belonged. When I was first sergeant, she was my Company Clerk. Cheryl recalled my concern for the POW/MIA's and getting the PMOF for Maggie. Melodye promised to keep in touch with Cheryl since they live near each other.

Noonie Fortin and Cheryl Patterson at Burbank book signing, September 1996. Photo by Melodye Condos.

As we chatted, a man looked at the cookbooks.

"Didn't Martha Raye have an affair with some senator?" he asked. I thought Melodye would lose her cool.

"You have her mixed up with someone else," we said in unison. He walked away.

An older gentleman kept walking past us. He would look our way but each time I glanced at him, he quickly looked the opposite way. Melodye asked me about him. Many Veterans still can't face issues about their military experiences, but I knew that at some point he would look at the book even though it might not be until we had departed.

As 9:00 P.M. approached, we began to pack my displays. The older man reappeared. This time he came right up to the table. He said he had special memories of Maggie, but he didn't want to talk about them. I asked him where he served and he insisted he wasn't a Vet but rather just a fan. I believe he was a Vet who hadn't come to grips with it yet. I didn't press the issue. He asked for an autographed copy of the book. Melodye signed his book first, then as I signed it. I said to him, "Welcome Home." Gary Garrison walked away with his book in hand and a smile on his face.

After we returned to Melodye's, we stayed up late talking. It reminded me of teenage slumber parties. We had hoped that Susan Christiansen could have joined us—then the books would have had all three signatures from the women authorized to write about Maggie. But she was unable to travel to Los Angeles.

During the course of the week, Melodye and I learned we liked many of the same things: simple homes, casual clothing, similar foods, music, and television shows. We could have been sisters or cousins. I learned so much about Melodye and Nick, as well as their relationship with Maggie. Melodye shared more information about Maggie's parents, brother, and sister, and about her relationship with Maggie, her father Nick Condos, and her stepmother. We entered a strong friendship that will last throughout our lifetime.

Thursday we headed for a signing at a bookstore in West Los Angeles. On the way, Melodye drove to BelAir. She wanted to show me what had become of "Maggie's Team House." As she proceeded down Roscomare from Sepulveda, I recognized some of the houses. I had been on that street many times in 1990 and 1991. I kept looking for Maggie's red ranch house with the white picket fence and flag pole.

"There it is. Look Up," Melodye said.

I couldn't understand why she said to look up— Maggie owned a one-story house. In the flash of a second, I realized Maggie's house was gone. In its place was a two-story structure being built for her last husband.

MAGGIE'S TEAM HOUSE

I felt sick. The home so many Veterans came to know and love was gone. The home Maggie said was to go to Melodye and Nick was gone. Nothing remained of the old structure. The military memorabilia that was to go to the JFK Special Warfare Museum at Fort Bragg was gone. Nothing was left of Maggie but memories. Now I'm *really* glad my first book was published.

Some folks have asked that I describe Maggie's home before her final marriage. Although she was a star of vaudeville, radio, movies, stage, and television, this Hollywood actress believed in the simple life. At different times Maggie had homes in California, Florida, and Connecticut. Sometimes she had maids or housekeepers and a gardener. Most of the time she did everything herself.

The home she loved the most, her final living quarters, was located in BelAir, California. The only thing separating this simple ranch-style house from the street was a tiny white picket fence, a flag pole where she proudly displayed an American flag, and the city sidewalk. There were no high security fences or gates, although she did have an alarm system throughout the house.

To the right of the foyer was a small bathroom, then Nick Condos' room or spare bedroom, the master bathroom, Maggie's bedroom, and two hall closets. The small bathroom had just a toilet bearing a bumper sticker that said something nasty about Jane Fonda.

Nick's room had a bed, dresser, closet, exercise bike, photos on the walls, a desk and chair. I stayed in Nick's room on my second trip to California. Many of the pictures were of Nick, Melodye, and Maggie. An autographed photo of President George Bush and Barbara Bush was on the desk.

Maggie's bedroom was simple with her heated waterbed, dresser, chest of drawers, television and the VCR Rock Hudson had given her. A photo of her mother hung on the wall. I was quite taken by it as Maybelle Hooper Reed resembled my favorite aunt, Elaine Hazzard. On her dresser was an autographed photo of Margaret Truman Daniels.

Nick's room, the master bath, and Maggie's room were all connected. Between them was a closet for her linens and a closet where she kept her outer garments and military uniforms.

Her large combination living room, dining room, and bar contained two fireplaces. The living room area had a sofa, chairs, end tables, desk, computer, television, piano, and a fireplace. A photo of President John Kennedy and Jackie graced the wall along with other photos and paintings. Stacks of military memorabilia were on the floor.

The dining area held a beautiful table and chairs, cabinets, and a huge fireplace. This was where Maggie kept a collection of stuffed and ceramic clowns and dogs.

The twelve-foot long bar was well stocked for parties or guests. Most of the back wall consisted of glass windows with a view of the small back yard and the mountain behind the house. Directly next to the bar was a large photo of Bob Hope presenting Maggie with the Jean Hersholt Academy Award. There was a sliding glass door that led out to the patio where she had some plants.

Off to the left of the front foyer was her den, better known to many Veterans as the "Team Room" and her eat-in kitchen. The Team Room had a fireplace on one wall directly opposite a large bay window with a window seat. Maggie kept most of her military memorabilia in this room. Her walls were covered with plaques, photos, and letters, wall to wall, floor to ceiling, and stacked on the floor behind the sofa and love seat. She had an impressive collection of coffee mugs on one wall. The Oscar she received for her humanitarian efforts with the troops was on a coffee table near the bay window. In this beloved room Maggie spent the most time. As you entered the kitchen from the Team Room, there was a small dry bar and a table with benches.

There was a small guest room in which I stayed during my first visit. When I opened the window, the security guards rushed to the house to be sure there wasn't a burglary in progress. The guest bathroom walls sported posters from her movie *Jumbo.*

Nick's office area was the room where Maggie kept her Hollywood memorabilia. It had a hidden doorway on the wall. Behind the wall Maggie kept all her movie scripts, sheet music, and reel-to-reel copies of her movies.

Although the garage was large enough for two cars, it contained stacks of boxes of Maggie's clothing—and the Mercedes-Benz, which Nick had given her. The car was seldom in the garage as Maggie would loan it to her friends, housekeepers, nurses—and even to me. The small back yard had a hot tub and was surfaced mostly with concrete. The only shade came from the mountain.

There was nothing gaudy or pretentious about Maggie's home. Those of us who have been there loved it—and Maggie. We know how much Maggie's Team House and Maggie will be missed.

The JFK Special Warfare Museum received 2,300 pounds of material. Much of it was damaged furniture. There was little military memorabilia in the shipment. Roxanne Merritt, curator of the museum, and I had an inventory of Maggie's things that was current up to September 1991. Among the items the museum did not receive were Maggie's seventy-fifth birthday present, a gold and diamond Airborne pin, and the Presidential Medal of Freedom or its citation.

We headed towards the Westwood Pavilion. We drove past Matteo's Restaurant. It brought back memories of Maggie and the meals I shared with her there.

A few blocks down the street was the three-story bookstore. The manager escorted us to the second floor. A sign advertised my presentation and listed Melodye as a special guest. As I made the slide presentation, Melodye noted that her Aunt Eileen was on one of the slides. The woman identified in Joe Janisch's photo in *Memories of Maggie* as Maggie's secretary was actually Melodye's aunt. [20]

I had invited some Hollywood stars to join us for our signings. Entertainer Steve Allen wrote a note saying he was unable to make it. Later I received a beautiful autographed photo from Vicki Lawrence on which she wrote "So sorry I missed your signing." Vicki is another woman who deserves credit for going to Vietnam without fanfare.

Miss Fireball

Vicki went to Vietnam with Johnny Grant in 1968. She soon learned of the Hollywood community's resistance to the war—it was very strong. Vicki was in Vietnam for three weeks, along with Melody Patterson and Karen MacQuarrie. Melody was co-starring on television's comedy "F Troop." Karen was a Miss World pageant runner-up. They spent their first night in Saigon. From there they flew on all types of aircraft to visit troops in DaNang, PhuCat, CamRanhBay, BienHoa, and many other sites.

Vicki's group, like Maggie's, stayed in-country and went wherever the troops were located. Vicki returned stateside with phone numbers from troops to contact their families. She made numerous phone calls, just as Maggie had done. Vicki talked about her experiences in Vietnam in her book, *Vicki: The True-Life Adventures of Miss Fireball* and once on her television talk show, *Vicki*. She obviously did not go to Vietnam to make a name for herself, and she seldom talks about her experiences there.

As Melodye and I left the bookstore, we said in unison, "Let's stop at Matteo's." Matteo's had changed since 1991. Gone were the Italian landscape paintings from the walls—replaced by modern pictures. Gone was the train set that ran along the ceiling rafter. Gone was Matty Jordan, the owner. He is confined to a wheel-chair.

We were escorted to a table and handed a menu. Prices had gone up. The menu selections seemed smaller. I pointed to the table where Maggie, Belle, and I sat in 1990 and the larger one at which Maggie and her guests, including me, celebrated her seventy-fifth birthday in 1991. I showed Melodye where Tony Curtis sat that same night. We reminisced about Maggie.

When we opened the door to leave, we stopped and stepped back. There on a shelf in a glass cabinet was a picture of Maggie. She seemed to be looking right at us. Melodye was shocked to see her mother's photo there. We stood looking at it a few more minutes, then quietly left.

THE NINETY-FOURTH AERO SQUADRON

Friday evening was going to be special. And special it was! It was supposingly a send-off party for me. Army

Major Randall "Randy" Muenzberg picked up Melodye and me. He was wearing dress blues. We were having drinks and dinner at the Ninety-fourth Aero-Squadron in Van Nuys.

The Ninety-fourth Aero-Squadron is a restaurant decorated as though it were a World War II military post. It has a room appearing as though it was bombed-out with airplane parts, Jeeps, ambulances, trenches, and other military memorabilia hanging from the ceiling. There are several of these theme restaurants across the nation. I had been in the one in Orlando in 1987.

As we walked down the ramp to the bar, I could see two men in dress greens sitting there. The expression of disbelief came over their faces when they looked at Melodye. She wore her mother's field jacket, one of Maggie's jumpsuits, and her Green Beret. She looked so much like Maggie when she wore the Beret her mom had given her. Lieutenant Colonels Michael Teilmann and Earl Smith envisioned Maggie coming down the ramp.

After a round of drinks we went into the dining room. There we were joined by Colonel Mal Harper and Major Steve Hall, both men wearing dress blues. They too were amazed about how much Melodye resembled her mother.

Melodye and I learned that Mal had been a POW. Steve said he didn't know that Melodye existed. That evening, touted to be in my honor, was really for Melodye. Michael Teilmann presented Melodye with a picture frame containing Maggie's ribbons, patches, rank, and name tag. She wasn't expecting that! What fun!

Michael gave a short speech about a presentation that was done shortly after Maggie passed away. A new medal had been issued for entertainers who cared for our troops during World War II. He then presented

Melodye with the Hollywood at War medal posthumously for her mom. The front of it read:

Hollywood at War 1941-1945

The back read:

> *This medal commemorates the USO and theater personnel that devoted their time and effort to helping the moral of the U.S. fighting forces.*

Melodye was so proud, finding out first hand just how much the troops cared about Maggie.

How I hated that week to be over. Early Saturday morning Melodye drove me to the train station. We tried to keep it light; after all, I would be returning to Los Angeles someday. Still it was tough to say good-bye. We gave each other a hug and I asked Melodye to return to her car while I waited for the train to San Diego.

As I sat in the station I thought about the events of the week. Melodye and Nick were so delightful. Melodye is her mother's daughter. She has her mother's compassion and love for her fellow man. Where did the stories originate that Melodye was an alcoholic and a drug user? I saw nothing that indicated either of those rumors to be true. I thought about Melodye and her relationship with her mother. Many people had told me they didn't know Melodye existed or that Maggie and she didn't get along. I think that Maggie tried to protect Melodye from media exposure, kidnapping, or other tragedy. Some who knew about Melodye thought she was a bad seed. Maggie had told them terrible things about Melodye so they wouldn't get close to her— another form of protection, although perhaps distorted. As I shared those thoughts with Melodye, I hope she began to understand why her mother did certain things.

Like Maggie, I'm proud to call Melodye and Nick my friends.

En route to San Diego, I sat across from a couple who both remembered Maggie and wanted a copy of the book. I also recalled that Beth Goodman was from the San Diego area. She was the wife of a retired Navy serviceman. She told of Maggie's foreign stints while her husband was overseas during World War II. I had corresponded with so many generous people, it was no wonder their stories kept popping into my head.

SAN DIEGO

When I reached San Diego, I hailed a cab to the hotel. It was noon and my room wasn't ready. I had a signing at 2:00 P.M. and needed to shower and change clothes. Fortunately the bookstore was located in the Mission Valley Mall near the hotel.

Retired Army Sergeant First Class Robert Moro of San Diego appeared with a picture of Maggie and him. He was mentioned in *Memories of Maggie*. [21] Howard Cohen said he saw Maggie on 5 December 1967 in BanMeThout. Howard recalled her saying, "Doc, I'm a nurse if you need help." Later, I had another signing at the Rancho Bernardo shopping mall.

Sunday morning I boarded the northbound train to Los Angeles heading back to El Paso. In my sleeper berth I had time to prepare for speaking engagements, book signings, and another trip to the Northeast. I wrote my thoughts about the California trip.

It was daylight when the train sped through New Mexico and barren desert ground. I could see Mexico. I was astonished at the squalor in which some of the residents lived. I was even more amazed when the train crossed the Rio Grande River. I expected a wide and rushing river, but instead it was narrow. The geography lessons on these train trips were eye-openers.

I looked forward to returning to the southwest in the future.

10

ANOTHER NORTHEAST TRIP

A pile of mail awaited me when I returned to El Paso 9 September. The nicest "welcome home" gift was a copy of the Fall issue of *The NCO Journal* in which Jim Collins wrote a favorable review of *Memories of Maggie* .

> This is an inspiring book about a remarkable woman whose heart was larger than her nickname of "Big Mouth."

There was little recuperation time, as two days later I addressed Chapter 574 of the Vietnam Veterans of America (VVA.) Then I taped a television program on KCOS-TV13, a Public Broadcasting Station located at El Paso Community College. Lois Hobart interviewed me for the show "Mature Living," which is primarily for senior citizens. Lois is an author, playwright, senior citizen,—and she remembered Maggie. Lois also reviewed my book for the *El Paso Herald Post*.

> Fortin's book pays tribute to a great lady who had become a dear friend.

Robbie Farley-Villalobos interviewed me for "State of the Arts," a weekly program on KTEP-FM 88.5 radio about happenings in the local community. This National Public Radio station is located at the University of Texas at El Paso.

Hyatt Moser attended my first book signing in El Paso. Hyatt met Maggie during World War II; his story appeared in *Memories of Maggie.* [22] When he retired from the Army, he returned to his home in El Paso to raise horses. One of his horses was sired by the horse that starred in the movie *The Black Stallion.*

Writers groups can be excellent for networking in this business. I met Caroline Freisen, a screenwriter, who expressed an interest in writing a screenplay based on my book. A few months later I suggested her name to a Hollywood motion picture company that was considering turning *Memories of Maggie* into a film or TV movie.

When I explained the process of getting published to one writers group, the president expressed appreciation for that reality check. She explained some writers receive a couple of rejections and stop sending out query letters. No one should ever give up writing to publishing companies just because they get some rejection letters. I'm glad I didn't stop trying.

HEADING NORTHWARD

Once again I was headed for the Northeast. I departed El Paso aboard Amtrak headed to San Antonio where I would change to a northbound train. In Chicago I changed trains and headed east to Albany. Yes, it's a long train ride. But I still hate flying!

Carolyn Shapiro, a reporter for *The Record* in Troy, New York, interviewed me. I grew up in the northern section of Troy called Lansingburgh and had attended the public school system there. Carolyn's article appeared in the Sunday paper. She said I was a home town author who had come back for a bookstore signing and that I would be addressing students at my alma mater, Lansingburgh High School.

I drove to Connecticut to visit my family before boarding a train to Providence, Rhode Island. As usual, I began thinking about people from surrounding areas. I had notified some special folks from Massachusetts that I would be in the area.

Gil Young of Brookline, Massachusetts saw Maggie in Grafenwohr, Germany in 1948. [23] In 1966, nearly two decades later, he saw her again as she performed in LongBinh, Vietnam. He was determined to thank her for being there. He told Maggie that he saw her in Germany earlier. As they shook hands, she looked at his gray hair and in her best "pigeon Vietnamese" she said, "You same sing me," meaning her gray hair.

William Balderson, Jr. from North Dartmouth was a member of a U.S. Navy Advisory Team. He was stationed in NhaTrang and lived there with a large group of Americans in what was called the Military Assistance Command-Vietnam (MAC-V) Compound from May 1965 to May 1966.

One night I had gone to bed early as I had the midnight to 7:30 A.M. duty. About 10:00 P.M. one of my colleagues wakened me "Martha Raye is down in Tadpole's room with a group having a party." I said, "I don't believe you." My friend insisted. I got out of bed, quickly pulled on my trousers and seconds later entered the room. I was somewhat embarrassed at this point as I was the only one of about twenty that was not wearing a shirt.

As I entered, Martha came right over, introduced herself to me and rubbed her hands through my hairy chest. My colleagues found this to be most amusing. I will never forget that event that happened over twenty-four years ago. She was truly one of our great treasures.

Retired Air Force Master Sergeant Harold Burns now lives in Dedham. In 1965 he met Maggie in Thailand, where she was entertaining troops. Harold recalled that it was a small base where he met her. Maggie spent the day with his group, put on a show, and took a tour of their facility. "She was outgoing and very accessible to all who wished to talk to her."

Paul Ferola, Sr. of Hull saw Maggie in Vietnam. He was attached to Company A, Fifth Special Forces (A-323) during 1967-1968.

Retired Army First Sergeant William McManus currently lives in Southwick. He has often thought of Maggie. He referred to her as "The Old Lady of the Boondocks." He served in Vietnam 1968-1969. Maggie visited his unit at DakTo in the Highlands: Company B, Twelfth Infantry Battalion, 157th Brigade, Fourth Infantry Division. William said that Maggie knew the terrain better than he did.

Maggie visited William's firebase during that time. With due respect to Bob Hope, William said he served in Korea and Vietnam but never saw Mr. Hope. He was upset that Bob Hope has a picture dedicated to him at Thayer Hall in West Point. He believed that Maggie deserved the same honor, if not more. His heart and thoughts will be with her till his day comes to be with her.

Army retired Lieutenant Colonel Robert Downey, Jr. now resides in Braintree. As a member of the Americal Division in 1969, he knew the positive effect this grand lady had on our soldiers' morale. "She ranked with the best!"

GIL, GOD BLESS HIM

As I left the train in Providence, former Marine Corps Sergeant Gil Woodside Jr. of Seekonk, Massachusetts was waiting for me. Gil had met Maggie in ChuLai in June 1965. [24] Many years later he was too ill to attend her performance when she came to his home town. He sent a card to Maggie thank-ing her and telling her how much she had brought America to him and his fellow Marines when they were in ChuLai. When he left the Marines, he completed his education and became a teacher.

Gil earned his Doctor of Education degree from LaSalle University in Vietnam Studies. His dissertation was about why the American high school and college education systems were not teaching students about Vietnam. He included methods of introducing courses to schools as well as where to find class materials, speakers, and appropriate video resources for classes. Talk about a worthwhile graduate project!

Gil, who has more than twenty-four years experience as an educator, continues teaching classes about Vietnam and Western Experience at Rhode Island College in Providence as well as classes in American History, World History, Anthropology/Archaeology, and Vietnam, at Seekonk High School. He was honored to be selected as the 1997 Massachusetts' Daughters of the American Revolution (DAR) American History Teacher of the Year. I am so honored that Gil consented to write the Foreword to *Potpourri Of War*.

He keeps himself very busy with community and Veteran organizations. During the past few years he has done a lot of good for his area. Gil was the creator, director, and host of the cable TV show "LZ Greensmoke" during 1992. As a member of Vietnam Veterans of America he has been President of Chapter 273, a member of the Discipline Board of Region 1, and part of their Speakers Bureau. He was also the Public Information Officer for American Legion Post 311. He continues to be an active member in the Greater Attleboro Vietnam Veterans Association.

Gil is Founder and Chairman of the Seekonk Vietnam Veterans Memorial Committee. They plan to honor Seekonk's sons and daughters who served in Vietnam. Groundbreaking for the memorial is scheduled for June 1998.

When Dave McCarthy of *The Providence Journal-Bulletin* interviewed me, he wrote a lengthy article about *Maggie* and my scheduled speaking engagement at the Legion Post. Dave saw Maggie at work when she visited his unit in Vietnam.

> Maggie sought the boondocks to show the soldiers, Marines, sailors, airmen and nurses that somebody from back home cared....Her love for them and her valor were legendary. They will want to read about her.

Seekonk High School

Gil drove me from the Providence train station to his school in Seekonk. Fred Crippen, the head of the English Department, and Gil had arranged for me to speak to over three hundred students between 7:30 A.M. and 1:45 P.M. Addressing four eighty-minute classes was tough.

The students were from the drama, journalism, English, and history classes. I talked about my background, Maggie, and getting published. Upon completion of my slide presentation, I asked if anyone had questions.

Some asked about Maggie's personal life, some about her career, and others about getting published. During each class I found myself giving a history lesson about our nation's wars.

Three photographers took pictures. Doug Allan, a reporter from *The Providence Journal-Bulletin,* asked questions of the students and me. Gil later sent me the article Doug had written.

> When she ventures into the classroom the kids are learning things [about Vietnam] that mom and dad didn't tell them....The kids want to know what was in it for her (Maggie) and I tell them it was heart....Raye 'needs to be remembered for her big heart.'

Doug also interviewed students that day. A freshman boy said he didn't know much about the war because none of his relatives were there. He commented, "Ms. Fortin brought me through the whole life of Maggie." A tenth grade girl said, "I never heard of her [Raye] before this. She was a very courageous woman."

Soon after returning to El Paso I received a wonderful letter from Dr. Russell Goyette, principal of Seekonk High School.

> The faculty and students haven't stopped talking about your day long visit to Seekonk High School on November 1, 1996.
>
> It isn't often that our school is visited by such an accomplished and dedicated speaker. Your topic "Colonel Maggie and the Vietnam War" is not only fascinating, but very important. Our young people, in fact the nation, are sorely lacking knowledge about the War and those who served. The story of Colonel Maggie's service to this country is incredible. When we associate heroes and a war, we automatically think about a male

soldier gallantly attacking the enemy...not a Hollywood star!

The passionately endearing story of a woman giving herself to her country is one you tell with great emotion, intelligence and poise. It is a story every American should hear!

Of equal importance is the arduous struggle you faced researching, writing, publishing and finally marketing your beautiful book. Many of the 600+ students and 20+ faculty who were lucky enough to attend your presentation commented to me that they had no idea how hard it was to complete a journalistic endeavor of this magnitude. Additionally, they marveled at your energy and dedication when you announced that you had already started work on a sequel. They loved the topic, you and your presentation.

Please feel free to use this letter as an endorsement to any educational institution or group (Veteran or civic) looking for a dynamic speaker with two amazing and highly interesting topics (Colonel Maggie and the trials and tribulations of authorship) rolled into one spellbinding presentation.

Please accept our sincere thanks and appreciation.

AN EVENING WITH MAGGIE

Gil had arranged "An Evening with Maggie" at American Legion Post 311. He invited the press, other Veterans groups, and the public. Those who attended were the best I could have hoped for.

I talked about how I became involved with Maggie, the Presidential Medal Of Freedom (PMOF) project, and the publishing process. After my slide presentation, I explained some of the problems we were having getting the book into the base exchanges (AAFES), Veterans Affairs (VA) Medical Centers, and the Military Book Club (MBC).

The Veterans were outraged. They found it hard to believe that AAFES said their book departments were too small for any more books and that the VA said their patients didn't read books. When I told them the Military Book Club said their readership was male and that they didn't read books by women or about women, the group really got upset. Gil told the Veterans he wrote a letter to the MBC and told them he was discontinuing his membership because they wouldn't carry my book.

Gil and Jewel Woodside Jr. at Marine Corps Ball in 1995. Photo contributed by Gil Woodside Jr.

Students, teachers, civilians, and Veterans learned about Maggie and the publishing process. I made new friends and hated to leave Gil and Jewel again. Following hugs and kisses, I boarded the train back to New London. I had been up nearly twenty-three hours, talked almost the entire time—and still had my voice. Thank God for Gil and Ocean Spray Cranberry Juice!

With only a few hours of sleep, I drove back to Albany Saturday morning. In the Berkshire Mountains I encountered snow showers—not a relaxing drive. I prayed a lot. Sunday afternoon I did a presentation and book signing at a bookstore in Colonie. Some of my friends were even there. As I was preparing to leave, a woman asked, "Are you the author?" Linda told me that her dad had been corresponding with me during the PMOF campaign. His name was Robert Setchfield. I said, "Phyllis must be your mom." Phyllis had autho-

rized me to use Robert's story in *Memories of Maggie.* [25]
Linda was elated. She asked that I sign a copy for her
mom. Linda had no idea I was going to be there. She just
happened to be in the store and saw the sign advertising
my signing. Had I not been a little late leaving the store,
we would not have met. My guardian angel Maggie was
still on the job.

MY ALMA MATER

Three days later I went to Lansingburgh High School
to address the students. Fred Erickson, the vice principal, had arranged for me to speak to the junior and
senior English classes. I did my slide presentation, spoke
about Maggie, getting published, my three friends who
died in Vietnam, and why they should honor Veterans
every day, not just on Veterans Day.

Charles Fake came to my presentation. He was my
history teacher when I was in school. Charles said he
was going to look in his things from school. If he found
anything that I had written back then, he would send it
to me. I mentioned to the students that I was in Charles'
class the day another student came running in saying
President John F. Kennedy had been shot. Some things
you don't forget!

In talking with the students, once again, I was per-
plexed. They didn't seem to know dates of the different
wars or much about them. They didn't even know that
three boys from their area had died in Vietnam. What
was worse—they didn't seem to care.

Although I was born in Schaghticoke, New York I
lived in North Troy during my school years. I grew up at
a time when it was safe to walk the streets alone. Three
of my friends who went to Vietnam didn't return alive.

MY THREE HEROES

Photo of engraving on The Wall in Washington, D.C.

Raymond Tymeson Junior was born on 31 March 1948 in Troy. He had been an altar boy in church and loved sports. After graduating from Catholic Central High School, he joined the Marine Corps in 1967 and was sent to Vietnam in 1968. Less than ten months later, his company came under intense fire near DaNang. They were caught in an enemy ambush. Ray went in trying to silence one machine-gun and was caught in enemy machine-gun crossfire.

Ray was shot in both legs and his neck. A bullet severed his carotid artery. A medic went to help him and got killed. Another medic went in but by then both young men were dead. Ray was a twenty-year-old corporal when he died on 2 December 1968 in QuangNam Province. For his actions he was posthumously awarded the Bronze Star. He was buried in Troy on Christmas Eve 1968. His name is located on Panel 37W at Line 22 on the Vietnam Memorial in Washington, DC.

Photo of engraving on The Wall in Washington, D.C.

Paul Baker was born on 23 August 1948 in Troy. After graduating as the valedictorian from Catholic Central High School, he attended Massachusetts Institute of Technology on a full-tuition scholarship. During his second year of college, he quit and enlisted in the Marine Corps. As a member of the Ninth Marines located north of DaNang in QuangTri Province, his unit encountered the enemy and had a running gun battle for five days. Paul was a twenty-year-old corporal when he died on 29 March 1969. His name is located on Panel 28W at Line 78 on The Wall.

Catholic Central High School's Class of 1966 collected two-thousand dollars to start the Tymeson-Baker Memorial Scholarship.

Photo of engraving on The Wall in Washington, D.C.

Peter Guenette was born in Troy on 4 January 1948. If I remember correctly, he graduated from LaSalle Institute in Troy. He enlisted in the Army in 1967. While serving with Company D, Second Battalion (Airborne), 506th Infantry, Third Brigade, 101st Airborne Division (Airmobile) in the QuanTanUyen Province of Vietnam, he died on 18 May 1968 at age twenty. His name is located on Panel 62E at Line 18 on The Wall.

Pete was a machine-gunner and had been sent on a mission to assist a Long Range Reconnaissance Patrol (LRRP) which heavily engaged a company-sized enemy unit that had an extensive bunker and tunnel complex in the province. He and his assistant gunner had been laying down suppression fire to allow the rest of his platoon to move ahead. Meanwhile, two other soldiers joined them. Suddenly there was an enemy grenade thrown at them which landed next to Pete. He realized the grenade would kill or wound at least the four of them and disable his machine-gun. He yelled "GRE-NADE," then smothered it with his body, absorbing the blast. For his actions that day he was posthumously awarded the Congressional Medal of Honor. Along with some of the information above, his citation read:

> For conspicuous gallantry and intrepidity in action at the risk of his life above and beyond the call of duty, Specialist 4 Guenette distinguished himself....Through his actions, he prevented loss of life or injury to at least three men and enabled his comrades to maintain their fire superiority. By his gallantry at the cost of his life in keeping with the highest traditions of the military service, Specialist 4 Guenette has reflected great credit on himself, his unit, and the U.S. Army.

In 1970 these friends were honored when a marble monument was erected at the corner where the Little League field used to be at 110th Street and 8th Avenue in Lansingburgh. Their names were engraved on it. I was at its dedication. How tragic that vandals destroyed the monument and that the community removed what was left of it.

In 1988 a bronze plaque was made in their honor and presented to the Lansingburgh Boys Club at 113th Street and 4th Avenue. It was placed inside the building where only members of the club could see it. I took part in the Honor Guard that day.

In 1991 I was the keynote speaker at an unveiling of another plaque to honor these three brave men. It was attached to a flag pole at the same  corner where the Little League field used to be. The Rensselaer Park Elementary school now stands on that corner.

In 1992 I attended a ceremony as part of the Honor

Guard once again. The community renamed a street "Peter Guenette Lane" near the skating rink we all went to.

My mother sent me an April 1997 newspaper clipping which said the bronze plaque from the Boys Club was moved to the Veterans of Lansingburgh Hall headquarters in North Troy. It would be indoors where all Veterans could see it.

Their names are embossed on The Wall, on the plaques in my hometown, on the Rensselaer County Vietnam Memorial located in Troy, and in the minds of all who lost these friends during the war.

STUDENTS CHALLENGED

There is little written in textbooks about the Vietnam War. During presentations I challenge students to do some research, study our wars and the people from their locality who served. Many don't know whether or not their parents and grandparents had served in America's armed forces. Vets often refuse to talk about their wartime experiences, except with other Veterans. Many do not realize it would be healthy for them to do just that.

Perhaps teachers could suggest having an essay contest. I have offered to read students' papers and select a winner. That individual could present the essay to the student body at an assembly or at a Parent Teacher Association meeting. It would be a good investment for an individual or group to offer an award or scholarship to a winner for the best essay about the war. Fred Erickson sent me a letter in which he wrote:

> I am writing to express my appreciation on behalf of the students and teachers for the heartwarming, informative, and inspirational presentations you made. You

were right on target with your comments and observations, and the students appreciated the anecdotes you shared with them. My only regret was that the time we allowed you was fairly short to properly do justice to a truly great American, Martha Raye. Thank you for sharing your time and for being so gracious, understanding, and sensitive with the students.

GOLD STAR MOTHERS

Many folks are unaware of what an American Gold

Star Mothers group is. I must say that this is not a group any woman would want to join. As American military personnel serve our country, all too often they die while on active duty, most often during hostilities in foreign countries.

Gold Star Mother, Joyce Billeaud, & Noonie at First Cavalry Division's Fiftieth Reunion, Killeen, TX, 1997. Photo contributed by Joyce.

During earlier wars, mothers would place a Blue Star in their windows when their sons went off to war. When their boys returned home they would remove the Blue Star from the window. The families who lost their sons would replace the Blue Star with a Gold Star. The objectives of the women who formed the American Gold Star Mothers are to:

- keep alive and develop the spirit that promoted world services
- maintain the ties of fellowship born of that service, and to assist and further all patriotic work

- inculcate (teach) a sense of individual obligation to the community, State, and Nation
- assist Veterans of World War I, World War II, the Korean War, Vietnam, and other strategic areas and their dependents in the presentation of claims to the Department of Veterans Affairs, and to aid in any way in their power the men and women who served and died or were wounded or incapacitated during hostilities
- perpetuate the memory of those lives sacrificed in our wars
- maintain true allegiance to the United States of America
- inculcate lessons of patriotism and love of country in the communities in which we live
- inspire respect for the Stars and Stripes in the youth of America
- extend needful assistance to all Gold Star Mothers and, when possible, to their descendants
- to promote peace and good will for the United States and all other Nations

The American Gold Star Mothers was organized on 4 June 1928 and chartered by Congress on 12 June 1984. As of September 1996 there were 2,200 members nationwide. These women, all dressed in white, sometimes participate in parades on Memorial Day, the Fourth of July, Veterans Day, or at other Veteran functions. Some speak to groups about patriotism to our country. Some chapters perform flag folding ceremonies explaining each movement to students.

While I was in the Northeast, there was a special display about the American Gold Star Mothers at the New York State Vietnam Memorial Gallery in Albany during November 1996. I had come to know many of these women, especially those from my hometown vicinity. I made a special effort to attend the opening ceremony to see them again. Dottie Rockenstyre lost her son Richard in Vietnam. She and I worked together when I first went to work for the Department of Motor Vehicles in 1970. Betty Hallock, Rita Volmer, Marie Ladouceur, Shirley Jones, and Marge Gilbert are members whose sons also died in Vietnam.

John Edwards (an Ex-POW) from Albany was also there that night. I had not seen him for a few years. Several months later he sent me an article from *The Stars and Stripes*. It was a review of my book by William West of Fort Myers, Florida.

> As a poem is supposed to do, this book begins in delight as we follow Maggie's development as an entertainer and ends in wonder, as we marvel at her self-sacrifice and commitment. It is worth reading.

I am grateful for each review and to those who sent me copies.

Once again I boarded a train headed southward. Time on the train afforded me an opportunity to work on a very important upcoming speech. I also wondered what winter in El Paso would be like.

Remembering...Our Veterans

Korean War Memorial, Washington, D.C.
Photo by Gil Woodside, Jr.

11

EL PASO

---◯---

In 1975 I moved to Albany and bought a house in Colonie three years later. With a population of approximately 100,000, Albany was the largest city in which I had lived. When I first decided to winter in Texas, I picked Copperas Cove with a population of 24,000. Fort Hood, our largest Army base, is near Copperas Cove. Surrounding communities are heavily populated with active duty personnel and Veterans.

In 1996, I moved to El Paso, a city of over 500,000. Many retired Veterans reside there. Numerous opportunities to speak to groups were open to me in El Paso.

Carlos Rivera invited me speak at El Paso's only ceremony to be held on Veterans Day. Fort Bliss and the U.S. Army Sergeant's Major Academy (USASMA) on Biggs Air Field are located there. White Sands Missile Range is within fifty miles and Holloman Air Force Base within eighty miles, so I was surprised there were not several ceremonies.

Most of our national holidays have been changed to Mondays so people can have long weekends. It's no wonder students today don't know important dates.

Presidents Washington and Lincoln's birthdays are no longer celebrated on the proper date; instead they have been combined into one day.

VETERANS DAY 1996

I was eager to see the turnout for the Veterans Day ceremony. In the Northeast, throngs of people attended parades and ceremonies.

Loaded with books and briefcase, I headed for the Veterans Outreach Center. I had no trouble locating a parking space; that was a clue! The Ysleta High School Junior (JrROTC) cadets were practicing for their part of the ceremony. A disc jockey played music from different war periods.

The color guard presented The Colors. The crowd joined in the Pledge of Allegiance. The invocation was given. Carlos identified special people in the audience. There were no elected officials, no representatives from Fort Bliss or the USASMA, and no Gold Star Mothers in attendance. Following introductions I addressed approximately four hundred people.

My talk included stories about my friends and classmates who had gone to Vietnam, the three young men who died there, the Korean War and their memorial in Washington, D.C., POW/MIAs that are still unaccounted for, and Maggie. I spoke about Lieutenant Colonel Frances Liberty's (Colonel Lib) passage in *Memories of Maggie* [26], the Nebraska Vietnam Veterans Reunion, and my motivation for writing my book to keep Maggie's memory alive. Veterans should be honored everyday, not just on Memorial Day or Veterans Day. I voiced the observation that our students need to learn more about America's wars. I threw out the challenge to instill patriotism in the hearts of our younger generation. The JrROTC group did a flag folding ceremony and presented the flag to William Leonard, an El Paso citizen who is an Ex-POW.

Bill arranged for me to address his Ex-POW Chapter a few months later. I was surprised to learn there were more than 120 Ex-POWs in the El Paso area but equally amazed that few of them attended the meetings. Bill Leonard had high praise for Maggie and my book. He said they all learned a lot that evening about a great American—Martha Raye. There were many folks who shared their memories of personal encounters with Maggie.

Esther Perez invited me to address the El Paso School District and VFW Post 5615 about patriotism and the lack of wartime knowledge among students. The Post was honoring surviving Veterans and those who died at Pearl Harbor in 1941, as well as members of Company E (mostly El Pasoans whose National Guard unit was mobilized for the war). Young Marines in the audience that day were attentive. The older generation shook their heads when I said the students weren't being taught much about our wars.

Bob Greenwood invited me to speak to the Pearl Harbor Survivors Association on Pearl Harbor Day and to attend a meeting for the El Paso War Veterans Museum.

Jose Robles told me he was a Veteran of both the Korean and Vietnam Wars. He met Maggie while he was serving near DaNang with the Third Marines.

Carlos Garcia is now a private investigator. In 1968 he was at Camp Eagle in Vietnam with the 101st Airborne Division. He was part of Psychological Operations when he saw Maggie there.

Retired Lieutenant Colonel Lou Lopez remembered that Maggie visited his team on 30 December 1970. He was with B-Fifty-five, part of the Fifth Special Forces Group. He brought along a painting of Maggie, which she had autographed for him.

Ralph Dominguez invited me to attend the next Special Forces Chapter IX meeting in El Paso, but a schedule conflict put this off to early 1997.

Retired Army Nurse Colonel Ramona DeLaney remembered Lieutenant Colonel Frances Liberty and wanted to know how to reach her. Ramona was the Chief Nurse 1970-1971 at the Twenty-fourth Evacuation Hospital in Vietnam.

A gentleman introduced himself as Franklin. He was in NhaTrang in 1963-1964 as an advisor to a Long Range Reconnaissance Patrol (LRRP) when he met Maggie for the first time. During his two other tours of duty in Vietnam, 1966-1967 and 1969-1970, he saw her often.

Christina Graves, Chief of Volunteers at the Health Care Center, invited me to be the keynote speaker on Valentines Day 1997. That day is devoted to saluting hospitalized Veterans and the volunteers who help care for them.

Joe and Irmgard Britt invited me to address The Retired Enlisted Association/Northeast El Paso Chapter 71 at their Christmas Dinner. Several members had seen Maggie in Vietnam.

Noonie and Joe Britt at The Retired Enlisted Association/Northeast El Paso Chapter 71 Christmas dinner, December 1996. Photo contributed by Joe Britt.

The Veterans Day event helped to open many doors for me in El Paso. I addressed civic groups as well as Veteran organizations. At the Five Points Lions Club, two men recalled encounters with Maggie. George Charity saw her in ChuLai. He commented that "Maggie's show was better than Bob Hope's." Retired Lieutenant Colonel Mel Adams served in Vietnam in an Intelligence (G-2) section. He met Maggie several times.

Bob Greenwood invited me to attend a meeting and become a member of a committee working on the El Paso War Veteran Museum. Here I met Erwin "Butch" Koehler, a retired sergeant major, who was in CanTho on a support mission when he saw Maggie. He was going to NhaTrang on a Caribou plane. Their paths crossed several times.

Several friendships developed at Fort Bliss and the U.S. Army Sergeant's Major Academy (USASMA). Master Sergeant Betty Pearce, Sergeant Major Maureen "Mo" Johnson, and Sergeant Major Angie Battista were soldiers. Betty was with Military Intelligence, had been stationed at Fort Devens, Massachusetts, and was an instructor for the Battle Staff Course at Fort Bliss. Angie, originally from the Boston area, was a faculty advisor at the Academy.

MSG Arden Davenport, CSM Maureen "Mo" Johnson, and 1SG Susan Naplachowski. USASMA Graduation Day, 1997. Photo by Noonie.

Mo was also with Military Intelligence; however, she was a student at the Academy. We quickly realized we were both from the Capital District area of New York state. She was born, raised, and educated in Watervliet, right across the river from Troy. We had so much in common. We both studied psychology in college. Both been first sergeants.

These three women understood my desire to have Maggie, as well as other women Veterans, recognized. Upon graduation, Mo was reassigned to Fort Hood, Angie was sent to Germany, and Betty remained at Fort Bliss.

Other friendships developed at Fort Bliss. LeEtta Waldhausen had accompanied her husband from

Culbertson, Montana to the USASMA. She chauffeured me to my destination to address members of the El Paso Chapter of the Eighty-second Airborne Association. LeEtta read *Memories of Maggie,* then sent it to her friend in Idaho as a Christmas gift. A few months later she handed me a page from *The Silver Valley Voice,* which contained a review by her friend, Belvina Bertino.

> This remarkable book...details the incredible legend of actress-comedienne-humanist Martha Raye...*Memories of Maggie,* rated fourth among the ten best sellers about military affairs, is classed as a collector's edition along with such books as Colin Powell's *My American Journey,* Scott O'Grady's *Return With Honor,* Gen. Perry Smith's *Assignment: Pentagon.*

ANY HEROINES PLEASE?

A friend suggested that young girls need a "role model" woman they can look up to and that Maggie might provide them with such a model. I wondered what other women were considered heroes. I remember the Nancy Drew mystery series, Wonder Woman, Super Girl, and now Xena Warrior Princess. But none of these women came close to what Maggie accomplished. Is it possible that we can help turn Maggie into a heroine for young girls to admire? We'll see.

After addressing the Military Veterans Coalition meeting in El Paso, I expressed the dream of having a Navy ship named for Maggie. These comments got a few heads nodding. The president of the Desert Sun Society of Military Widows became interested in the idea. I addressed this group in February 1997.

On Pearl Harbor Day 1996, I spoke at the two ceremonies held in El Paso. I told about Maggie visiting our troops before the war as well as after the bombing at Pearl Harbor, and her trips to England and Africa, her Hollywood career, family life, and how she gave up everything to be with our troops wherever they were. I also encouraged them to talk to their children and grandchildren about their wartime experiences. The president of the Pearl Harbor Survivors Association, Robert Lally, said Maggie visited his unit when he was in San Diego before shipping out to the South Pacific.

Dolores Lenko of Las Cruces has a weekend program where she features local people and their activities. When she heard that Martha Raye was the subject of my book, she invited me to be on her show. I went to the New Mexico State University campus in Las Cruces where she taped the program, "Que Pasa with Dolores" at the KWRG-TV22 (PBS) television studio. The show was scheduled to air several times throughout New Mexico and West Texas for a month.

ADDRESSING TEACHERS AND STUDENTS

In April 1997, Barbara Snyder, whom I had met at an Optimist Club meeting in El Paso, asked if I was available on short notice to speak at her school. The school district was having a teachers' seminar at Burges High School and one of the presenters had cancelled. What a wonderful opportunity for me to address teachers!

Their theme was "Climbing the Mountain to Success." Had I climbed some mountains since 1987? I spoke at two forty-five minute sessions. Those teachers were amazed at what Maggie had done as well as what an uphill fight it had been to get her recognized.

Kimberly Walsh, the Women's Resource Center Director at the University of Texas at El Paso (UTEP), arranged for me to speak during March 1997 for Women's History Month. Among other things, students were interested in what it took to get *Memories of Maggie* published. Later Kimberly sent me this note:

As part of our programming during Women's History

Month, your presentation appropriately introduced the audience to a significant piece of history and an amazing heroine...those in attendance expressed great amount of interest and enlightenment. I'm still amazed at how such a woman as Martha Raye, with all her wartime efforts, could go uncelebrated and unrecognized for so long.

Thank you again for a moving, enlightening, and inspiring presentation on the life of Martha Raye.

In the El Paso I met Janice Woods Windle, who wrote the historical novel *True Women*, based on her family's background and diaries. Janice's novel traced her family's life from before the siege at the Alamo into the twentieth century. Janice's book was made into a television mini-series, which starred Dana Delany.

Dana Delany is also known for her starring role in the television series "China Beach." Through that program, Dana became close to many women Veterans and became involved with Veterans' issues. She frequently can be seen at Veteran functions.

Dana Delany attending the DMZ to Delta Dance in Washington, D.C. Photo by Susan Christiansen.

Few Americans know about women of long ago who not only helped settle America, but also defend it.

12

BRAVE WOMEN

Women who served our nation either in the military or in civilian support roles are seldom recognized for their contribution and sacrifices. The first women to receive Purple Hearts for injuries in Vietnam were Navy nurses. Christmas Eve, 1964, Lieutenant Commander Ruth Ann Mason and Lieutenants Ann Reynolds, Frances Crumpton, and Barbara Wooster were injured when Viet Cong bombs hit their quarters in Saigon.

Most people know that male casualties exceeded 58,000 in Vietnam. However, few know much about the women who died in Vietnam. Eight American military women's names are listed on The Wall. But many more American women were killed in Vietnam. Since they were there as civilians, they are not listed on The Wall.

Seven women served in the U.S. Army:
   Second Lieutenant Carol Ann Elizabeth Drazba
      (Panel 5E, Line 46)
   Second Lieutenant Elizabeth Ann Jones
      (Panel 5E, Line 47)
   Captain Eleanor Grace Alexander
      (Panel 31E, Line 8)

First Lieutenant Hedwig Diane Orlowski
   (Panel 31E, Line 15)
Second Lieutenant Pamela Dorothy Donovan
   (Panel 53W, Line 43)
First Lieutenant Sharon Ann Lane
   (Panel 23W, Line 112)
Lieutenant Colonel Annie Ruth Graham
   (Panel 48W, Line 12)

Second Lieutenant Carol Ann Drazba, born in 1943, was from Dunmore, Pennsylvania. Second Lieutenant Elizabeth Ann Jones from Allendale, South Carolina, was born that same year—1943. Both women were assigned to the Third Field Hospital in Saigon. They died in a helicopter crash near Saigon on 18 February 1966.

Captain Eleanor Grace Alexander from Westwood or River Vale, New Jersey was born in 1940. She was twenty-seven and assigned to the 85th EVAC. First Lieutenant Hedwig Diane Orlowski from Detroit was twenty-three and at the 67th EVAC. Both women were located in QuiNhon. They were sent to Pleiku to assist during a major push. Their plane crashed on the return trip to QuiNhon 30 November 1967. Both were awarded Bronze Stars posthumously. Killed along with them were two male nurses, Jerome E. Olmstead of Clintonville, Wisconsin and Kenneth R. Shoemaker Jr. of Owensboro, Kentucky.

Second Lieutenant Pamela Dorothy Donovan, born in 1942, was from Allston, Massachusetts. She was assigned to the 85th EVAC in QuiNhon where she died of pneumonia on 8 July 1968.

Born in 1943, First Lieutenant Sharon Ann Lane from Canton, Ohio was one month short of her twenty-sixth birthday. She died of shrapnel wounds when the 312th EVAC at ChuLai was hit by a rocket attack on 8 June 1969. Posthumously, she was awarded the Vietnam

Gallantry Cross with Palm and a Bronze Star for Heroism. In 1970, the recovery room at Fitzsimmons Army
Hospital in Denver was dedicated in her honor. This
was where she served before going to Vietnam. In 1973
the Aultman Hospital in Canton, where she attended
nursing school, erected a bronze statue in her honor. At
the statue's base is a plaque listing the 110 local people
who were killed in Vietnam. In 1996 the new volunteer
center at Fort Hood, Texas was named for her.

One of Gil Woodside's friends who had met Sharon
in ChuLai was on perimeter detail the night of the attack
and learned later of her death. Years later when Gil
visited The Wall, he made a rubbing of Sharon's name
and took it to his friend.

Hostile Fire is the first book about Sharon's life. Written by Philip Bigler, it was published in 1996. Why do
people have to die first before books are written about
them?

Lieutenant Colonel Annie Ruth Graham of Efland,
North Carolina, born on 7 November 1916, was fifty-
two. She was the Chief nurse at the 91st EVAC in
TuyHoa. She suffered a stroke in August 1969 and was
evacuated to Japan where she died four days later. She
was also a Veteran of World War II and Korea.

One of the women who sacrificed her life served in
the U.S. Air Force. Captain Mary Theresa Klinker from
Lafayette, Indiana was twenty-seven when she died.
She was a flight nurse assigned to Clark Air Force Base
in the Philippines. She was on a C-5A Galaxy plane that
crashed on 4 April 1975 outside of Saigon. The plane
was on a mercy mission known as Operation Babylift,
evacuating Vietnamese orphans. She was posthumously
awarded the Airmen's Medal for Heroism and the Meritorious Service Medal. Her name is located on Panel 1W,
Line 122 of The Wall.

Many male and female American civilians died in

Vietnam. The Wall is reserved for military members who died while in-country, or since then due to their injuries or illnesses from the war, and those listed as POW/MIA. There is no memorial for all the civilians working for our country who died in Vietnam. However, there are currently two memorials that list the civilian women who died there: one in Fresno, California, and the other in Angel Fire, New Mexico.

Captain Mary Klinker was not the only person to perish that fateful day. In all, sixty-five Americans died: fifty-six civilians and nine military. Thirty-eight were women who were trying to get the orphaned Vietnamese children out of the country. Except for one child and a teacher, all worked for U.S. government agencies in Saigon at the time of their death.

The women who died that day were: Barbara Adams, Clara Bayot, Nova Bell, Arleta Bertwell, Helen Blackburn, Ann Bottorff, Celeste Brown, Vivienne Clark, Juanita Creel, Mary Ann Crouch, Dorothy Curtiss, Twila Donelson, Helen Drye, Theresa Drye (the child,) Mary Lyn Eichen, Elizabeth Fugino, Ruthanne Gasper, Beverly Herbert, Penelope Hindman, Vera Hollibaugh, Dorothy Howard, Barbara Kauvulia, Barbara Maier, Rebecca Martin, Sara Martini, Martha Middlebrook, Katherine Moore, Marta Moschkin, Marion Polgrean, June Poulton, Joan Pray, Sayonna Randall, Anne Reynolds, Marjorie Snow, Laurie Stark (the teacher,) Barbara Stout, Doris Jean Watkins, and Sharon Wesley.

Theresa Drye was not the only American child to die that day. Her brother was also on board.

Sharon Wesley had previously worked for both the American Red Cross and the Army Special Services. She chose to stay on in Vietnam after the pullout of U.S. forces in 1973.

Other American women civilians also died in Vietnam. Two female journalists were killed. Georgette

"Dickey" (sometimes spelled Dickie) Chapelle was on patrol with a group of Marines outside of ChuLai in 1965 when someone hit a trip line booby trap and she was hit in the throat. She fell into a field of hundreds of punji sticks. She was working for *Readers Digest* when she died on the second day of Operation Black Ferret. Gil Woodside was in ChuLai at that time and had met her.

The Marine Corps League later established an award in her name. The Dickey Chapelle Award is intended to extend recognition to a woman who has contributed substantially to the morale, welfare, and well-being of the United States Marine Corps. Past recipients include Martha "Colonel Maggie" Raye, Marjorie Merriweather Post, Kate Smith, Sally Ride, Jeanne J. Kirkpatrick, Lucy Caldwell, Sister Veronica, O.S.B., Yvette Sommers, Congresswoman Beverly B. Byron, Rear Admiral Grace Hopper, Robin M. Higgins, Hazel E. Benn, Esther Clark, Elaine Rogers, Carmella LaSpada, and Susan Braaten.

The other woman journalist was Phillipa Schuyler. She was killed during a firefight in DaNang in 1966.

Barbara Robbins worked for the Central Intelligence Agency. She died in the Christmas bombing of the American Embassy in Saigon in 1966. Barbara was a twenty-year-old stenographer from Denver. After the Viet Cong bomb hit her building, she was found dead at her desk still holding a ballpoint pen.

The United States Agency for International Development employed Marilyn Lourdes Allan, better known as Lynn Allan, from Albany, New York. Lynn was murdered by a U.S. soldier in NhaTrang in 1967. Although she could not be listed on The Wall, her name was added to the names listed on the Albany County Vietnam Memorial. The soldier who murdered her then committed suicide and, ironically, his name is on The Wall.

Two women who worked for the Army Special Services perished in accidents in-country. Dorothy Phillips died in a plane crash at QuiNhon in 1967. Rosalyn Muskat died in a Jeep accident near LongBinh in 1968.

The Catholic Relief Services had many workers in Vietnam. Gloria Redlin from Oshkosh, Wisconsin was one of them. She was shot to death in Pleiku in 1969.

Volunteers for the American Red Cross also died in-country. Hannah Crews died in a Jeep accident at BienHoa in 1969. Virginia Kirsch was murdered by a U.S. soldier in ChuLai in 1970. Lucinda Richter died from Gillian-Barre disease at CamRanhBay in 1971.

Even though they were missionaries, women and their children also died. Janie Makeel was five months old when she was shot to death in an ambush at DaLat in 1963. Killed during a 1968 Tet raid on a leprosarium in BanMeThout were Carolyn Griswold, Ruth Thompson, and Ruth Wilting.

There are at least four civilian women listed as POW/MIA. Eleanor Ardel Vietti was captured at a leprosarium on 30 May 1962. She is still listed as a POW. Elizabeth "Betty" Ann Olsen was captured during a 1968 Tet raid on a leprosarium. She died in 1968 and was buried somewhere along the Ho Chi Minh Trail by her fellow POW, Michael Benge. After his repatriation Michael reported that he had personally buried Betty and had witnessed the burial of another male POW. Unfortunately neither of their remains were ever recovered. Both Evelyn Anderson and Beatrice Kosin were captured in 1972. They were burned to death in Kengkok, Laos. Their remains were recovered and returned to the United States.

Barbara Black from the Australian Nurse Corps also died at VungTau in 1971.

BRAVE WOMEN

VIETNAM WOMEN'S MEMORIAL

Unveiled on Veteran's Day
Washington, D.C.—1993

Some of this information came from the Internet and some from a variety of books I have read. But I have found no one place where it is all written down until now. These civilian women were either working for or associated with the agencies mentioned above. If you know any further circumstances or information about these women, please contact me or A Circle of Sisters/A Circle of Friends.

A Circle of Sisters/A Circle of Friends is a coalition of women who served as civilians with various organizations in Vietnam during the Vietnam War. This group had compiled some of what you just read. It is a private nonprofit educational group founded to create an archival collection documenting civilian service in war and to honor the memory of American civilian casualties of the Vietnam War. For information about the organization or to make additions or corrections to their compilation please contact Jolynne Strang, 1015 S Gaylord, Suite 190, Denver, CO 80209, (303) 575-1311.

Many more male and female American civilians probably died in Vietnam. As you can see, Maggie was not the only one who did not receive recognition for her endeavors. All of these women deserve to be recognized in some way.

NINETEENTH-CENTURY WOMEN IN SERVICE

We have all heard of Clara Barton and the Red Cross, Betsy Ross who made our first flag, and nurse Florence Nightingale, but few people remember Mary Edwards Walker, who was born in Oswego, New York on 26 November 1832. She was a feminist long before that term was coined. She was active in the women's suffrage movement, and she worked toward reforming women's clothing. You would think those two reasons were enough for her to be remembered and recognized, but they weren't.

In 1855 she graduated from Syracuse Medical College in upstate New York. She entered the Union Army at Louisville, Kentucky. During the Civil War she served as a nurse. She was present on the battlefield during the Battle of Bull Run on 21 July 1861. She worked at Patent Office Hospital during October of that year in Washington, DC. She continued service to her country between 1861 and 1863. She was in Chattanooga during September 1863 following the Battle of Chickamauga.

In 1864 she became the first woman commissioned as an assistant surgeon in the Union Army. She wore men's clothing. Assuming this doctor was a man, the Confederate Army captured her on 10 April 1864. She was kept as a Prisoner of War in Richmond until 12 August. After her release she continued caring for the wounded. She was on the field during the Battle of Atlanta in September 1864.

She served her country with pride. For her heroic medical work and efforts of aiding our wounded, President Andrew Johnson presented her with our nation's highest military award—the Congressional Medal of Honor—on 11 November 1865. The citation says it all.

Whereas it appears from official reports that Dr. Mary E. Walker, a graduate of medicine, "has rendered valuable service to the Government and her efforts have been earnest and untiring in a variety of ways," and that she was assigned to duty and served as an assistant surgeon in charge of female prisoners at Louisville, KY, upon the recommendation of Major Generals Sherman and Thomas, and faithfully served as contract surgeon in the service of the United States, and has devoted herself with much patriotic zeal to the sick and wounded soldiers, both in the field and hospitals, to the detriment of her own health, and has also endured hardships as a prisoner of war four months in a Southern prison while acting as contract surgeon; and

Whereas by reason of her not being a commissioned officer in the military service, a brevet or honorary rank cannot, under existing laws, be conferred upon her; and

Whereas in the opinion of the President an honorable recognition of her services and sufferings should be made:

It is ordered, That a testimonial thereof shall be hereby made and given to the said Dr. Mary E. Walker, and that the usual medal of honor for meritorious services be given her.

Given under my hand in the city of Washington, DC, this 11th day of November, AD 1865

Mary became the first—and to date the only—woman to receive this prestigious medal. After the war she worked as one of the first women journalists in the United States. She authored a book of essays in 1871 titled, *Hit.* Unfortunately she became an object of ridicule in her late life, partly because she continued to wear men's clothing.

In 1917, her Congressional Medal of Honor was rescinded along with 910 other Veterans of the Civil War. The reasons given for the action differed. Mary was informed she could not have it because she was a woman and at that time women couldn't serve their country in the military.

Mary died on 21 February 1919 at the age of 86. This physician and feminist had been a pioneer for women of her time. During the 1970s women's movement, those women who knew what had happened to her were outraged. They petitioned Congress and The White House to right the wrong. It took a long time, but the Medal was finally restored to her by President Jimmy Carter on 10 June 1977.

I've known about Mary for years, but then I'm originally from upstate New York. Her life was similar to the Texas women portrayed in Janice Woods Windle's book and the television mini-series by the same name, *True Women*. Janice's novel was based on her family's real life journals. These women and many others like them served their country in ways most people don't recognize.

WOMEN'S EQUALITY DAY

Women's Equality Day has been celebrated on 26 August every year since 1848. Elizabeth Cady Stanton presided over the first Women's Rights Convention which adopted their declaration stating the limitations to women's equal participation in society and listed the means they intended to use to bring about change.

In 1997 I wrote a speech for my friend, newly promoted Command Sergeant Major Maureen "Mo" Johnson, to give on Women's Equality Day. Women's history is so important but often overlooked. Here are some of the facts I shared with Mo.

Women have served our country both in and out of the military since its beginning. During the Revolutionary War, many women stood by their husbands' sides— some dressed like men, used a man's name, and fought with the American forces against the British. Sisters— Rachel and Grace Martin—did just that. Likewise Deborah Sampson of Plymouth, Massachusetts called herself Robert Shirtliffe and fought the Red Coats. She was wounded twice before her gender was identified.

During the War of 1812, Lucy Brewer served on board *Old Ironsides*. She had passed herself off as George Baker and no one was the wiser.

During the Civil War, at least six women donned men's clothing, used different names, and fought for their land. Sarah Emma Edwards called herself Franklin Thompson. Jennie Hodgers went by the name Albert

Cashier. Loreta Velazquez was known as Lieutenant Harry Buford. A woman named Emily passed herself off as a man and joined a Michigan Regiment. She later died at a battle in Chattanooga. Sarah Rosetta Wakeman, alias Lyons Wakeman, joined the 153rd Regiment of the New York State volunteers and went south to fight for the Union forces.

Some records of the Spanish American War indicate that about 1,500 women served our country. Record-keeping was poor during World War I, but an estimated 30,000 women served in one capacity or another.

HEROES OF THIS CENTURY

On 14 May 1942, former Texas First Lady, Oveta Culp Hobby became the first Director of the Women Army Auxiliary Corps (WAAC). Records may not have been all that accurate, but nearly 400,000 women served our country during World War II, both at home and overseas. It is reported that 5,600 women were in the South Pacific Theater of Operation. Six were killed in action, four were wounded, and sixty-seven taken as Prisoners of War. Between the South Pacific and European theaters, it is estimated that over two hundred women died serving our country.

Among those who served were Grace Lally, Elizabeth Murphy, Annie Fox, Betty Grable, and...Martha Raye. Grace Lally was Chief Nurse on the USS *Solace* early in WW II. She and her Navy nurses tended some of the first casualties. Elizabeth Murphy was an Army nurse stationed at Trippler General Hospital at Pearl Harbor on 7 Dec 41. She worked twelve-hour days, unable to bathe or change her clothes for weeks. Army nurse Annie Fox received a Purple Heart following the Pearl Harbor attack. Betty Grable was a movie star and pin-up girl for the troops during WW II. Meanwhile Martha "Colonel Maggie" Raye became a USO volunteer. She also pitched in to help nurses and doctors through three wars. These women all served during World War II.

By the time the Korean War began and throughout its course, records show that more than 120,000 women were serving our country both stateside and overseas. One such woman was Frances Liberty, a member of the Army Nurse Corps. She had joined the Army during World War II, continued to serve during the Korean War, and was still on active duty during the Vietnam War. Along with more than 10,000 women, she was in-country during the Vietnam War. If it weren't for such nurses fewer of the 2,709,965 men sent there would not have made it back alive.

Bonnie O'Leary served with the Air Force and retired as a major. Mary Stout and F. Martha Green were Army Nurses who served in Vietnam. Mary is a former president of the National Vietnam Veterans of America. Actress Connie Stevens was one of the many female entertainers who went to Vietnam to be with our troops.

F. MARTHA GREEN, RN

F. Martha Green joined the Army Nurse Corps in 1967. She was sent to Vietnam in 1968 shortly after she

married a physician and was stationed at the Sixth Convalescent center in CamRanhBay. When her husband, John, arrived in-country in March 1969 Martha was reassigned

1LT F. Martha Green, U.S. Army Nurse Corps, NhaTrang, Vietnam, November 1968. Photo contributed by F. Martha Green.

with him to ChuLai to the 312th Evacuation Hospital.
The 312th frequently came under attack. Martha and
many other nurses worked twelve-hour shifts, six days
a week in Vietnam. She was there in June 1969 when
Sharon Lane was killed by enemy rockets. It was a
turning point in Martha's life.

L-R: F. Martha Green,
actress Connie Ste-
vens, and John A.
Green, at the New
World Hotel, Saigon
(Ho Chi Minh City),
Vietnam, November
1995. Photo contrib-
uted by F. Martha
Green.

Martha and John joined Connie Stevens for a return
trip to Vietnam in November 1995 with other Vietnam
Veterans. Connie took a camera crew with her and
recorded this historical event. She turned the film into a
documentary called *A Healing*. The movie was shown to
the public during WIMSA Memorial dedication festivities. Martha and John now have a Bed and Breakfast
home in Adams, Massachusetts.

I found the following poem when I was visiting The
Wall in Washington, D.C. in 1988. Nurses were there
passing it out to people. Once read, I couldn't forget it.
In 1992 I bought the book *Visions of War, Dreams of Peace*
edited by Lynda Van Devanter and Joan A. Furey. I was
so glad to find this same poem in the book and even
happier to find out where it was first published. BUT
better yet, I actually located the original author of the
poem in 1997. I'm so glad I found the woman who wrote

this poem. Once we communicated I realized that our paths had crossed before—in 1996 when Susan and I were signing copies of *Memories of Maggie* Memorial Day weekend at The Wall—Dusty asked us for an autographed copy. Dusty, from Chicago, has granted me her permission to share this special poem with you.

∾ HELLO, DAVID ∾

Hello, David—my name is Dusty.
I'm your night nurse.
I will stay with you.
I will check your vitals
    every 15 minutes.
I will document
    inevitability.
I will hang more blood
    and give you something
    for your pain.
I will stay with you
    and I will touch your face.

Yes, of course,
    I will write your mother
    and tell her you were brave.
I will write your mother
    and tell her how much you loved her.
I will write your mother
    and tell her to give your bratty kid sister
    a big kiss and hug.
What I will not tell her
    is that you were wasted.

I will stay with you
    and I will hold your hand.

I will stay with you
   and watch your life
   flow through my fingers
   into my soul.
I will stay with you
   until you stay with me.

Goodbye, David—my name is Dusty.
I am the last person
   you will see.
I am the last person
   you will touch.
I am the last person
   who will love you.

So long, David—my name is Dusty.
David—who will give me something
   for my pain?

Dusty
1986

During the Persian Gulf War, 1,704,770 Americans were serving in the armed forces. Of those, more than 40,000 women served in key support and active military positions throughout the Gulf region. Several women died. Three were listed as POW/MIA, two of the POWs were recovered. There are still thirty-five names listed as Missing In Action, one of those is thirty-one-year-old Army Staff Sergeant Crystal Rickett.

In all nearly two million women have served during our nation's armed conflicts. Some were pilots, nurses, clerks, photographers, or filled other support roles. Some were not in the military but served with the Red Cross, USO, and Special Services. All these women have earned their place in history and should be honored and saluted today and every day.

Although the nineteenth Amendment giving women the right to vote was ratified in 1920 and the Women's Rights Movement began in 1848, American women have been serving much longer than that. None of these fine American women should be forgotten.

It was time for me to move again. I decided to go to the heartland of our country in July 1997. This proved to be a good move. New opportunities were opened to me for speaking and meeting interesting people.

No sooner had I arrived in Wichita than the Kansas Vietnam Veterans held their annual reunion. They had arranged for The Moving Wall to be in El Dorado at the same time. They invited me to attend and do a book signing.

FORT RILEY

I was only an hour's drive from Fort Riley so I contacted the U.S. Cavalry Museum Gift Shop manager. We arranged a book signing on a Saturday afternoon. I'm so glad we did, as two of the men I had corresponded with about Maggie attended that day.

Retired Army Command Sergeant Major James Trepoy [27] walked in wearing his Colonel Maggie T-shirt. He had served in World War II, Korea, and Vietnam. After we talked he asked for two books, one for himself and the other for his daughter who is a nurse. James is now in his seventies. As I was beginning to pack my things, retired Army nurse Richard Seymour [28] walked in. He apologized for being so late and insisted on having me sign books for each of his six children and stepchildren. It's hard to believe that I had been corresponding with these folks for so long and yet never met before this day. What a pleasure it was to meet these Veterans who had helped get Maggie honored.

I received a call from *The Wichita Eagle*. Phyllis Jacobs Griekspoor interviewed me and wrote about Maggie, *Memories of Maggie*, and me in her article. It was featured on the first page of the "Arts and Leisure" section of the Sunday paper. Phyllis included three pictures of Maggie with the article. She gained additional comments from James Trepoy.

Arrangements were made for me to give a two-hour slide show at the McConnell Air Force Base Library. Mine was to be the base's main presentation on the Air Force's 50th anniversary.

It was rewarding to receive so many speaking invitations. As a guest speaker at the annual meeting of the Wichita YWCA, my theme was how Maggie's devotion to our troops could impact children. She was one they could look up to for the empowerment of young women.

The Wichita Chapter of the Kansas Authors Club asked me to speak about problems I had with getting published, promoting, marketing, and distributing *Maggie*. After an hour on the subject, they had many questions. They learned it takes more than an hour to cover some of the problems many authors face with publication. If they want to write a book, they have to be prepared to promote it themselves.

ON THE ROAD AGAIN

Britt Small had asked me to attend and speak at Freedom Fest 97. I loaded my truck with supplies and books. Arriving in Skidmore, I went to visit The Moving Wall. It was set up behind the local school. After touching my three friends' names on The Wall, I knew I was ready for anything that might come my way that weekend. I met Carla Wetzel who had made all the arrangements, then headed for the hotel room in Maryville to rest up for the next day's events.

Saturday turned into a long day. After setting up my materials, a woman asked when I was going to be in her home state of Connecticut. Her family was from there and some remained in that area. She belonged to VVA Chapter 633 from Waynesville, Missouri near Fort Leonard Wood. They were having their reunion in October and had begun to plan for the reunion in 1998. She would like me to be a speaker.

During the day I signed many copies of *Memories of Maggie*, two to Veterans who had been on my mailing list for several years. The opening ceremony began at 11:00 A.M. and Britt led the festivities, introducing each speaker and entertainer. Jerry Hayes performed Country and Patriotic music; his songs were powerful and brought tears to my eyes.

Britt introduced me by telling the audience about his friendship with Maggie—and her last tattered flag. I spoke for fifteen minutes about Maggie's love for the troops and how I'm trying to keep her memory alive. I also talked about the importance of teaching children about history, our wars, and individual experiences. When Britt returned to the stage I noticed him wiping his eyes.

Others had stories to share with me about seeing Maggie. Some wanted me to speak elsewhere. And, many wanted copies of *Maggie.*

It was an honor to speak at the same Veterans function as: Albro Lundy III—son of a POW, Bob Heft—originator of the 50-star flag, Nelda Alexander—from Nebraska and spouse of a Vet, and Sammy L. Davis—CMH recipient.

One couldn't help but listen intently as Albro talked about going to Vietnam with his brother to try to locate their father. They came so close to his last known location, but their guides refused to take them any further. Albro has been involved with the POW/MIA issue all his life.

I talked with Bob Heft about the flag, patriotism, and how he approaches schools to talk about why he designed the flag the way he did.

Nelda and I first met at the Nebraska Vietnam Veterans Reunion in 1996. I feel close to people who value our Veterans as I do.

I've attended other Veteran functions where Sammy has spoken. He always has an inspirational message to share and continues to fight for the POW/MIA cause.

Other speakers and entertainers were in town for this special weekend. The evening's entertainment was topped off by Britt Small and Festival. Sunday morning there was a church service led by the Reverend John Steer, followed by closing ceremonies at The Moving Wall. Those three days in the Skidmore area were emotionally lifting and draining.

My drive back to Wichita was filled with thoughts of Britt and Freedom Fest 97. I played his tapes the whole trip. His music lifts my spirits. I wondered what lay ahead as I planned another major trip to the East coast.

13

WIMSA

The past ten years have been phenomenal! Until *Maggie*, I had expected that retirement years would happen in a house on Cape Cod for summers and a home somewhere in the south for winters. When I became a published book author and speaker, that all changed. I have become more heavily involved with Veterans' groups and their issues.

It was exciting to attend several events at the Vietnam Veterans Memorial in Washington, D.C. including the groundbreaking and dedication of the Vietnam Womens Memorial. However, there was one more dedication: a memorial for which I felt a kinship.

In 1983 a call went forth to recognize women from the past, present, and future for serving our country. Ohio Congresswoman Mary Rose Oaker and Alaska Senator Frank H. Murkowski introduced legislation for a memorial. Public Law 99-610 authorized a group called The Women In Military Service For America (WIMSA) Foundation, to build a memorial on Federal land in the Washington, D.C. area—without Federal funds. This law was not authorized until 1986 when President

Ronald Reagan signed it. The Memorial was to be financed solely by private donations.

On 18 October 1997 the WIMSA Memorial was to be dedicated at an entrance to the Arlington National Cemetery. That date happened to be my fiftieth birthday. I began yet another train journey—this time from Wichita.

First I went to Albany, where I attended the monthly meeting of my group, Tri-County Council Vietnam Era Veterans. I hadn't been to a meeting in almost three years. President Joe Pollicino asked me to address the group. Following the meeting, several Vets wanted autographed copies of *Memories of Maggie.*

I also touched base with Benita Zahn at WNYT-TV13 and filled her in on the status of *Memories of Maggie* as well as how *Potpourri Of War* was coming along. Benita arranged for another television appearance when this book is released.

Washington, D.C. took the next five days. WIMSA personnel invited me to do a book signing there, since *Memories of Maggie* was written by a woman Veteran about a woman who served our country.

Transportation to and from dedication events, however, was a nightmare. Except for the afternoon of the dedication, the weather was wet and cold.

GALA CELEBRATION

Thursday evening 16 October 1997 there was a gala black-tie dinner and dance held at the Washington, D.C. National Guard Armory. Actress Loretta Swit, who played Major Margaret "Hot Lips" Houlihan on television's " MASH," performed. Actress Connie Stevens, who had been to Vietnam several times for the USO, attended. Tipper Gore, the vice president's wife, spoke; Hillary Rodham Clinton was unable to attend since she was in South America attending a state function with President Clinton. The armory was packed, and they ran out of table space and hot meals. Many folks were seated in the balcony and served box lunches. Since tickets were expensive, many people were understandably upset.

Friday noon there were luncheons for each branch of the military and the civilians who served with the Red Cross, Special Services, airlines, etc. Again transportation proved to be a problem. At least one busload of women Veterans never made it to their luncheon, while another arrived at their location only to learn there was no food left. This was another costly event with *more* folks becoming upset.

THE REUNION

I went early to the Friday evening Reunion celebration to make certain I was on time to sign copies of *Memories of Maggie.* I had called the WIMSA staff several times before I left Kansas to verify that they had plenty of books on hand. I suggested that they order more as I was confident they would sell quickly.

When I sat down to sign books that evening, I was handed three copies and informed there were more in the back room. Those three books disappeared in a few minutes. I requested more books and was told there were no more. I couldn't believe it! Neither could the other authors who were there with me. They faced the same problem.

Since over six hundred of my brochures were picked up, efforts weren't in vain. When more people asked how they could get copies of *Maggie,* I handed them my business card so they could send for signed copies when they returned home.

I met several women with whom I had been corresponding about Maggie: Donna Fournier [29], F. Martha

Green, and Bonnie O'Leary. Our book shortage did free up time to meet some of the other authors who were there.

A Yeomanette

In 1991 Hilda Orleans, who sat next to me, wrote a book about her mother, Charlotte Winslow Winkler, titled *Lottie's Legacy*. Lottie had enlisted in the U.S. Navy on 29 May 1918 as a Yeomanette. She began her service to our country on 17 June 1918 when she was assigned to the commissary in charge of a group of younger Yeomanettes.

Their duties were to keep supplies ordered and moved upon request at the Marine Barracks in Norfolk. Lottie worked long hours until she was discharged from the Navy on 8 December 1920. Following the bombing of Pearl Harbor on 7 December 1941, she volunteered to work with the Red Cross.

When Lottie passed away following a cerebral hemorrhage on 16 December 1954, she received a military memorial service from the Melvin Rhoades American Legion Post 1231 in Rennselaer, New York—not far from my home town. Lottie and her children had lived in the Capital District area of New York a long time. Hilda is now spreading the word about her mother's service to our country. She has invited me to address the Writer's League of Washington, D.C. and is hoping to have me speak to the Washington Independent Writers. I look forward to making the trip back to our nation's Capitol to speak to writer-colleagues.

Jean Ebbert, an author who sat on my other side, is a Navy Reserve Veteran. She had a book called *Crossed Currents: Navy Women from WWI to Tailhook* published about Navy women. It was co-authored with Marie-Beth Hall. Jean also is one of several women who co-authored *In Defense of a Nation: Servicewomen in World War II.* It was available for the first time at this Reunion and six of the women autographed it for me.

THE DEDICATION WE HAD WAITED FOR

The WIMSA Memorial was dedicated Saturday afternoon 18 October 1997. While the U.S. Parks and Services Department estimates 30,000 were in attendance, I believe closer to 100,000 were there. After looking at the aerial coverage, it reminded me of the crowd that converged on our nation's Capitol during the civil rights movement when Dr. Martin Luther King made his famous "I Have a Dream" speech on the steps of the Lincoln Memorial, 28 August 1963.

Many dignitaries were on hand for this special day honoring women. There were speeches. Vice President Al Gore stood in for President Clinton. The president and First lady's pre-taped speeches were aired for the crowd. My pal, Herschel Gober, Deputy Secretary of Veteran Affairs, spoke. He had a special story about Maggie [30] to tell in *Memories of Maggie.* Another speaker was Robert Stanton, head of the Parks and Services Department.

But the emphasis was on women who served. WIMSA personnel had scheduled one woman from each war period to speak. Speakers covered World War I, World War II, Korea, Panama, Somalia, and Bosnia but no one represented or even mentioned Vietnam or the civilians who served! I was upset!

Susan Christiansen was to cover the Vietnam period. Although the WIMSA staff asked her to speak, they never communicated further with her—no schedule, no verification of the invitation, no travel expenses. They dropped the ball.

That evening a candlelight march moved from the

Lincoln Memorial and Reflecting Pool across Memorial Bridge to the new memorial. Following a short service, fireworks were set off.

Sunday morning a service for giving thanks was conducted at the Arlington National Cemetery's Amphitheater. Former Senator Bob Dole was the guest speaker. Then a new memorial honoring nurses was dedicated not far from the Tomb of the Unknown Soldiers. I did not attend those ceremonies because, at the same time, the WIMSA Memorial was open for viewing. There were already lines forming when I arrived.

THE WIMSA MEMORIAL

The Exhibit Gallery has fourteen alcoves holding memorabilia of the architects' plans, as well as artifacts, text, and memorable images to illustrate women's contributions to our nation's defense—from the American Revolution through Bosnia. The final alcove had books available for visitors' signatures. Some of these alcoves will be permanent exhibits while others are temporary. This is one of the ways we can honor all the women who have served our country.

The starkness of the plain concrete pillars was a disappointment to me. I was under the impression the whole memorial was going to be marble. On the other hand, the opposite wall was fresh cut, polished marble with nothing on it. There was a room that displayed the flags of the fifty states. Eventually a Hall of Fame will be created for recognition of women who have served, sacrificed, and achieved throughout history. The distinguished list of women will include those who have been killed in service, suffered as prisoners of war, taken heroic actions in our nation's defense, or displayed distinction as exceptional role models and leaders.

The next room holds the computer system that will include a database for all women who have served as military or civilian members, as well as an education center. Believe it or not, the U.S. Government failed to keep records of the women who have served our country.

If you qualify and have not yet registered with WIMSA, I urge you to do so immediately. There will be a computerized register in the center of the Memorial that will hold information women provide about themselves. You also should be able to find friends, if they registered, or read about many others who have served.

Another room houses a theater with seats and a stage where films will show the roles women have played in our military history. This theater will also provide meeting areas for lectures, speeches, and conferences. The gift shop is relatively small and was poorly stocked when I was there (after waiting an hour and a half to get inside the doorway).

While walking through the Memorial, I spoke with some of the women. I was curious as to when they served and why. Leslie Fischer enlisted in the Navy for two years and was discharged in December 1942. Leslie said she was in the first group of women to serve at Newport, Rhode Island. She wanted to serve her country in time of war. "It was the right thing to do." Leslie now lives in Brooklyn.

Marilyn Belshe from Olathe, Kansas served in the Marine Corps 1957-1960; then she joined the Navy Reserve 1960-1963. She entered as a private and departed as a corporal. Marilyn grew up wanting to be a member of the military to serve her country. While in the Marines she was stationed at Camp Lejeune working in supply. When asked why she got out when she did Marilyn said, "I might have stayed in if circumstances were different."

Ramona Orum enlisted in the Air Force in February 1974 and served in Vietnam May 1974-1975. She entered as a airman first class and still serves as a sergeant. Ramona is a medical technician in an Emergency Room. When asked why she joined Ramona said, "I thought it would be fun."

Before leaving the area, I walked upstairs. The roof is partially made of glass, in some places etched with comments from people who have become well known. The comment I liked best was by Army Major Rhonda Cornum. Rhonda served with the Medical Corps during Operation Desert Storm, was captured by the Iraqi troops, held as a Prisoner Of War (POW), and later released.

> The qualities that are most important in all military jobs, things like integrity, moral courage, and determination—have nothing to do with gender.

That statement is as true today as it was years ago when the first women took a stand to serve their country—with or without recognition.

I am proud to be an American and I am proud of all my sisters and brothers who served their country. What a privilege to communicate with audiences listeners and readers about those who served and to talk about Martha "Colonel Maggie" Raye's efforts and her devotion to our troops.

SOUTHBOUND

Following the dedication of the WIMSA Memorial, I was on another lengthy train trip headed for Texas by way of Florida. When I made reservations, I didn't pay much attention to the fact that I would be sitting in Jacksonville for ten hours. That gave me far too much time to think. I began remembering people from Florida who had provided comments about their encounters with Maggie.

Paul Portner of Sebring recalled his memories of being a lonely GI on a hillside somewhere in either Algeria or Tunisia between January and March of 1943. He clearly remembered a troupe of USO personnel consisting of Bob Hope, Jerry Colona, Frances Langford, and Maggie. They did so much for troop morale. The entertainers performed from the back of a six-by-six-foot truck. That performance was a highlight in Paul's service career.

John Schuelke is a retired Army first sergeant living in Fort Myers. He was stationed in CaMau in 1965. He always went to mass, where the usual attendees were the Chaplain, one Captain and himself. However, on Sunday 7 November 1965, there was another person in attendance—Maggie. She was visiting the advisors on the outposts around CaMau. She landed at the air field he was overseeing. "A great moment in my RVN first tour."

Rudi Hamvai from Bradenton met Maggie in the Officers Club at the 173rd Airborne Brigade near BienHoa during the late summer of 1966. They had some drinks and some laughs.

Jon Phipps of Oviedo was overseas when he first wrote to us. He enjoyed Maggie's visits to three Special Forces camps during 1969. He was chagrined when he learned the personal price she paid when blacklisted by Hollywood (as chronicled in *Memories of Maggie*.)

"THE MAGGIE"

And then there was Tom Eggers Jr.! He shared his experiences with Maggie. Tom was a member of Special Forces but that's not what brought him to mind while waiting for the next leg of this trip. The train would go through Crestview where Tom lived. He wanted me to visit there someday to speak to ROTC students and others. Tom is an inventor. One of his creations is quite special. It is a stethoscope that could be used on patients through their clothing instead of having to be placed directly on the skin. This makes it especially useful on burn victims. His stethoscope also can be used in extreme temperatures and in chemical environments. He named it "The Maggie" stethoscope in honor of Colonel Maggie! He also has a smaller version for use with pediatric patients which he dubbed "The Chrissy" in honor of Chris Noel.

When I finally arrived in San Antonio, Lois Qualben (President of LangMarc Publishing) was there to meet the train. The purpose of this stopover was twofold. First we planned to do some preliminary editing on this book and envision its cover. It was great brainstorming with her and to meet Michael Qualben, graphics designer of *Memories of Maggie* and the *Potpourri Of War* covers.

Lois had arranged for a table at the Texas Book Festival in Austin that weekend. Sponsored by Texas First Lady Laura Bush, this was their second annual festival. Many authors were on hand for the occasion including well-known Broadway personality, Tommy Tune. It was stimulating to speak with other authors, discuss marketing strategies and meet some interesting people. One author complained that her publisher had only sold 85,000 copies of her book. She wanted to know what Lois and I did to sell my book. *We* wanted to know why she was complaining!

When a woman from Oklahoma saw Maggie's photo on the book cover, she said her husband, Amos Ewing, also helped get Maggie honored. I showed her his story in the book. [31] She just had to have a copy autographed to him. A couple of weeks later I received a note from Amos thanking me for the book and what it said about him.

One of the most rewarding aspects of this adventure has been connecting Veterans with their long-lost buddies. Many who donated their photos and stories in *Memories of Maggie* didn't know what became of their friends. When they saw someone's name they recognized in *Memories of Maggie,* they contacted me for their pal's address. (You will find many names listed in the "Buddy Search" section. If you know any of these people, perhaps you can help locate them; perhaps I can help you locate one of your long lost buddies from my files. Feel free to contact me and we'll try to match you up.

I have visited every section of the country, met so many people and made many new friends.

My own labor of love continues to be so satisfying.

LABORS OF LOVE REMEMBERED

L-R: Major Eileen Bonner, Maggie, and Captain Martha Flack as the Army Reserve nurses present Maggie with a special plague and make her an honorary nurse in New York, May 1969. Photo contributed by Rick Phillips.

14

MORE MEMORIES
OF MAGGIE

So much had to be cut from *Memories of Maggie*. Her activities prior to and during World War II—the places she went and things she did—never cease to amaze me.

John Mjos adored Maggie years before World War II. He first saw her in person in Hawaii. He couldn't recall her co-star because he only had eyes and ears for Maggie and her singing. He had a few of her recordings and loved the way she would say "Whoa Boy"! Years later he saw her at the Policeman's Ball in Minneapolis.

Miles Glazner Jr. served in World War II. He was a B-26 pilot in the 432nd Bomb Squadron, Seventeenth Bomb Group in North Africa from November 1942 through November 1943. During the summer of 1943, Kay Francis, Carole Landis, Mitzi Mayfair, and Maggie paid them a visit and put on a show for the troops. Miles met them just long enough to thank them for an excellent performance. He said Maggie was one year and five months older than he was. She was born on 27 August 1916.

Miles will never forget Maggie's first movie *Rhythm on the Range* in which she sang "Mr. Paginini." Her rendition of that song has remained a favorite of his (and many others) even though he has never been able to find a recording of it. He even remembers some lyrics of this classic. He got a kick out of her Polident television commercials when she called herself the "Big Mouth."

Abel Tesdall of Jewell, Iowa served in the 899th Tank Destroyer Battalion, 1941-1945. In January 1943 his battalion landed in Casablanca, North Africa. His group had been on a hike and found Maggie performing way out in a wooded area on a makeshift stage.

Egon Andersen, now from Wayzata, Minnesota, traveled overseas in November 1942 with the 347th Fighter Squadron, 350th Fighter Group operating P-39 and P-47 fighter planes. The 347th served in Corsica, Sardinia, Italy, North Africa, and Tunisia. Their group finally came together in Africa to begin operational flying. General Mark Clark's Fifth Army was there undergoing a rigorous training program.

The 347th landed at Casablanca at the Cages Air Drome. Egon's squadron were transported to the North African town of Oujda on forty-by-eight foot boxcars loaded with horse manure and rotten vegetables. The train took three days and two nights to get to their destination. They found gross runways and no living quarters except pup tents. Yet, they were blessed by Maggie's USO program in the middle of that miserable January of 1943. Egon remembered the troupe's wonderful performance. He got to thank Maggie for bringing a little of America to him and thousands of other GI's far from home.

From May to October 1944 Reverend Bob LeRoy of Langley, Washington was in New Guinea, where he was serving with the Eleventh Airborne Division. USO shows visited their camp area often. Maggie came one weekend. "She had a great sense of humor and cracked jokes that really helped us get our minds off the problems of the war we faced daily."

William B. Brown always enjoyed Maggie in movies, on television, and in person. He saw her when he was in the Oakland Naval Hospital in early 1945. She was performing in a USO show. "It was a hilarious part."

Formerly of Spokane, L. Perkins Sr. met Maggie the first time prior to entering the military when he was working with Metro Goldwyn Mayer (MGM.) He has a great sense of humor. He said the Navy made him a Chief during the war. He was stationed close to an Army Hospital, where he was hospitalized for two months after he had a run-in with a five-hundred-pound personnel bomb. He overheard the staff say he wasn't going to make it. They were proven wrong with the help of a fairy godmother named Maggie, whom he believed helped him survive.

Maggie traveled to many places throughout World War II, Korea, and Vietnam. More stories of her exploits in Vietnam are in order.

Retired Lieutenant Colonel Robert Thomas saw Maggie when she stopped over at QuiNhon while he was the 315th AD TMC Chief (in April or May 1965.)

Retired Marine Master Sergeant Robert Dyer still holds the highest respect for this lady. She gave him a few hours of enjoyment and laughter during a bad period in his life. Robert told of his tribute to her. "She is one heck of a lady."

In 1965 to 1966 I was a Platoon Sergeant with Company A, First Battalion, Ninth Marines. In August of 1965 I was sent to the S-2 Section (Intelligence) of Headquarters Ninth Marines. It was during August or September, that Lieutenant Colonel Raye visited our compound. There were about 200 of us plus some Red Cross workers there.

General Lewis Walt introduced her. She said, "I'm sorry—but, Ann Margret did not make the trip." She was accompanied by an elderly gentleman who played, I believe, the bass violin. It was just the two of them. She had changed from fatigues into a flowered muumuu dress. She told us, "The draft dodgers back home aren't good enough to lick your boots." We were pulled off the line to see her show, and I was a lucky one to go.

I was fortunate to see her again in 1968 when I was security chief at the Marine barracks, Washington, D.C. from 1967-1969. She was rehearsing for a White House show with the band. She came into the Staff NCO Club and wrote in lipstick on the wall; "To the greatest guys in the world."

Retired Army Chief Warrant Officer 3 Philip Owen lives in Mount Clemens, Michigan. He was assigned to the Thirteenth Aviation Battalion in CanTho from August 1965 to August 1966 when Maggie visited the villa and Officers Club. She had just come in from VinhLong, which had suffered a mortar or artillery attack. She had spent somewhere between eighteen and thirty-six hours on duty as a nurse caring for casualties. Philip believed Maggie was an Army nurse first and foremost, a comedian and entertainer next. "A wonderful person to talk to."

Don P. Livingston wanted to be counted as one of the troops who greatly appreciated Maggie and her group's visit to BearCat off Route #1 in the III Corps area of South Vietnam in November 1965. As a member of the First (Big Red One) Division's First Battalion, Eighteenth Infantry, Company A, they had just returned from a five-day field operation. Maggie and her escorts sang and joked with their small group. Having an entertainer of Maggie's star status entertaining them made it all the more meaningful. One song Maggie sang to the troops will always be a special one for Don—"The Girl from Ipanema." Whenever that song is played, his thoughts return to that group of guys sitting in the dirt being entertained by some real heroes.

Don said that Maggie was loved by all her troops. He, for one, was happy to have the opportunity to express his feelings. "I'm very grateful for Martha's efforts throughout the Vietnam War years." He added a special thanks to General William Westmoreland for his recognition of Maggie on behalf of all those she entertained.

Jerry Mason is a Vietnam Veteran who was in the Navy. He lives in Allerton, Iowa. He was on the USS *Kitty Hawk* with Aviation Attack Squadron VA-85 in 1965-1967. Maggie entertained on his ship just before Christmas in 1965. They were always happy to have company since they had been at sea thirty days with many long, hard hours.

Colonel W. J. Gotschall wrote that he had seen my letter to the editor in the *Army Times*. He wanted to add these remarks about Maggie and her tours in Vietnam.

I met Miss Raye on two separate occasions in 1965. I was visiting GiaNghia, the provincial capital of QuangDuc. This is an interior province that lies next to the Cambodian border in central Vietnam and about as out of the way as you could possibly get. Miss Raye was holding court in the messhall and I was introduced as an out-of-town visitor from MAC-V Headquarters in Saigon.

Six months later, once again I was visiting GiaNghia, and to my surprise Miss Raye was in the messhall. She looked up, recognized me, and said something to the effect, that we should stop meeting like that or people would start to talk. I've told this story many, many times. And I might add, that where ever I went incountry, the comments about Miss Raye, were always in the highest regard.

James Hughes of Vancouver wrote a note to me. "I met with this individual at a military headquarters some fifty kilometers west and to the south of Saigon in 1965." He went on to say that he has some 35mm slides from the area of MyTho, Vietnam. The main subject is Martha Raye. He sent these slides along with documentation (as to where they were taken) to the office that was assisting in the award of a Bronze Star for Maggie. James thought he did that ten or twelve years prior to 1993.

Retired Army Captain William Fitch received a news clipping from the *Air Force Times* from his daughter, an Air Force sergeant stationed at McCord Air Force Base, Washington. She learned of his admiration for Maggie after seeing his eight-millimeter home movies of Maggie taken in DaNang in 1965 and listening to the stories he told about her.

William served in the Army during World War II, Korea, and Vietnam. He was the only Senior Army Pilot in DaNang in 1965 and was assigned to all of Maggie's flights into Special Forces Camps all over Vietnam. The Army aircraft, The Otter, could carry up to ten people and land on runways under 1,000 feet. He couldn't recall how many Special Forces camps they visited over a period of the year. His copilot and he flew Maggie, her manager, a three-piece combo, and an assigned Special Forces officer wherever she wanted to go. On a number of occasions William saw her perform humane acts at the risk of her own life. As pilot in-charge, he frequently had to tell her, "We are not safe here. We must go."

Jerry Bell served with the 101st Airborne Division in 1965 in PhanRang when he met Maggie. He lives in Hampshire, Tennessee. He saw our request for comments and personal experiences in the *Static Line*. Jerry had never heard of Maggie before—and he never forgot her afterward. One night nearly everyone had gone to the base camp to see her show. His platoon didn't get to attend because they were on perimeter guard. Although they were in an unsafe area, a chopper came in carrying Maggie, Eddie Fisher, and Jackie DeShannon. This group of entertainers made their day. "I have never forgotten the three people who took time out to come see thirty people when they had such a busy schedule."

James Sushak of Bemidji, Minnesota saw Maggie at Takhli, Thailand in 1965 when she performed. She opened the "Cobra Lounge" for them. "She was a Class-A person and entertainer. I'll always remember her with the fondest of memories. She was aces!"

Lieutenant Colonel William Flenniken was the Commanding Officer (U.S. Army Captain) of the Twenty-second Finance Disbursing Section in NhaTrang during 1965-1966. During his tour he had an occasion to meet Maggie and provide her with some military money. He commented that somewhere in his files he had a picture of them taken in front of his tent. William retired and lives in Liberty Lake, Washington.

Ernest Rhyne was stationed in DaNang in late 1965 through 1966 on an auxiliary, personnel, living ship (APL-27) when Maggie and Ann Margret came aboard to entertain the crew. Ernest recalled that Maggie was great. "She made us all laugh and we loved her." When he wrote in 1990, he was serving aboard the USNS *Narragansett*.

Joseph Foster was in the Air Force in June 1965. He saw Maggie in the Officers' Club at Clark Air Force Base. He recalls that she was in tiger fatigues, her Special Forces Beret, and lieutenant colonel insignia. She was having lunch with a group of Air Force and Army "folks." At that time Joseph was a C-133 aircraft commander flying out of Dover Air Force Base in Delaware.

I volunteered for Vietnam and flew as an C-123 pilot with the Nineteenth Air Commando Squadron in Saigon between July 1966 and June 1967.

In October 1966 I picked up Martha at an Army field in the Delta (III Corps) and flew her and three USO musicians to a small Special Forces unit also in the Delta. It had a short 1,800-foot-long dirt airstrip which was about our minimum for landing the C-123. Miss Raye had on typical jungle fatigues, which were very big and baggy.

When she got off the aircraft, she gave me the World War II "thumbs up." My operations officer, who was a WW II type, was flying as my copilot. Martha made both of us feel special.

About two minutes after I took off to return to Saigon, we got a call on the Frequency Modulation (FM) radio from the camp. Martha, the three musicians, and the musical instruments were okay, but they had forgotten their bags and clothing. We didn't have them either...they had never been put on board when we first picked her up. The Special Forces guys got a chopper to pick them up.

I read in *Stars & Stripes* and heard about Miss Raye many times during 1966-1967 in Vietnam. She was A First Class Lady who loved the troops. She was indeed deserving of recognition.

J. V. Brown recalls how Maggie visited the Third Brigade, Twenty-fifth Infantry Division during the Fall of 1966 at Pleiku. She was there with a USO group. After entertaining them, Maggie spent that evening talking and playing cards with a number of the troops. J. V. still has her autograph on the back of a photo of his (then) three-year-old son.

Ken Lovell was somewhere inland from ChuLai in the Fall or Winter of 1966 when Maggie and her troupe entertained his group of Marines. Ken was in Company H, Two, Seven, First Marine Division at the time.

John Wohlwend, a Senior Chief Air Traffic Controller, is retired from the Navy and resides in Millington, Tennessee. He remembered that Maggie was with the First Air Cavalry during the Winter of 1966 at AnKhe. She was a regular passenger on his CV2 (C7A) Caribou aircraft out of and into the AnKhe airfield. John was one of many who suggested that I compile all the letters I received into a book for Maggie. He thought she would like that more than getting a medal.

In complete battle dress, with an M-16 rifle, I didn't know her at first. She would sit quietly up front in the Very Important Person (VIP) seat, right side forward, reading a paperback book. I knew she was important. I was an Avionics Man and my radio rack was just in front of her seat. She always spoke to me.

One day a buddy of mine asked me if I had seen Martha Raye on the plane I had just worked on. I told him no. When he told me where she was sitting, I knew who she was.

Over the years I have remembered her and told my family about how great she was compared to other show people who came to visit. Martha Raye knew how it was. She lived it with us.

God bless her. She has my love.

Retired Navy Lieutenant Commander Ron Elrod served three tours of Vietnam as a Naval aviator (Phantom pilot), with Fighter Squadrons VF-1, VF-14, VF-41, and VF-84. He served his tours in 1966, 1969, 1974-1975. He was carrier based, as well as shore based at DaNang, and other outfits. Ron had an opportunity to catch Colonel Maggie's act twice during his tours, once in 1966 and again in Saigon in 1974. Although he never met her personally, the lasting impression left by her has stayed with him all the years since then. Ron's jet was shot down in 1975 as his squadron provided air support against the advancing Communists during the fall of Saigon. He spent the next two years in hospitals for his injuries and was discharged from the Navy in March of 1977.

First Sergeant Dwaine Selk of LoLo, Montana had the opportunity to talk to Maggie in 1966. The helicopter in which she was riding landed for refueling at ChiLong National Training Center. ChiLong was located in the Delta. Dwaine was assigned to Advisory Team Sixty-one at the time. The twelve-man team consisted of six officers and six enlisted. He was the team's first sergeant and it was his day to refuel the aircraft. Maggie did not debark from the aircraft, but he remembers talking with her.

The last time I heard from Lieutenant Colonel Bill Pooley he was overseas again. He recalled that Maggie visited his Advisory Team in the Mekong Delta either late 1966 or early 1967.

Robert Kholos lives in Eugene, Oregon. Between 1966 and 1967 he was a combat correspondent with the Fourth Infantry Division in Pleiku. He helped put together a show to welcome Maggie back to Vietnam.

Sergeant First Class Arthur Morrill from Meredith, New Hampshire recalls that Maggie was at the Ninety-third Evacuation Hospital in LongBinh in late 1966 or early 1967. She was entertaining patients and hospital staff.

Richard Krueger of Neenah, Wisconsin met Maggie in TayNinh sometime during 1966-1967. She had just been evacuated from a Special Forces camp that came under fire. Richard's unit was F Troop, Seventeenth Cavalry, 196th Light Infantry Brigade.

Army retired First Sergeant Fred Ybanez talked to Maggie for a brief period while stationed in Vietnam in the Spring of 1967. He became a loyal fan of hers from that point.

Al Blanche wrote that during the summer of 1967 he was in the South China Sea about ten miles from DaNang on the USS *Hermitage* (LSD-34.) He was a Navy photographer when Maggie and the *Hello, Dolly!* troupe came on board for two performances. He has dozens of color slides of her and the troupe interacting with the crew. All these years he has wanted to thank her and tell her how much it meant to all of them. She and the entire cast ate with the officers and crew and were an "incredible boost" to the morale of everyone there. A few days later Al went on an operation in-country and heard that one of the helicopters Maggie was on had been hit; but there were no injuries. Al was only twenty-three years old then, but Maggie won his heart and admiration on the spot. She will always be "Dolly" to him.

Army retiree First Sergeant Luis Rexach was overseas when he contacted me. He was wounded by an enemy mine on 31 October 1967 and evacuated to the hospital in DongTam. It just happened to be a day when Maggie was performing *Hello, Dolly!* Luis remembered that when he woke up in the hospital, Maggie was by his side. They had a friendly chat. She was helping with the wounded.

Major General (then Major) Joe Lutz was the Commander of Detachment B-Thirty-five, Fifth Special Forces at the time. He also was present that day in the Advisory Team Ninety-nine compound.

Colonel Maggie's entourage was down to one other brave soul. The rest of her group had skipped out for fear of losing their hides. Even so, she promised one of our team members to visit our A-Team in TraCu. The team was delighted. We purchased her favorite scotch and Mateus wine. We were informed later that she was refused transportation because of the danger.

That Thanksgiving, 1967 we toasted with our glasses

of Mateus to a super trooper, Colonel Maggie. This was the first time I drank Mateus. I am still drinking it twenty-three years later and still remembering someone special who loved Special Forces because she was one of us!

Michael Patrick from Cottage Grove, Oregon was playing in a band at PhanRang in 1967. His group backed up Maggie and her troupe for two shows. Michael said it was "a very memorable experience."

Retired Army Major Arthur Williams was also overseas when he wrote to me. He saw Maggie in DucHoa in 1967. She was wearing a Green Beret with a Fifth Special Forces Group flash and full colonel insignia on it.

Retired First Sergeant William McGrane served with the Marines. During his tour in 1967-1968, he had the good fortune to see Maggie's show when it was in the HuePhuBai area. "It was a wonderful show and she was the only big-name entertainer that I saw in the northern I Corps area." William called her a dedicated lady who served this country by entertaining our troops during World War II, Korea, and Vietnam. "It is time our country honored her for her service!"

Jack McHale also is a Vietnam Veteran. He was an Army field artillery officer from 1967 to 1969. He still has fine memories of Maggie visiting his very remote forward A-team camps in northern III Corps where he was stationed.

During his tour in Vietnam, now retired Army First Sergeant Bruce Longnecker had the pleasure of seeing Maggie between February 1968 and October 1969. He also saw her during his later tour in Germany between 1973 and 1977.

Thomas Palmateer served as the first sergeant of Company B, 716th Military Police Battalion in Saigon from July 1968 to July 1969. Maggie had entertained his

troops for a whole evening. They thought she was ter-
rific.

Steve Backus was in Vietnam from September 1968 to
October 1969, serving with the Second Battalion, First
Marine Division. His unit was located approximately
ten miles south of DaNang. Steve spoke briefly with
Maggie in 1969. She was in their enlisted club talking
with troops.

Jack Naughton met Maggie at CanTho. He was at the
Civil Operations and Revolutionary Development Site
(CORDS) of the U.S. Agency for International Development (USAID). It was sometime between October 1968
and October 1969. Maggie lifted their spirits with her
humor. She showed him and his group proper ways to
use chopsticks.

John Mitchell's photos taken between December 1968
and January 1969 appeared in *Memories of Maggie,* but
not his story. [32] He said that we could add a firebase at
AnLoc to the list of places Maggie visited. He was a
Medevac pilot while Maggie was visiting Company C,
Fifteenth Medical Battalion, First Cavalry Division.
Maggie personally talked with all of the Medevac crews
and medical personnel. As always, she was a very welcomed "trooper." She cheered them up. John's pictures
were taken after a long, hard day for both Maggie and
the rest of his crew. She was a pleasant respite from a
weary war and a reminder of home. John will always
remember Maggie and never forget Jane!

Gene Gavigan of Laughlin, Nevada met Maggie in a
"Mike Force" bunker outside DaNang in 1968. She was
on her way to a camp that had been under siege for over
thirty days. Rumor had it that there were over two
hundred enemy dead in or on the defensive perimeter
wire. The fact she was going into a "heck of a firefight"
made her even more insistent on visiting this location.

The camp was commanded by an Officer Candidate School (OCS) classmate of Gene's.

Senior Chief Photographers Mate (Air Crewman) Robert L. Lawson from Dammeron Valley in Utah retired from the Navy. The photos he sent appeared in *Memories of Maggie.* [33] They were taken at the club during 1968 at the Fifth Special Forces Camp, Forward Operating Base Four, DaNang East, near Marble Mountain. Robert said, "She was not at that club as an entertainer. She was truly one of the guys."

Air Force Colonel Ruth Anderson remembered Maggie going to TanSonNhut while she was there in 1968. "She was a real morale booster."

Rene Gagnon lives in Manchester, New Hampshire. In 1968 and 1969 he was a Chief Petty Officer with Mobile Construction Battalion Twelve (MCB 12) stationed at Camp Adenir in DaNang East by Marble Mountain. He recalls that on the night of 4 January 1969 Maggie popped into the CPO Club. After visiting the Officers Club and Enlisted Men's Club, she was "full of the devil and had a line of jokes." Her picture wound up in their Tour of Duty Battalion Book. Rene wrote a letter home in which he said:

> If I told you that right now Martha Raye is standing about three feet from me, you would think that I was crazy. I was sitting here at the Chief's Club writing this letter and all of a sudden, in comes Martha Raye. I had her sign the back of this page. I suspect she may be a little under the influence. But she was appearing at a USO show down the road and some people talked her into stopping at this hard-working Seabee camp. So here she is. She is a pretty good trouper.

Master Sergeant George Tabor is retired from the Army and lives in Tulsa. When he was assigned to Company B, First Battalion, 503rd Infantry, 173rd Airborne Brigade (Separate), Maggie visited Landing Zone (LZ) Uplift in late 1968 or early 1969. She didn't stay long, but she ate a meal with his group and took time to talk to them and pose for pictures.

> This isn't probably any different than any other story you've heard except that she also took pictures with our monkey. Colonel Maggie was not too comfortable with the monkey, but she went out of her way to try to please us. I know I never forgot the kindness that she showed to me and the other guys in my unit.
>
> I also had a chance to speak to Martha while I was assigned to Cal-Poly University as the Senior Non-Commissioned Officer (NCO) with the Army Reserve Officer Training Corps (ROTC) detachment. I invited her to speak at our commissioning ceremony. A cadet called after office hours with a message that a Colonel Raye had called. She left her home number so I returned her call. She explained that she would be out of the country during the time of our ceremony but would be glad to speak at a later date. She was very gracious and we had a nice conversation.

January 1971 found Maggie visiting troops on Okinawa while Colonel John Maher was attached to the First Special Forces. She was aiding those unit members by mending their wounds and also showing the U.S. personnel a great time by being a generous person. It was hectic trying to keep up with Maggie. John has retired and lives in Bainbridge Island, Washington.

During Christmas of 1971, Neil Mastrud was a young civilian advisor with the U.S. Air Force's Ninetieth Special Operations Squadron in NhaTrang. Maggie found time to spend the entire day with his group. She was a great encouragement for a lot of guys a long way from home. He has always been grateful to her.

Chief Warrant Officer 3 Charles Rogers was still serving in the Army when he contacted us. In 1971 he was in the Special Forces Club in CanTho waiting for a flight on Air America that would take him back to MocHoa. That's when he heard a familiar voice at the table behind him. He turned, and there she was! He said it was really hard to believe because other entertainers always had their presence announced by fliers, on Armed Forces Radio Network, or in *Stars and Stripes*. Wearing jungle fatigues she was joking and kidding like one of the troops. He couldn't muster the courage to talk to her but felt good knowing she was there. When Charles was at Fort Riley in Kansas ten years later, he came across an address for writing to Maggie. He wrote to her about that incident at CanTho and how much he appreciated her efforts. By return mail he received a thank you note from her. "That lady is all class."

Frederick Kent Carter met Maggie once—at NhaTrang. He commented, "To those who knew her then and now, she's a saint!" John Larimer was one of those lucky ones chosen to accompany Maggie while he was in Vietnam.

Mrs. Robert Stephens of Fort Worth recalled that her husband saw Maggie when he was in Korea and Vietnam. She knew how much Maggie did for our servicemen.

Chief Warrant Officer 2 Robert Dilley retired from the Army and settled in Killeen, Texas. He met Maggie on several occasions in the United States and while serving in Vietnam. "She was a lady in all respects and devoted her life to supporting the United States military."

In Appreciation—

Martha Raye thoroughly changed my life. I have come to know so many fine people along the way and continue to receive mail and phone calls from Veterans associated with the PMOF campaign and *Memories of Maggie*. I collect stories as I go around the country meeting people and addressing groups about her, about what she stood for.

Recently, Melodye Condos sent along an article that appeared in the August 1985 issue of *State Military Reserve*. In it was a picture of Maggie with Brigadier General Ronald Markarian. Maggie had just been inducted into the "Armenian Air Force" during the National Sojourner Convention that was held at the Disneyland Hotel. Here was another piece of the puzzle about Maggie's legend—her sense of humor about troops' roots.

One day while I was surfing the Internet, I learned about another award Maggie received. In 1985 she was selected to receive the Living Legacy Award from the Women's International Center in San Diego. The director of the Center and I corresponded; she has memorabilia available that Maggie had signed years ago.

Major Ronald Winkles of Whitesburg, Tennessee was so pleased with M*emories of Maggie* that he wrote a letter to the editor of his local paper.

> I highly recommend this book...the author did a wonderful job at capturing Ms. Raye's frontline dedication to entertaining our military men and women as well as providing them with nursing care. If I could, I would see that every Veterans' organization had a copy. I know this book would have been Martha's greatest gift.

Ronald later contacted me and said he was taking copies of my book to Europe with him to let people there know about Maggie.

Each time a correspondent does something like that, I am reassured I did the right thing to work on Maggie's story. Is there anything better that I can do?

Epilogue

Between December 1995 and November 1997, I traveled more than 35,000 miles by truck, car, bus, or Amtrak. *Why?* To spread the word about a great American legend.

From October 1987 to November 1989, I devoted my life to researching Martha Raye's life to see if she deserved to be honored. I was totally involved with the Presidential Medal of Freedom campaign from November 1989 to November 1993. From then on I concentrated on writing Maggie's story.

Throughout 1995, I tried to write the best book I could. Fortunately, so much help was forthcoming from my editors and publisher. Upon signing a contract with LangMarc Publishing, I began a new journey: marketing, traveling, speaking, and book signings. I was never so proud as I was on Pearl Harbor Day 1995 sitting in San Antonio autographing the first copies of *Memories of Maggie.*

People will be richer for learning about Maggie. To be sure, she was a complex—even troubled—person throughout her lifetime. Many of us are like her. But she had discovered her mission in life, nonetheless—a life that began in the charity ward of a Montana hospital.

Some may be tempted to frown at her many marriages, her troubles with alcohol, neglecting her own personal life and relationships. But we cannot forget this other fact: Maggie accomplished her Mission. And the lives of thousands of America's troops were richly blessed because of that. I wrote *Memories of Maggie* for that reason.

The best way to tell her story is to travel our country and speak to diverse groups to tell them what it was like researching her life, working to get her honored, writing her biography from the Veteran's point of view, and our difficulties in getting her story noticed.

In the past couple of years I've been asked many questions. Some were about Maggie. However, most questions were about why it was so difficult getting Maggie the Presidential Medal of Freedom and having her story published. My own efforts link with those of so many others' in this labor of love—for Maggie's Mission.

I am encouraged that no group, including students, has "tuned me out" when I am speaking about Martha Raye and her troops. Hopefully someone, someday will make a movie about Maggie's Mission. Her story needs to be told.

I nominated Maggie for induction into the National Woman's Hall of Fame in Seneca Falls, New York for 1998. Since she was not selected, I will resubmit her name.

My dream is for groups to set up awards or scholarships in her name. Clayton Hough of Holyoke, Massachusetts founded a Martha Raye Nursing Scholarship at his high school. Charles Thomann of Annapolis sponsors a Drama Award in Maggie's name at his local high school. Perhaps others will be moved to fund some form of award or scholarship to honor her unique life and Mission.

I dream of incentive awards in Maggie's honor set up at high schools based on essay contests about our wars, local service personnel, or patriotism. I hope my own high school will do something like this. Gil Woodside is seeking the same in Seekonk, Massachusetts.

General Westmoreland said that *Memories of Maggie* recorded American history. My aim is for *Potpourri Of War* to serve a similar purpose. Fellow citizens should be aware of the men and women who have served our country proudly—including those who are still listed as POW/MIA.

Several events have been scheduled for Veteran-related groups and civilian organizations. The Wisconsin Association of Concerned Veteran Organizations Incorporated had their Thirty-second Annual Reunion around the time this book went to print. When Matt Stevenson called to invite me to be their guest speaker, I mentioned that Melodye, Susan, and I have never appeared together. They invited the three of us and paid our travel expenses. A book signing at the Wisconsin Veterans Museum, a slide presentation and lecture, and comments by Susan and Melodye were scheduled.

Jess Jespersen, Susan Christiansen, Noonie, Melodye Condos.
Photo contributed by Ray Payne.

Bob Buhr and Melodye Condos.
Photo contributed by Ray Payne.

Bob Buhr and Melodye Condos.
Photo contributed by Ray Payne.

The second event involves a train trip to Providence, Rhode Island, where I'll be guest speaker for the groundbreaking of the Seekonk (Massachusetts) Vietnam Veteran Memorial on Flag Day, 14 June, 1998. Gil Woodside is Founder and Chairman of the committee that has worked to get this memorial. Seekonk will be the first place to have *Potpourri Of War* available.

After a trip to Cape Cod for a long overdue Whale Watch aboard the Dolphin Fleet vessel, I will head to Albuquerque to speak to members of the Special Forces Association during their 1998 Reunion. I look forward to visiting the Vietnam Veterans Memorial in Angel Fire, New Mexico as part of the SFA's bus tour.

Every day there are new speaking opportunities for Maggie's story. I am grateful to be given a voice to speak on issues related to Maggie, to writing and publishing, about other women Veterans, and the POW/MIA issue. My guardian angel "Maggie" watches over me and continues to bless these efforts.

What a rare honor it has been to know Maggie—for me, for so many others. She will live forever in the hearts and minds of many Veterans. Until we meet again:

BLESS YOU, COLONEL MAGGIE.

Appendix A

References

A Circle of Sisters/A Circle of Friends, c/o Jolynne Strang, 1015 South Gaylord, Suite 190, Denver, CO 80209 phone (303) 575-1311.

——*Above and Beyond*. Editors of Boston Publishing Co. 1985.

Altbach, Philip G. Student Movements. Grolier/Grolier/Meta0278920-0. Grolier Multimedia Encyclopedia. Online. America Online. (19 August 1997).

Ambrose, Stephen E. *Nixon*. New York. Simon and Schuster, 1989.

—— *American Gold Star Mothers, Inc.* Online. America Online. (9 September 1997).

Biemiller, Lawrence. "Tragic Days Remembered." *The Chronicle of Higher Education*, May 5, 1995.

Brandon, Heather. *Casualties*. St Martins Press, 1984.

——"Build-up To Tragedy at Kent State." *US News & World Report*, May 25, 1970.

——*Chronology*, May 1-4, 1970. Online. America Online. (26 August 1997).

Clark, Gregory. *Words of the Vietnam War*. Jefferson, North Carolina. McFarland & Company, Inc, 1990.

——*Congressional Medal of Honor Society*. United States of America.

Dolan, Edward F. *America After Vietnam*. New York. Franklin Watts, 1989.

Duiker, William J. *VIETNAM: Revolution in Transition*. Boulder, CO. Westview Press, 1995.

Fortin, Noonie. *Memories of Maggie:* Martha Raye-A Legend Spanning Three Wars. San Antonio, Texas. LangMarc Publishing, 1996.

——Edited by Marvin E Gettleman. *VIETNAM*. Greenwich, CT. Fawcett Publications, 1965.

Golden Ink, Inc. "Welcome to North Georgia Letters to the Editor." World Wide Web, Golden Ink, Woostock, GA, 1997.

——"Guard Fired in Self-Defense." *US News & World Report*, November 2, 1970.

Healy, Patrick. "Death on a Starry Night at Jackson State College." *The Chronicle of Higher Education*, May 5, 1995.

——Edited by Major General Jeanne M. Holm. *In Defense of a Nation: Servicewomen in World War II*. Arlington, Virginia. Vandamere Press, 1998.

——"In the Aftermath of Kent State Indictments." *US News & World Report*, November 2, 1970.

Isserman, Maurice. "Four Dead in Ohio, 25 Years Later." *The Chronicle of Higher Education,* May 5, 1995.

Keating, Susan Katz. *Prisoners of Hope.* New York. Random House, 1994.

Kotah, Mr and TchrOnCall, AAC staff. "Question: What was the Kent University Massacre? How did it compare to the Boston Massacre?" Document ID: HHC8209. AOLís Academic Assis tance Center. Online. America Online. (26 August 1997).

——Edited by Philip B. Kunhardt Jr. *LIFE, The First 50 Years 1936-1986.* New York. Time Inc, 1986.

Lawrence, Vicki with Marc Elliot. *VICKI: The True-Life Adventures of Miss Fireball.* New York, New York. Simon and Schuster, 1995.

Mason, Patience H. C. *Recovering From the War.* New York, New York. Penguin Books, 1990.

McNamara, Robert S. *In Retrospect: The Tragedy and Lessons of Vietnam.* New York Times Books, 1995.

Mullins, John F. "Code Name Gerry." *The Retired Officer Magazine,* October 1994.

Murphy, Edward F. *Vietnam: Medal of Honor Heroes.* Ballentine Books, 1987.

——"Notable Events in Ohio History." *Compton's Living Encyclopedia.* Compton's Learning Company, 1997. Online. America Online. (19 August 1997).

Noel, Chris. *Matter of Survival.* Boston, Massachusetts. Branden Publishing Company, 1987.

Olson, James. *Dictionary of the Vietnam War.* Westport, Connecticut. Greenwood Press, 1988.

Orleans, Hilda. *Lottie's Legacy.* Edisto, South Carolina. Edisto Press, 1991.

Plonka, Michael. *New York State Vietnam Medal of Honor Recipients.*

Roth, David, abridged and edited by Linda Lee Maifair and Lori Walburg. *Today's Heroes: Colin Powell.* Zondervan Publishing House, 1993. Abridged from *Sacred Honor* copyright 1993.

Scruggs, Jan and Joel L Swerdlow. *To Heal A Nation.* Harper & Row Publishers, 1985.

Sitkoff, Harvard. "History of the United States (III)." Online. America Online. (19 August 1997).

Sizgorich, Thomas. "25 years ago this month: Long Beach reacts to Kent State." Forty-Niner Online. *Compton's Living Encyclopedia.* Compton's Learning Company, 1995. Online. America Online. (19 August 1997).

Snyder, Jim. "A Professor Explores the 'Legacy of May 4.'" *The Chronicle of Higher Education,* May 5, 1995.

Taylor, Sandra C. "Vietnam War." *Grolier Multimedia Encyclopedia.* Online. America Online. (19 August 1997).

——Edited by Lynda Van Devanter and Joan A. Furey. *Visions of War, Dreams of Peace*. New York, New York. Warner Books Inc, 1991.

——"Vietnam War." Online. America Online. (26 August 1997).

Vietnam Women's Memorial Project, 2001 S Street NW, Suite 302, Washington, DC 20009 phone (202) 328-7253.

——"Walker, Mary Edwards." *Grolier Multimedia Encyclopedia*. Online. America Online. (19 August 1997.)

WIMSA Memorial Foundation, 5510 Columbia Pike, Suite 302, Arlington, VA 22204-3123. Phone 1-800-222-2294.

APPENDIX B

FOOTNOTES

These Footnotes refer to pages in *Memories of Maggie.*

[1] Ed Baron's story appears on page 10.
[2] Meeting with Chris Noel appears on pages 231 and 233.
[3] Story of Ty Herrington and Chris Noel appears on pages 165-166 and 187.
[4] Brenda Allen of Lincoln is on page 286.
[5] John Sullivan's photo of Maggie appears on page 68.
[6] Bill Miller's story and photo are on pages 199 and 205-206.
[7] Darwin Edwards story appears on page 167.
[8] Julio Rodriguez's story appears on page 76.
[9] Robert Siebenmorgan's story appears on page 158.
[10] Michael Moehlenkamp's story appears on page 210.
[11] Sam and Joe Patton's story appears on page 8.
[12] Some of Charles Olson's stories of meeting Maggie are on pages 116-118.
[13] Ken Plante's story is on page 313.
[14] Clayton Hough Jr. is mentioned on pages 185-187, 189, and 300.
[15] Olive Justice's story about her brother Michael Dooley is on page 174.
[16] Chuck Folsom appears on page 228.
[17] Harlan Jencks first two stories are on page 122.
[18] Belle Pellegrino's poem "Colonel Maggie" is on pages 249-250.
[19] Fred Wise contributed a photo on page 26.
[20] Joe Janisch's photos are on page 40.
[21] Robert Moro's story appears on page 177.
[22] Hyatt Moser's story appears on page 29.
[23] Gil Young is mentioned on page 44.
[24] Gil Woodside's story and photo appear on pages 72-74.
[25] Robert Setchfield's story appears on page 38.
[26] Lieutenant Colonel Frances Liberty's (Colonel Lib) story is on pages 48-49.
[27] James Trepoy's section is on page 168.
[28] Richard Seymour's story is on page 146.
[29] Donna Fournier's involvement is on page 263.
[30] Hershel Gober's story is on pages 105-106.
[31] Amos Ewing is mentioned on page 298.
[32] John Mitchell's photos appear on pages 198 and 213
[33] Robert L. Lawson's photos appear on pages 124 and 164.

Appendix C

Buddy Search

Some of the following individuals are those I have lost contact with. Some are people that others are searching for. When known I have listed the branch of service, their last known ranks, and their last known location. If you know them, please contact me by email (NFortin@aol.com), through LangMarc Publishing (1-800-864-1648) or my web site (http://members.aol.com/NFORTIN/index.html).

Rennie Grant's photo appeared on page 112 in *Memories of Maggie* but not his story. He met Maggie and her group in November 1966 when she visited his advisory team and spent two nights with them. That was in the II Corps area of South Vietnam while he served with the Army. Rennie now lives in Dallas, but he is still trying to locate his buddy Specialist VanHook.

Lieutenant Colonel George Massey retired from the Army. He was last known to reside in Fayetteville, Tennessee. His picture appeared in *Memories of Maggie* on pages 132-133. Many are looking for him.

Major Kenneth Robert's photo of Maggie standing by a truck was in *Memories of Maggie* on pages 200 and 207. His last known location was Hinesville, Georgia.

Reggie Hurd, owner and manager of The Sandpiper in Laguna Beach, and his relationship with Maggie was mentioned in *Memories of Maggie* on pages 225-227.

COL Ruth Anderson, U.S.A.F.—Tucson, AZ
CPT Charles Bastin—Burbank, CA
COL Daryl Baxter, U.S.A. (Ret)—Alexandria, VA
Al Blanche—Elmira, NY
CWO4 Charles Boyle, U.S.C.G. (Ret)—Fenton, MO
SFC Ernest Bradley—Colorado Springs, CO
MAJ Dale Brown, U.S.A.—Berkeley, CA
J. V. Brown—Staten Island, NY
William B. Brown—Stuart, FL
SGM Franklin Bryan, U.S.A. (Ret)—Corpus Christi, TX
Joseph Cappozzoli—Orange Park, FL
CPT Dan & Jenny Castillo—Roswell, NM
Bill Castro—Chula Vista, CA
LTC Philip Choate, U.S.A. (Ret)—Augusta, ME
Edward Clough—Lafayette, CA
Steve Clute—Sacremento, CA
MAJ Pat Coulter, U.S.M.C. (Ret)—Hollis, NH
Jim Cutler—San Diego, CA

Ruth Endlar Cyphers—Hazleton, PA
Marge Davis—Cisco, TX
MSG Timothy Doherty, U.S.A. (Ret)—Huntsville, AL
MSGT Robert Dyer, U.S.M.C. (Ret)—Gadsden, AL
Harry Edwards—New York City, NY
LCDR Ron Elrod, U.S.N. (Ret)—Decatur, IN
SGT David Fawcett, U.S.A. (Ret)—Minneapolis, MN
CPT William Fitch, U.S.A. (Ret)—Pensacola, FL
CPT Dick Flynn—Eau Claire, WI
Joseph Foster, U.S.A.F.—Seal Beach, CA
COL Carl Gaddis (Ret)—Ninety Six, SC
MG Donald Gardner, U.S.M.C.—Camp Lejeune, NC
Loretta Gibson—Arlington, VA
DCC William Gillingham, U.S.C.G. (Ret)—Battle Ground, WA
Miles Glazner Jr.—Santa Fe, NM
MSG Robert Glemaker, A.U.S. (Ret)—Fayetteville, NC
COL W. J. Gotschall, U.S.A. (Ret)—The Dalles, OR
Geoffrey Hancock—Copperas Cove, TX
Rod Hinsch—Santa Rosa, CA
Chuck Howard—Woodcliff Lake, NJ
Wilfred Hunt—Sparta, GA
David Jackson III—Phoenix, AZ
CPT Francis Jepson, U.S.N.—Washington, DC
SGT Rocky Kelley, U.S.A.—Scott Air Force Base, IL
Judy Knopp, A.N.C.—Lincoln, NE
CPT Robert Knowles, U.S.A. (Ret)—Lillburn, GA
Dan Laino, U.S.M.C.—Purdys, NY
John Larimer—Acworth, GA
CPT H. Lavin—Coronado, CA
COL Knute Lawson, U.S.A.F. (Ret)—Albuquerque, NM
COL Monte Lewis—Plattsburgh, NY
SFC Edward Linker, U.S.A.—Fort Polk, LA
Don P. Livingston—Memphis, TN
1SG Bruce Longnecker, U.S.A. (Ret)—Seattle, WA
Ken Lovell—Jacksonville, AR
LTC Richard Lynch, U.S.A.F. (Ret)—Virginia Beach, VA
Malcolm Marsh—Mineola, TX
JOC George Marshall, U.S.N. (Ret)—FPO AP
George Martin—Riva, MD
TSGT Richard Martin, OH.A.N.G.—Columbus, OH
Neil Mastrud—Santa Clara, CA
1SG William McGrane, U.S.M.C. (Ret)—Jacksonville, FL
Jack McHale—Latham, NY
Scotie McLennan—Tacoma, WA
John Mjos—Minneapolis, MN

MAJ Robert Morelan II—Ft. Sheridan, IL
Jose Natal—Wallkill, NY
Jack Naughton—Chicago, IL
CPT E. P. Nicholson, U.S.N.—Indian Head, MD
Thomas O'Connor, U.S.A. (Ret)—Staten Island, NY
Norman Pearson—Washington, DC
1SG Luis Rexach, U.S.A. (Ret)—APO, NY
LTC Paulette Risher, U.S.A.R.—Pensacola, FL
CWO3 Charles Rogers, U.S.A.—Fort Polk, LA
SFC Elmer Rogers, U.S.A. (Ret)—Augusta, GA
LTC Bill Shelton, A.U.S. (Ret)—Las Vegas, NV
LT (jg) George Simon, U.S.N.R.—Oakville, Ontario, Canada
COL Carl Sitter, U.S.M.C. (Ret)—Midlothian, VA
Joe Ed Spargur—Dickinson, ND
COL Harry Stevenson—Yorktown, VA
Gary Tallman—Ft. Bragg, NC
LTC Robert Thomas, (Ret)—Pearl City, HI
COL Duncan Thompson, U.S.A.R., SF—Reynoldsburg, OH
MGYSGT J R Todd, U.S.M.C. (Ret)—Tucson, AZ
BG Richard Toner, U.S.A.F. (Ret)—Arlington, VA
COL Harry Tower, U.S.A.F. (Ret)—Georgetown, TX
Fred Trafton—Augusta, GA
LT Michael Turner, U.S.N. (Ret)—Virginia Beach, VA
Rusty Warren—Paradise Valley, AZ
SMSGT Jerry Watkins, U.S.A.F.—APO NY
MAJ Arthur Williams, U.S.A. (Ret)—APO AE
1SG Fred Ybanez, U.S.A. (Ret)—Galveston, TX
MAJ Benjamin Yudesis, U.S.A.—Morrow, GA

Glossary

AAFES: Army Air Force Exchange System, similar to a department store.

ABC: American Broadcasting Company, also Audio Book Connection.

AFFA: Americans For Freedom Always, a group keeping the POW / MIA issue in the forefront.

APL-27: auxiliary, personnel, living ship—a big barge built on an LST (Troop landing ship) hull used as a floating base which includes an operations center.

APO: Army post office, overseas mailing address.

ARVN: Army of the Republic of Vietnam.

Barracks: a building(s) for lodging soldiers; living quarters.

Base camp: also known as the rear area; a resupply base for field units and a location for headquarters units, artillery batteries, and airfields.

Bird: chopper; helicopter; colonel.

Boonies: backwoods, jungles, or swampy areas far from civilization.

Bouncing Betty: a land mine that when triggered shoots an explosive charge up to waist level before detonation spraying shrapnel.

Bunkers: a protected embankment or dugout.

Cav: Cavalry, sort term for 1st Cavalry Division.

CBS: Columbia Broadcasting System, radio and television.

Chaplain: a member of the clergy attached to a military unit.

Chopper: helicopter; bird.

CIA: Central Intelligence Agency; coordinates governmental intelligence activities.

CIDG: Civilian Irregular Defense Group consisting of Montagnards, Nungs, or Cambodians.

CMH: Congressional Medal of Honor; the highest U.S. military decoration awarded for conspicuous gallantry at the risk of life above and beyond the call of duty.

CORDS: Civil Operations and Revolutionary Development Site.

Creosote: an oily liquid obtained by distillation of coal tar and used in preserving wood.

DMZ: Demilitarized Zone; dividing line between North and South Vietnam established in 1954 by the Geneva Convention; also divides North and South Korea.

DMV: Department of Motor Vehicles, New York State.

Drop zone: area where airborne soldiers exited their plane or chopper and landed by parachute.

Elephant grass: tall, razor-edged tropical plant indigenous to certain parts of Vietnam.

ETO: European Theater of Operation.

EVAC: Evacuation Hospital; where wounded were treated.

Evac'd: evacuated.

FBI: Federal Bureau of Investigation; investigates certain types of violations for theAttorney General.

Fifty Dong note: Vietnamese money.

Fire base: an artillery base set up to support combat ground troops.

Flak gear: heavy fiber-filled vest and other equipment designed to protect soldiers from shrapnel wounds.

Freedom Bird: the plane that took soldiers from Vietnam back to the U.S.

Gams: slang for women's legs.

GI: an Army enlisted soldier, the term dates back to World War II, and originally stood for Government Issue.

Green Berets: a highly trained and specialized corps in the US Army, usually assigned to especially hazardous roles; the name refers to their distinctive uniform hat.

Group: combined into a unit; more than two.

Grunts: lowest ranked foot soldiers; infantrymen in ground combat units of the Army and Marine Corps.

Gunny: a Marine sergeant.

Hawk: a person who advocates war.

Huey: nickname for the UH-1 series helicopters; also called Jolly Greens, gunships, and slicks.

I Corps, II Corps, III Corps, IV Corps: four military regions into which South Vietnam was divided, with I Corps the northernmost region, and IV Corps the southernmost (Mekong Delta).

ID: Identification papers or dogtags.

In-country: serving in Vietnam.

Infiltration route: the route followed by soldiers to penetrate the enemy's line in order to assemble behind the enemy position.

IV's: Intravenous injections of medications.

JrROTC: Junior Reserve Officer Training Corps, found at high schools mostly located near military bases.

Kilometer: a unit of length equal to 1000 meters, 6/10 mile, 3280 feet or 1090 yards; ballistic measurement of distance used for map distances, contours, and elevation; also called klick or click.

KSU: Kent State University, Kent, Ohio.

L.O.V.V.E.: Loved Ones of Veterans are Very Enterprising.

LRRP: Long Range Reconnaissance Patrol; an elite team usually comprised of five to seven men who would go deep into the jungle to observe enemy activity without initiating contact.

LST: Troop Landing Ship; an ocean going military vessel used by amphibious forces for landing troops and heavy equipment on beaches.

LZ: Landing Zone; where helicopters land to take on or discharge troops or supplies.

MAC-V: Military Assistance Command, Vietnam; the main American military command unit that had responsibility for and authority over all US military activities in Vietnam; based at TanSonNhut.

M-14: rifle used in Korea and Vietnam before the M-16.

M-16: standard semiautomatic rifle of the U.S. Army.

Medevac: medical evacuation from the field by helicopter; also called a "dust-off."

Mike Force: Mobile Strike Force Command consisting of Special Forces 12 man A-team, several Civilian Irregular (e.g. Montagnard) Defense Group battalions, a reconnaissance company, and a Nung or Cambodian airborne company.

MM: millimeter, unit of length.

MO: Modus Operandi, motive; method of working.

Monsoons: seasonal wind from the southwest in summer and northeast in winter marked by heavy rains.

Montagnard: a Vietnamese term for several tribes of mountain people inhabiting the highlands of Vietnam near Cambodian border.

NCO: Non-Commissioned Officers, enlisted personnel.

NCOIC: Non-Commissioned Officer In Charge.

O-Club: the Officers Club

OCSA: Office of Chief of Staff Army at The Pentagon.

Paddy: a rice field.

Perimeter: outer limits of a military position; the area beyond this belongs to the enemy.

Platoon: a subdivision of a company-sized military unit, normally consisting of two or more squads or sections.

PMOF: Presidential Medal of Freedom, the highest civilian award authorized by President.

POW: Prisoner of War.

POW/MIA: Prisoner of War/Missing in Action.

PTSD: Post Traumatic Stress Disorder.

Pungi sticks: long sharpened sticks designed to pierce a soldier's body when he falls into a pit or trips a booby trap.

PX: Post Exchange, where military members and families shop—like a department store; also known as BX—Base Exchange on Air Force bases and NEX—Navy Exchange on Navy and Marine bases.

Rear Area: the hindmost portion of an army; removed from the combat zone and responsible for administration and supplies Recon.

Regiment: a military unit usually consisting of a number of battalions.

ROK: Republic of Korea.

ROTC: Reserve Officer Training Corps, found on college campus.

SAC: Strategic Air Command, part of the Air Force.

SDS: Students for a Democratic Society.

Seabee: Naval Construction Battalions; engineers.

SFA: Special Forces Association.

Shrapnel: metal fragments from an explosive device.

Shtick: slang for routine such as comedy.

Six-by-six: a 2 1/2 ton standard military cargo truck.

Snipers: individuals who shot at the enemies from concealed positions.

Squad: a small military unit consisting of less than 10 men.

Squadron: an operating unit of warships, cavalry, aircraft, etc.

Stand Down: a period of rest for a military unit when all operations other than security are curtailed; also used for Veteran reunions.

Stubby pencil: handwriting everything instead of typing or using computer.

Tet: Buddhist lunar New Year.

Tet Offensive: a major uprising of Viet Cong, VC sympathizers, and NVA characterized by a series of coordinated attacks against military installations and provincial capitals throughout Vietnam. It occurred during the lunar New Year at the end of January 1968.

The bird: flipping the bird—a hand gesture using middle finger; also—helicopter.

The Colors: US Flag and other flags.

The Wall: The Vietnam Veterans Memorial in Washington, DC.

The Weathermen: a faction of SDS.

The World: slang for America used while in-country; home.

Top: a slang word for first sergeant, sometimes used for highest ranking NCO.

Tour of duty: an extended period in a military zone. In Vietnam, three phases were noted:

1—new troop in-country; basically fearful of the unknown, enemies capabilities, his own limitations;

2—in-country for awhile; learned some survival tricks, more confident, callous, even a little crazy in his personal disregard for the dangers of war;

3—ultimate paranoia; knows enemy's capabilities and random factors controlling his life; does all he can to insure he survives his tour, knowing full well his limitations and vulnerability.

Triage: the procedure for deciding the order in which to treat casualties.

Triple canopy: the thickness of overhead tree cover where one cannot see the sky from below or ground from above.

Trundle cover: usually a leather or metal covering for automobile convertible tops when top is in closed (top down) position.

USAR: United States Army Reserve.

USMC: United States Marine Corps.

USO: United Services Organization.

Vaudeville: a stage entertainment consisting of unrelated acts such as acrobats, comedians, dancers, or singers.

Vertex: the point opposite to and farthest from the base of a geometrical figure; the highest point; apex; intersection of two sides.

Vet Forum: an advice column of sorts.

Veteran: a former soldier or other service member, also Vet.

VVA: Vietnam Veterans of America.

WIMSA: Women in Military Service for America.

Yeomanette: a female Navy petty officer having mostly clerical duties; term used mostly during World War I.

0200 hours: military time for two o'clock a.m.

0300 hours: military time for three o'clock a.m.

INDEX

Army Special Services, 196-197
AShau Valley, VN, 112, 129
Australia, 51
Australian Nurse Corps, 198
Austria, 26
Backus, Steve, 235
Baez, Joan, 117
Baker, George, 202
Baker, Paul, ix, 177
Balderson Jr., William, 169
Bangkok, 29, 46
BanMeThout, VN, 166, 197
Baron, Ed, 14, 248
Barr, Onnie, 28
Barton, Clara, 199
Bath VA Hospital, 80
Battista, Angie, 189
Baxter, Daryle, 86
Bayot, Clara, 196
BearCat, 226
Bell, Jerry, 228
Bell, Nova, 196
Bell, Sharleen, 15
Belshe, Marilyn, 217
Benavidez, Roy, 4-6
Benge, Michael, 198
Benn, Hazel E., 197
Bensenhaver, Clyde, 140
Berg, Charles & Susan, 147
Bertino, Belvina, 190
Bertwell, Arleta, 196
BienHoa, VN, 78, 96, 151, 162,
    197, 219
Bigler, Philip, 195
Billeaud, Joyce, 181
BinhThuey, VN, 135
Bishop, Joey, 61
Biskra, North Africa, 151
Black, Barbara, 198
Blackburn, Helen, 196
Blackhorse Forward, 105
Blanche, Al, 233
Blanket Hill, 121
Blinded Veteran Assn, 137
Boguszewski, Jim, viii, xiv
BonSong, VN, 19

Bosnia, 215-216
Bottorff, Ann, 196
Braaten, Susan, 197
Bradbury, L., 94
Bradley, Ernest, 132
Brewer, Lucy, 202
Britt, Joe & Irmgard, 188
Bronx VA Hospital, 85
Brown, Celeste, 196
Brown, J. V., 230
Brown, Patty, 28
Brown, William B., 225
Buford, Harry, 202
Buis, Dale Richard, 127
Burges High School, 191
Burns, Harold, 170
Burr, Raymond, 138
Bush, Laura, 220
Bush, President George &
    Barbara, 160
Byron, Congresswoman
    Beverly B., 197
Cages Air Drome, 224
Caldwell, Lucy, 197
California State Guard, 27
California Vietnam Veterans
    Memorial, 33
CaMau, VN, 219
Cambodia, 5, 44, 47, 54, 114,
    118-119, 122, 227
Camp Adenir, 236
Camp Eagle, 187
Camp Enari, 23
Camp Goodman, 23
Camp Halloway, 79
Camp KienQuan II, 141
Camp McDermott, 96
Camp Robert's, 27
Camp Shield, 86
CamRanhBay, VN, 81, 115, 132,
    144, 162, 197, 204
Canada, 51, 91, 122
Canfora, Alan, 121
CanTho, VN, 79, 189, 226, 235,
    238
Cappozzoli, Joseph, 85

Nixon, President Richard, 5, 44, 114, 118, 125
Noble, Jerry, 14
Noel, Chris, 21-22, 25, 34, 220, 248
Nunn, Senator Sam, 99
NYS Vietnam Memorial Gallery, 182
O'Grady, Scott, 190
O'Leary, Bonnie, 139-140, 203, 214
O'Brian, Hugh, 138
Oaker, Mary Rose, 211
Oakland Naval Hospital, 225
Ocean Spray Cranberry Juice, 175
Ohio Riot Act, 120
Okinawa, 237
Old Ironsides, 202
Olmstead, Jerome E., 194
Olsen, Elizabeth "Betty" Ann, 198
Olson, Charles, 102, 248
Olson, Ken, 19
Operation Babylift, 195
Operation Black Ferret, 196
Operation Desert Storm, 218
Operation Homecoming, 126
Operation Varsity, 150
Operator #47, 40-41, 43, 56
Orleans, Hilda, 214
Orlowski, Hedwig Diane, 194
Oropallo, Marcia, ix
Orum, Ramona, 218
Oujda, North Africa, 224
Ovnand, Chester Melvin, 127
Owen, Philip, 226
Palmateer, Thomas, 234-235
Panama, 51, 215
Patrick, Michael, 234
Patterson, John & Cheryl, 157
Patterson, Melody, 162
Patton, Dr. Sam & Joe, 99, 248
Pearce, Betty, 189
Pearl Harbor Survivors Association, 187, 191

Pearl Harbor, 3, 11, 187, 191, 203, 214, 241
Pearl, Minnie, 27
Pellegrino, Belle, 2, 29, 88, 136, 148, 151, 163, 248
Pentagon Book Store, 87-88
Peoples, John, 124
Perez, Esther, 187
Perkins Sr., L., 225
Persian Gulf War, 18, 83, 207
PhanRang, VN, 228, 234
Philippine Islands, 91, 102, 195
Phillips, Dorothy, 197
Phipps, Jon, 219
PhoQuoc, VN, 81
PhuBai, VN, 142-143
PhuCat, VN, 162
PhuYen Province, VN, 108
Pine, Eddie, 19
Pitrone, Jean, 156
Plante, Kenneth & Kathleen, 107-108, 248
Pleiku, VN, 23, 77, 79, 82, 94, 101, 132, 144, 151, 194, 197, 230, 232
Polgrean, Marion, 196
Pollicino, Joe, 212
Pondy, Tina, 100
Pooley, Bill, 232
Port of Jubail, Saudi Arabia, 82
Portner, Paul, 219
Portugal, 91
Posch, Herman, 150
Post Traumatic Stress Disorder (PTSD), 24, 32, 35, 135
Post, Marjorie Merriweather, 197
Poulton, June, 196
Powell, General Colin, 12, 115, 129, 190
Pray, Joan, 196
Presidential Medal of Freedom (PMOF), 2-4, 29, 67, 101, 136, 150, 157, 162, 174-175, 239, 241-242, 259-260
Presley, Elvis, 21
Price, Ernest, 27, 151
Prisoner of war/Missing in

269

96, 98-99, 101-102, 107-108, 111-116, 119, 125, 132, 134-135, 138-139, 141, 143, 151-153, 162-163, 170-171, 176-177, 187, 189, 193, 196-198, 203-205, 210, 212, 215, 218, 225-227, 229, 231-232, 235
Vietnamese Special Forces, 142
Vietti, Eleanor Ardel, 198
VinhLong, 226
Vocelka, Mayor Jim, 147-148
Vollmer, Rita, 183
Vung Chua Mountain, VN, 23
VungTau, VN, 96, 198
Wakeman, Lyons, 202
Wakeman, Sarah Rosetta, 202
Waldhausen, LeEtta, xix, 190
Walker, Dr. Mary Edwards, 199-201
Walt, General Lewis, 152, 225
War of 1812, 202
Warner Robins Air Force Base, GA, 97
Washington Independent Writers, 214
Washington, D.C., 29, 32-34, 61-64, 85, 87-90, 92, 100, 108, 117, 126-127, 133, 138, 177, 186, 192, 198-200, 205, 211-212, 214, 226
Waterston, Terry & Pam, xix, 82-84
Watkins, Doris Jean, 196
Weber, Lieutenant Colonel, 17
Weir, Richard, 150
Wesley, Sharon, 196
West, William, 183
Western, Johnny, 28
Westmoreland, General William, 4, 23, 227, 243
Wetzel, Carla, 209
White Sands Missile Range, NM, 185
Wilkerson, Marty, 22
Williams, Arthur, 234
Williams, Bill, 107

Williamson, Dick, 151
Williamson, MaryAnne, 151
Wilson, Milton, 16
Wilting, Ruth, 197
Windle, Janice Woods, 192, 201
Winkler, Charlotte Winslow, 214
Winkles, Ronald, 239
Winters, Jonathan, 143
Wise, Fred, 151, 248
WNYT-TV13, 3, 84, 212
Wohlwend, John, 231
Women's Equality Day, 201
Women's International Center, 239
Women's Rights Convention, 201
Women's Rights Movement, 207
Women in Military Service for America (WIMSA), 42, 72, 84, 139, 205, 211-213, 215-217, 219
Woodside Jr., Gil & Jewel, xix, 171-173, 175, 186, 195-196, 243, 248
Wooley, Sheb, 27-28
Wooster, Barbara, 193
World War I, 1, 182, 202, 215
World War II, 1, 3, 6, 22, 25, 77, 80, 83, 85-86, 93, 100, 103, 112, 136, 147, 152, 164, 166, 168, 182, 195, 202-203, 208, 215, 223, 225, 228, 230, 234
Wrentmore, Douglas, 121
Wyatt, Elvin, 132
Yankee Station, 129
Ybanez, Fred, 232
Yeager, Chuck, 136
Yeager, Jerry, 136
Ying Lin, Maya, 127
Young, Gene, 124
Young, Gil, 169
Young, Peggy, 97
YWCA, 208
Zahn, Benita, ix, xix, 3-4, 84, 212
Zepeda, Maurice, 153

SUGGESTED ACTIVITIES FOR STUDENTS

1. Draw (or use) a map of the United States. Plot Noonie's travels and explore the country. Discuss the different states, cities, rivers, mountains, and oceans that she saw.

2. Draw (or use) a map of the World. Plot Maggie's travels mentioned in *Memories of Maggie* and *Potpourri Of War*. Discuss the different countries, communities, deserts, mountains, and bodies of water that she saw.

3. Ask your family and friends if they served in the military (or as a civilian) during any of our wars. Ask them to talk about their experiences. Write an essay about their experiences.

4. Ask your family and friends if they have any medals, photos, or memorabilia related to their time in the military. Ask them to show them to you. Write a story about these items. Bring them to class for show and tell. Better yet, have your family member or friend talk to your class.

5. Do a history project about women and men who served our country. Use charts, scales, graphs, photos, stories, or anything to help show what you have learned from reading not only *Potpourri of War* and *Memories of Maggie* but others as well.

6. Write a composition (like a book report) about what you learned from reading *Potpourri or War*, *Memories of Maggie*, or other books about women or men who served our country.

7. Imagine you are in the military, far from home, and lonely,—maybe even a Prisoner of War. Write a letter to someone telling them how you feel.

ABOUT THE AUTHOR

Noonie Fortin reveals her struggle to get women and men, both military and civilian, some recognition for their efforts on behalf of the U.S. armed forces. She writes how her life has changed in the years since being asked to help get Martha "Colonel Maggie" Raye honored with a Presidential Medal of Freedom. Noonie's is a sharing of love's joys and tears from many people including herself. This woman Veteran, community volunteer, speaker, and author shares a bit of herself with a hope her readers will share a remembrance of many labors of love so generously given.

Noonie has done an outstanding job of researching and gathering primary-source information about women and men who have served our country. She has found that journal writing is not only a tool for self-knowledge but a process for healing.

Her optimistic viewpoint is evident as she writes of people who have served our country. She shares her impressions and reminisces as she travels across America speaking to students and adults. Her firsthand account of the challenges of getting her first book, *Memories of Maggie*, published and marketed is an eye opener.

Originally from upstate New York, Noonie now has a home in central Texas. She is a Vietnam Era Veteran who attained the rank of First Sergeant in the Army Reserve before retiring with twenty-two years service.

Noonie has authored three newsletters, several book reviews, and numerous articles published in newspapers, journals and magazines including *Forty & Eighter*, BRAVO *Veterans Outlook, The Scottish Rite Journal*, Canada's *199 News*, and *VIETNAM* magazine. She has also written several book reviews for the Internet. Her first book, *Memories of Maggie*, was published in 1995.

She is a life-member of both Tri-County Council Vietnam Era Veterans and Tri-County Veteran's Alliance, a charter member of Women In Military Service For America Memorial Foundation, a member of The American Legion and The International Women's Writing Guild, National Speakers Association, and an Honorary member of The Association of U.S. Army Transporters in Thailand.

She writes an editorial column called "The Sarge" for the Military Network on the Internet at: http://www.military-network.com. Noonie also has her own home page at: http://members.aol.com/NFORTIN/index.html. She can be reached by email at: NFortin@aol.com.

To Order Copies

If unavailable in your local bookstores,LangMarc
Publishing will fill your order within 24 hours

✉ Postal Orders: LangMarc Publishing
P.O. Box 33817 • San Antonio, Texas 78265-3817

Potpourri Of War _____ copies
Memories of Maggie _____ copies
Each book is $15.95 (Canada $18.95)

Quantity Discounts: 10% discount for 3-4 books; 15%
for 5-9; 20% 10 or more copies.
Add Shipping: Book rate $1.75 for 1 book; 75 cents for
each additional book. $3.00 for priority mail (1-2 books).
Call for UPS charges on quantity orders.
☎ 1-800-864-1648

Please send payment with order:
_____ *Potpourri Of War* at $15.95   _____
_____ *Memories of Maggie* $15.95   _____
Less quantity discount -   _____
Total for books   =   _____
Sales tax (TX only)   _____
Shipping   +   _____
Check enclosed:

If this is a gift, we'll include a gift card and message.

Potpourri Of War • *Memories of Maggie (Circle choice)*
Name and Address for Order Delivery

_____
_____
_____
_____

Questions? Pick up the phone.

BOOKS PUBLISHED BY LANGMARC PUBLISHING

Ambushed at Sunset: Mature Adult Temptations

Angel on Trial (a humorous novel)

Are You Listening, Lord? Reflections for Christian Teen Girls

Ballad of Sara Doom: Myths, Messages and Markers from the Culture Zone (for teens-young adults)

Blue Garter Club: Ties That Bind Fourteen Christian Women For Forty Years

Bobbing for Apples—With Success: Practical How-To's for Congregational Leaders

Christ Care: A Purposeful Bible Study

Echoings From the Bible in Literature (meditations)

Guide-Lines and God-Lines for Facing Cancer: Mind, Body and Faith Connections

Illuminations: An Interweave of Thought, Identity, and Love (poetry)

Like Abigail (a novel)

Memories of Maggie—Martha Raye: A Legend Spanning Three Wars

Peace in the Parish: How to Use Conflict Redemption—Principles and Process

Potpourri of War: Labors of Love Remembered

Sand Castles and Fortresses: Bible Study on Relationships

Secret of the Viking Dagger (historical novel 5th-8th grades)

St. Murphy's Commandments (humor-cartoon)

The Complete Guide for Over-Protective Parenting (humorous advice with cartoon illustrations)

The Next Step: A Daily Walk in Recovery

Values Symphony: How to Harmonize Faith and Daily Choices in Everyday Living

When I Was First Alone: A Journey from Hurt to Healing

Whispering Stones (a novel)

You Might Be in a Country Church If...(humor-cartoon)